ALIENS ABOVE,
GHOSTS BELOW:
EXPLORATIONS OF THE UNKNOWN

By

Dr. Barry E. Taff

COSMIC PANTHEON PRESS
COPYRIGHT 2011

Aliens Above, Ghosts Below by Barry E. Taff

COSMIC PANTHEON PRESS

©Copyright 2011 Cosmic Pantheon Press and Dr. Barry E. Taff.

Aliens Above, Ghosts Below is a registered trademark of Dr. Barry E. Taff.

PUBLISHED BY COSMIC PANTHEON PRESS
www.cosmicpantheon.com

PROUDLY PRINTED IN THE USA!

"We shall not cease from exploration and in the end of all our exploring will to be arrive where we started and know the place for the first time."

"Time present and time past are both perhaps present in time future and time future contained in time past."

T.S. Eliot

ACKNOWLEDGEMENTS

Jeff Balanger, Bob Bastanchury, Art Bell, Doris Bither, Larry Brooks, Paul Dae Clemens, Ron & Wendy Cohn, Scott Colborn, Sharon Coyle, Frank De Felitta, Emil De Toffol @ Less EMF, Mark Downie, Don & Vicki Ecker, John Del Favero, Pete Davenport, Bart Ellis, Herbert Eveloff, M.D., Daniel Farrands, Barbara Gallagher, Christopher Garetano, Kerry Gaynor, Steve Glanz, Jolene Rae Harrington, Jim Hagopian, Jan Henderson, Jackie Hernandez, Daniel Hobbit, Rogers Johnson, Don Jolly, Sharna Kahn, Ted & Janet Klouzal, Stanley Krippner, Ph.D., Christine Lederman, Loren Lewis, Ron Magid, Abdi Manavi, Perry Martin, Richard Christian Matheson, Rodd Matsui, Lisa McIntosh, Dorthy Melvin, Tuesday Miles, Marcia Miller, Alex Mistretta, Thelma Moss, Ph.D., Bill Murphy, Steve Neil, Andrew Nichols, Ph.D., Tom Potier, Jeff & Deborah Radin, Jeff Rense, Frank A. Reveles, Steve Robin, Bill Roll, Ph.D., Steve Rubin, Andy Scheer, Dale Sobotka, M.D., Kenneth P. Stoller, M.D. John Streiff, Keith Swenson @ Pelican Products, Inc., Bonnie Vent, Jeff Wheatcraft, Brent Wolfberg, Chris Wingerd, Mort Zarcoff and Ron Ziskin,

With special thanks to Barry Conrad, Todd and Annie Faris, Laurie Jacobson, Russ Noratel, Jack Rourke, Dave Schrader, Pat Wheelock and Vince Wilson, whom without which this book would not have been written or published.

TABLE OF CONTENTS

FOREWORD

I first met Barry Taff in the early 1990s on the set of a paranormal-themed television talk show called *The Other Side*. As professional parapsychologists, we were both scheduled to appear on the show to discuss the merits of alleged paranormal photographs. At the time, Dr. Barry Taff was already almost a legend in the field of parapsychological research. His investigations of literally thousands of cases of alleged ghosts, poltergeists, UFOs and Extrasensory Perception were well known to me.

I had heard that the files of Barry Taff bulged with paranormal accounts from decades of research, including some high-profile investigations such as the Entity case (which had been novelized and produced as a popular film). I also knew that Barry's vast knowledge of psychic research stemmed from his years as a graduate student at UCLA, where he honed his scientific skills at the famous parapsychology laboratory, operated under the auspices of UCLA's Neuropsychiatric Institute, and under the watchful eye of the laboratory's director, parapsychologist Dr. Thelma Moss (who was something of a 1960s counterculture icon herself).

Barry had another unique quality of which I had heard. He was gifted with extraordinary extrasensory perception abilities. His ESP had been tested and verified at the UCLA lab, and for a time he served as the lab's leading test subject, as well as a scientific research associate. His reputation was such that I was thrilled to finally meet him in person in the "Green Room" of the television studio while awaiting our appearance on the show. As we talked, I realized that there is another aspect to the personality of Barry Taff which could not be appreciated by reading the dry text of the scientific journals: Barry Taff is not only a scientist of the highest caliber, an inventor and holder of numerous medical patents, and a visionary thinker. He is also a heck of a nice guy.

Nearly two decades have passed since my initial meeting with Barry Taff, and today I regard him as one of my closest friends and most respected colleagues. I look forward to our weekly telephone conversations, which must substitute for face-to-face interaction, since we live on opposite sides of the continent. Over the years, I have listened enthralled as he recounted some of his most fascinating paranormal investigations, many involving Hollywood celebrities; a non-stop stream of colorful anecdotes, corroborated with rigorous scientific data, and liberally flavored with wry humor. I remember thinking; "this guy really should write a book about his adventures." Finally, he has done so, and the result is the volume before you. You will not be disappointed.

Andrew Nichols, PsyD, PhD

Professor of Psychology, City College

Gainesville, Florida

March 2010

INTRODUCTION

So, you want to be a parapsychologist, huh? A scientist, who runs around chasing ghosts, poltergeists, apparitions and possibly even UFOs during the dead of night. A researcher who is the real-life version of Fox Mulder or Dana Scully of The X Files, or on the lighter side, perhaps Bill Murray or Dan Akroyd of Ghostbusters?

Or maybe your taste runs more to controlled laboratory research in telepathy, precognition or psychokinesis as depicted in the major motion pictures The Fury or Dreamscape. And if you really want to get serious, you might wish to enter the worlds of The Haunting (1963), The Legend of Hell House or even The Entity (of which I was the principal investigator and, to this day, is one of only two reality-based paranormal feature films ever made, as the Amityville Horror, its sequels and remakes were pure fiction).

Hopefully, you do not desire to follow in the footsteps of the majority of paranormally themed, alleged reality television shows such as Ghost Hunters, Ghost Hunters International, Ghost Hunter's Academy, Paranormal State, Psychic Kids, Ghost Adventurers, Ghost Lab and last, but not least, Extreme Paranormal. If you really believe what you're seeing and hearing on these shows, that they are anything other than misinformative, juvenile entertainment, there's a bridge I'd like to sell you that has several trillion barrels of oil trapped beneath its waters. Are you interested? What, you don't believe me?

This book is a compilation of unique articles I have written based on my forty years of research and investigations into a variety of paranormal events and experiences. Some of these articles have previously appeared in redacted form within journals and magazines dealing with parapsychology and UFOs.

Over the course of four decades, I have worked with numerous distinguished researchers and gifted individuals (those wonderful souls mentioned in the acknowledgements) with whom I have learned of and encountered a vast assortment of these types of events. I have also participated in several controlled scientific studies on Extra-Sensory Perception (ESP), all of which generated significant results. This collective body of work has led me to the following inescapable conclusion:

There are things happening to people that seemingly violate, defy and contradict our current understanding of how the physical world works----inexplicable things, that are understood by no one on earth. At present, these occurrences are defined as paranormal, however, they may eventually become classified as preternatural as opposed to supernatural.

In some ways my life has been a conglomeration of the previously mentioned television and motion picture characters and stories. From my parapsychological perspective, the last forty years have been a dream come true. For others, especially family, friends, acquaintances, associates and relationships around me, it's often been nothing short of a nightmare.

When you finish reading this book, you will have a better understanding why I have never been married, have not been in any long-term relationships and not even able to retain many of the same close friends for any lengthy period of time. Why? Perhaps this is because my priorities in life are fundamentally different from almost everyone I have ever known.

Parapsychology is an occupation (or perhaps an avocation according to some) unlike any other on earth. As someone who has dedicated their entire adult life to exploring the fringes of reality along the cutting edge of these unacknowledged scientific frontiers, I do not leave my insatiable curiosity, intrigue, fascination, hopes or dreams in an office to come home at night to an otherwise mundane ordinary existence.

And, believe it or not, there are many individuals who believe that a parapsychologist can actually bring phenomena home with them, which is one reason many people are so frightened by this entire field. Fortunately or unfortunately, depending on one's perspective, you need not worry, such events rarely, if ever, occur.

For all intents and purposes, my research is my life, with everything relegated to second place [other than my long-standing interest and involvement in advanced aerospace technology, biomedical technology, high-performance sports cars and science fiction films]. There are not many friends and acquaintances, let alone intellectually inspired, educated women, who have the patience, strength of will or grounding to endure a life dedicated to investigating things that few understand, and even fewer care about.

Face-to-face, most people are very polite and feign interest, or perhaps even belief, in paranormal phenomena and/or UFOs. However, once the party's over and you are no longer standing in front of them, most people's political correctness rapidly wanes and there is little, if any, tolerance for those who trek after things that go bump in the night, especially those who take it very seriously.

This closed-minded attitude is quite prevalent in high technology circles, whether it be electronic engineering, medicine or aerospace. Even though many such highly educated people have had profound, personal paranormal experiences, due to fear of ridicule and being labeled a crackpot or a quack, they do not discuss them. To be honest with you, I cannot blame them.

The television news media that has frequently featured these topics still finds it impossible to take such matters seriously. They always interject laughter or ridicule when closing out a news segment regarding this subject. They either feature individuals who are obvious frauds or quacks or they come forward with some absurd prosaic explanation to account for what occurred.

Do not forget, television news is essentially entertainment and it cares about one thing and one thing only...ratings. Guess what generates those ratings...sensationalism, controversy and fear. "If it bleeds, it leads" is the mantra of modern television news.

As this introduction was being written, a major UFO flap was occurring in Lansing, Michigan. One family observed an unknown aeroform hovering over their home and others were even somewhat successful at videotaping the objects. The tape showed the luminous object both close up and at-a-distance. As expected, the news segment closed by saying that the object was probably the moon or the planet Venus (hmm, haven't we heard this one before?).

I guess the folks in Lansing cannot differentiate between our moon, a planet millions of miles away that appears as a distant light in the sky [both of which they have seen all of their lives] and a huge enigmatic glowing object floating over the top of their house? Yeah, right. Give me a break!

Back in the late 1970's I had the opportunity to meet a well-known, local news reporter/journalist, who once co-anchored one of the nightly news shows for a major television network. I will not identify her by name but her description is self-revealing: a short Asian woman who is married to a talk show host.

When I was introduced as a parapsychologist, she laughed in my face asking if I really believed in "that bullshit" as "anyone with half a brain knows that it's all crap." Well, at least I knew I was not going to waste any of my time by debating the point with her.

Over the years I have had the opportunity to meet and speak with numerous news journalists. I believe I understand what is behind their severe skepticism and cynicism. Most people who work in the news media are painfully aware that their industry embellishes, distorts, slants, twists, hypes and otherwise manipulates the information they report on, which everyone erroneously calls the news.

If news journalists know that what they are reporting over the air or in the press is really not the truth, and this is what they do for a living, then why should they believe anyone's story about anything? In simple terms, if the news agencies they work for misrepresent information and occasionally (or perhaps, frequently) even lie to the public, why should news reporters themselves believe anything anyone else has to say?

Maybe they've heard the phrase "Everything I'm saying to you now is a lie. Oh, and by the way, I'm lying to you now as well." Talk about being jaded and conditioned to ignore facts and believe their own lies.

At the same time, let's not forget that the majority of individuals on this subject matter who appear on talk or tabloid shows, the nightly news or in the tabloid press are not respected researchers and investigators. Instead, they tend to be little more than space cadets and new age groupies. But they make for great ratings. With the predominance of such quackery, how would you expect seasoned and highly skeptical journalists to react? Most news journalists are trained to ignore everything and anything they themselves do not manufacture.

Given the foregoing, it is little wonder as to why most people in any position of status or power never discuss such matters. Maybe its because when they do, they are relegated to hair-brained talk or sleazy tabloid shows that portray these subjects as totally facetious. Most individuals with any level of critical thinking and judgment would not believe a word of such stories because of the way they've been conditioned by the media.

The most common behind-my-back response I have heard over the years is "Get a Life" or "Get Real." Generally, there appears to be three distinct groups of people when it comes to belief systems in this area.

The first group, are those I refer to as "New Age Groupies," those who tend to believe almost anything they are told, regardless of its strangeness or source.

The second type, the hard-nosed skeptics and debunkers, seem to have a particular agenda in their adamant denial of any and all phenomena and do not wish to be confused with details, evidence or facts.

The third group consists of those individuals who are extremely afraid of this entire area, generally due to their religious indoctrination. Believe it or not, even at the beginning of the 21st century, I still regularly meet individuals who say that anyone who investigates such phenomena is doing the devil's work unless they are doing it with a religious or spiritual orientation.

When I come across zealots of this degree or hard-nose skeptics and/or debunkers, I do not waste my time trying to persuade them as to the phenomena's reality because their minds are already made up and they obviously do not want to be confused with the facts.

To most people, parapsychology and ufology are subjects best reserved for discussions at cocktail parties, extension classes or following the latest big-budget theatrical film. Since the majority of people believe such matters do not generally relate to everyday existence; for example; job, family, health, etc., these topics are viewed as something better left to one's "spare time," when you have nothing else or better to do. I beg to differ.

Research strongly suggests that paranormal processes do, in fact, play an important, albeit subliminal role in everyday life, and they may be a guiding or mediating factor regarding decision making at an unconscious level. Just because we cannot, as yet, reliably replicate most of these phenomena in a controlled laboratory environment, does not preclude their existence.

One fact is accepted as true: paranormal phenomena do not appear to function as do machines. They cannot be turned on and off like a "switch." If such phenomena (telepathy, precognition, apparitions, etc.) never occurred, then there would be no cause or reason to investigate them.

Conversely, if they were regularly occurring events and were reproducible on command, they would be an accepted part of our reality and most likely explainable. Either way, the word phenomena would not be applicable.

The fact that these events occur only some of the time under certain conditions that are not scientifically understood or easily reproduced, tells us one thing: We are ignorant about a significant aspect of the world we live in, an aspect that probably dates back to the very beginning of civilization itself that may unknowingly influence every judgment and decision we make throughout the course of our lives.

It is safe to assume that psychic processes work within the boundaries of nature through principles and mechanisms that we have yet to discover. This is a reasonable assumption since paranormal events directly involve human perception in ways that mimic vision, hearing, touch, smell and taste, although seemingly independent of our known sensory mechanisms.

Unfortunately, the scientific community has always been, and still is, of the mindset that unless a model can be hypothesized which relies on known physical principles, such phenomena are rejected with knee jerk swiftness.

I submit that if someone went back in time to the middle of the 6th century and presented the concept of a laser, television, computers, cell phones or hypersonic travel in the space shuttle, they would have received the same closed-minded, chilly reception that most scientists give to paranormal research today. It's important to remember that just because we currently do not understand how a phenomenon or system operates does not mean that it does not exist. We just lack the knowledge or wisdom to explain its operational properties.

In a generic sense, paranormal phenomena should more accurately be referred to as preternatural, because the word implies that a process is unknown now but will eventually be understood, instead of supernatural, that suggests that a phenomenon lies beyond the scope of human understanding altogether.

I personally believe that when (not if) we finally unravel the mysteries and enigmas of the paranormal, we might not like what we find because it will force us to re-evaluate our place in the greater scheme of things, for better or worse. Perhaps that's why there is such intense, subconscious fear regarding the paranormal within so many people?

This is not to say that I believe everyone who claims to have had a paranormal or UFO experience. I am not going to bore you with the sordid details of my frequent encounters with individuals who appeared to be emotionally disturbed and deluded, believing something that never occurred. Moreover, they believed that this would make people pay attention to them and improve their otherwise dull and boring existence.

A perfect example of just how insane some people are who enter this field comes from an event more than two decades past. At that time (1987), I was part of a Mutual UFO Network (MUFON) support group that was formed here in Los Angeles in response to the fallout from

Whitley Streiber's book, Communion.

I met a young woman at one of these support groups by the name of Val, who talked about her alleged alien abductions. After listening intently, I personally felt that Val's experiences were little more than the product of a very troubled psyche. I politely thanked her for her time, but did not offer any kind of follow-up.

In all likelihood, she was seeking consensual validation of her alleged alien encounters from an academic researcher. In my opinion, all she really needed was psychiatric intervention and little else, although I would've liked to have been a fly on the wall of her family's home when she was growing up.

Some years later, I was on the Internet and came across a bizarre blog by Val. She started off by saying that when we met she instantly knew that I was sneaky and underhanded (she must have been a very astute woman?). Then, according to Val, I instantly hypnotized her and gained control of her mind.

Shortly thereafter, according to Val, I went home where I used numerous psychotronic devices hidden in my basement (that's odd, last time I checked, my apartment building doesn't have a basement?) to direct "evil entities" to repeatedly rape her as she walked down streets. Think this claim is a just a little weird? Wait, there's more and it gets a lot worse.

Val went on to write how I based The Entity book and movie on her public, paranormal sexual assaults, which of course, I caused. Beyond the obvious absurdity, if not insanity, regarding such a claim, her understanding of linear time was really distorted.

Let's see if reality, in any way whatsoever, conformed to Val's perception of it. The Entity case (Chapter 2) occurred in 1974-5. The Entity novel was published in 1978, and the motion picture was released in 1983. However, the first and only time I met Val (which was quite enough) was in 1987.

Do you notice a temporal discontinuity here? Well apparently, in her delusional state of mind, Val did not. Hopefully, she has sought and received psychiatric counseling with concomitant medication (maybe combined with some ECT).

There is a much more recent incident illustrating just how psychotic a seemingly normal person can become for no apparent reason.

It was 1998, and I was giving a lecture at the Learning Light Foundation in Anaheim, California, when an old girlfriend showed up to say hello. I had not seen Linda in more than fifteen years and was amazed to see how well she had aged; no fat, no lines or wrinkles. It appeared that Linda's exterior had not been ravaged by the passing of time.

After my talk, she came up and we spoke. Right off the bat she asked if I would join forces with her and Jesus Christ to defeat demonic aliens who were conspiring with the CIA and FBI to destroy the world, after of course, they destroyed her.

Hmm, I believe I've heard this story way too many times from way too many people? Needless to say, Linda never discussed anything even remotely resembling this when we dated in the mid-'70's. If she had, I never would have seen her more than once.

About one year after this lecture in Anaheim, Linda showed up at my home unannounced. She began rambling, even more irrationally than during our meeting in 1998.

Concerned that she was suffering from a psychotic break, I quickly pulled her out of my home where she continued her ranting. This time, however, her psychobabble sounded even

11

more fragmented and dissociative. Once again, I strongly suggested that she consult a psychiatrist, as she sounded suicidal.

I asked her if she had been physically or emotionally ill since we first knew each other in the 70's. She replied in the negative. I asked where these bizarre thoughts came from, as she never voiced anything like this way back when.

Linda said that she always had thoughts like these, but she was too shy to verbalize them. Too shy, or too worried, that I might have become aware of her psychosis? Again, I asked her to leave, as I had absolutely no interest whatsoever in anything she was saying as she sounded completely delusional. Fortunately she never returned.

However, Linda kept telephoning to inform me that objects in her trailer home, located up in northern California, kept disappearing. Items, such as computers, keys, phones and jewelry allegedly kept vanishing on their own. She also spoke of her computer's hard drive being erased as were all the files she backed-up with various storage mechanisms.

She of course, blamed the CIA/FBI/alien conspiracy for everything. Linda insisted that she knew too much about what was really going on in the world and who was really behind it all. Therefore, the powers that be were trying to drive her insane and/or kill her.

Well, it seems that in one respect she might be correct...she was insane, although I question her conclusions as to the cause. I wonder if she remembers the phrase; "paranoid delusions?"

Months later she contacted me by phone again and acknowledged that she had, in fact, attempted suicide, but had obviously failed. Linda said that something compelled her to walk into the path of an oncoming car, but she didn't know what that "something" was, but she was sure it must have been the alien/government conspiracy controlling her actions. Oops, there's that pesky mind control nonsense again.

Some time later, she again tried to terminate her existence in a similar fashion. Fortunately, this attempt also did not succeed. Or, maybe in her case, perhaps it was unfortunate that she didn't succeed! Both of these suicidal attempts resulted in her being held at a psychiatric hospital for a short time.

I told her to stop calling me, as I was not at all interested in what she had to say anymore if she refused to seek and receive psychiatric help. For the most part, she ceased in her efforts to inform me as to her hapless plight.

Thankfully, for the next several years I did not hear from Linda at all. Then, in early 2008, she called to inform me that the Earth was about to explode and that I had to help her.

I could not pass up the wonderful opportunity Linda had just provided me with, so without a second's hesitation I replied: "Excuse me Lara, I have to send baby Kal-El off to his new home before Krypton explodes?" There was a long pause, as Linda hadn't the foggiest notion of what I was referring to. Do you? I then immediately told her she was insane and hung up on her.

I guess that I see some humor in everything. Perhaps it makes dealing with such disturbed individuals much easier than it would be otherwise, or perhaps, it's my way of insulating myself from the constant barrage of emotionally ill people I've met over the decades?

Please remember that first and foremost I am a scientist. I am not looking for something that is not there. It is only after I rule out and exhaust all the prosaic and conventional causes and explanations for any occurrence that I even consider a particular event might be paranormal in nature.

If one is ignorant as to what constitutes normal physical reality in a scientific sense, it is then extremely difficult, if not impossible, to make the determination that an occurrence is paranormal in nature; that is, operating outside the boundaries of conventional physical laws as we know them today.

Over the course of my forty years of work, I have closely adhered to this particular methodology and protocol, just as it was drilled into my head during the course of my education. I have had no desire to be forever chasing the proverbial ghost only to later discover it was nothing more than someone's overactive imagination, a peculiarly cast light or shadow, or an individual's unhealed emotional scars.

As a parapsychologist, the question I am most frequently asked is; "What first got you into this area?" First and foremost, it was my insatiable scientific curiosity. I was also tantalized by the fact that it was an important area of scientific exploration that was not likely to supply answers to every posited question in a short time and, in one form or another, these questions have been around since the dawn of human civilization.

The most significant reason I pursued this line of work was my recurring personal experiences in telepathy, clairvoyance, precognition, psychometry and out-of-body experiences (OBE's). As a child, I had continual psychic experiences such as knowing what was medically wrong with people around me, knowing when there was a direct threat to me and being able to occasionally predict future events.

I had only three potential ways to view these phenomena since none of my friends or family shared these experiences. First, I could have chosen to believe that I was out of my mind, delusional or hallucinating. This was not a very pleasant thought since nothing else about me seemed that peculiar. The second alternative was to believe that everyone else was a little crazy and I was the only sane one. A dangerously paranoid attitude that I never gave thought to.

Or, third, that something truly amazing and unique was going on in my life, something that was not uniformly distributed in the population nor readily accepted by western society. For reasons that will become all too obvious throughout the course of this book, I chose the latter viewpoint, despite the fact that my experiences were totally alien to my family and friends, who, half the time looked at me through fearful eyes reminiscent of a scene out of the classic movie Village of the Damned.

It's somewhat sad to admit the many friends, acquaintances' and relationships I have scared away or bored to death over the years.

Nevertheless, I logically assumed that my psychic abilities were akin to any other talent or gift possessed by human beings. Not everyone shares equal abilities, but whatever is possible for one member of a given species is more or less possible for all members to a greater or lesser degree, barring any specific handicap.

We all have muscles, but only a scant few individuals become true athletes, even less Olympic champions. Most of us drive cars, yet few possess the hand-eye-foot coordination, stamina and endurance to professionally race a Formula 1 car.

Every chapter in this book was written from my own first hand, personal experiences or research over the last four decades. The numerous accounts comprising the chapters of this book range from the sublime to the humorous, although many are somewhat unnerving in that there are no simple answers or resolutions to their otherworldly occurrences.

Many of these events have dramatically altered my life, mostly for the better, but occasionally they tore the very fabric of my personal world to pieces in ways almost impossible to deal with.

When your dreams, hopes and aspirations translate into most other people's night terrors, how do you interrelate with others living a day-to-day existence totally blind as to the intricate complexity surrounding them?

Other than casual conversation at a party, can you imagine coming home to your family and discussing any of the following events? How long do you think people would stick around or treat you seriously if you investigated these kinds of events for a living:

- A ghost possessed the brother of a colleague and attempted to strangle me at a haunted house.

- An assistant was almost killed by hanging and then later was thrown into a wall by psychokinetic forces during the investigation of a poltergeist case.

- A former girlfriend, was abducted while we slept together in the same bed. Thereafter, her personality and sanity totally disintegrated and she became a religious zealot.

- A ghost crawled into bed with me while I was sleeping in a haunted house that I was house sitting for a friend.

- A friend precognized the Guatemalan earthquake of 1975.

- Two assistants passed out from fright during an apparition's appearance while investigating the real-life Entity case.

- Poltergeist activity (flying household objects) chased a Los Angeles television news crew from a haunted house while astonished onlookers gazed on in amazement.

- The suppression at a very high level of the U.S. military/government of hard physical evidence regarding extraterrestrial visitation including autopsies of alien bodies that suggest an entirely unique and unknown species of life is visiting our planet....reptilian humanoids.

The government denies the existence of UFOs because they fear such information would shatter our understanding of life on such a profound level that it could result in the socio-economic collapse of our society and perhaps the next world war. The government may also believe that the earth's anxiety prone population could not cope with what such knowledge would reveal about our past and future.

The really scary part is -- they may be right.

Of course, our subjective personal experiences are virtually impossible to prove or disprove in terms of their objective physical reality. In the end, you must be the sole judge about the validity and significance of ghosts, hauntings, poltergeists, apparitions and UFOs.

It's really not important what news anchors or professional debunkers think or believe is happening. It's irrelevant what famous astronomers say about the supposed impossibility of extraterrestrial life visiting Earth.

Again, playing devil's advocate, it is abundantly clear there is no shortage of people running around the world making the most outrageous claims imaginable -- everything from being able to directly talk with the dead as if they were in the chair next to you to having ongoing sexual relationships with benign, but beautiful, alien beings. It is important to remember that many of these individuals are essentially lonely, bored people desperately seeking attention. Or perhaps, they're badly in need of psychiatric intervention?

Others are merely con artists seeking to take advantage of people's naive nature in order to drain their bank account or to gain a twisted form of status and celebrity fame. Others may be suffering from serious emotional problems and really believe what they are saying.

What is important to understand and remember when examining the unknown is to focus on legitimate research by credible academically trained investigators so that the path to greater understanding is not muddled and confused by obfuscating or distracting misinformation and trivia. If you wish to explore the unknown, do so with a light, not through a dark and murky screen.

For the moment however, sit down in a very comfortable chair, take a deep breath and unwind for several hours because everything you are about to read is true. Then, prepare yourself for a ride into another dimension of reality, a dimension that to some is as strange as One Step Beyond, The Outer Limits, The X-Files and the Twilight Zone combined. Before buckling your racing harness as this might be a very wild ride, be sure that your bedtime is not too close at hand.

ENJOY.

Chapter 1:
A HAUNTING THOUGHT

"I ain't afraid of no ghosts!" was a memorable line from the motion picture Ghostbusters. However, given the current attitude of modern parapsychologists, a more appropriate phrase might be, "I don't believe in no ghosts!" Yeah, I know, bad English. Right?

It is a disheartening fact that the majority of contemporary academic paranormal researchers consider the possibility of discarnate intelligence about as likely as the moon being made of green cheese. Yet, less than a quarter century ago, such scientists openly investigated and debated the possibility.

Today, no parapsychologist worth their credentials would publicly exclaim that phenomena that were originally labeled as ghosts, hauntings, apparitions and poltergeists are anything more than manifestations of recurrent spontaneous psychokinesis (RSPK) generated by living human agents.

Curiously, even though the German word poltergeist translates into English as "noisy spirit," the vast array of phenomena associated with poltergeist outbreaks are now theorized to stem from all-too-human perpetrators, hence the term poltergeist/psychokinetic agent (PGA/PKA).

Moreover, there has been a dramatic paradigm shift within parapsychology to where the collective scientific opinion is that virtually all phenomena lumped under the aforementioned headings can be ascribed to mind-over-matter reactions, albeit unconscious ones.

Is there any evidence that contradicts this new world-view? YES! If such evidence is examined with a totally objective mind, the conclusions drawn are somewhat obvious: the belief in disembodied or discarnate intelligence (DI) cannot be totally dismissed!

Admittedly, perhaps ninety percent (90%) or more of the 4,400 cases investigated by this author since 1968 (initially out of UCLA's former parapsychology lab) meet most of the criteria for poltergeists, i.e., the presence of pubescent and/or adolescent children in a rather tense, conflict ridden, emotionally chaotic environment. However, that still leaves approximately 440 cases strongly suggesting the presence of discarnate intelligence.

Playing devil's advocate, it is readily apparent that the entire notion of discarnate intelligence or survival is, in and of itself, a totally untestable hypothesis and therefore cannot be proved or disproved, at least with modern scientific tools or methods.

On the other side of the coin is something known as Ockham's Razor that, simply stated, says that all things being equal, one must attempt to explain a given phenomenon with a theory that most easily, logically and empirically fits what is being observed, measured or recorded. Moreover, your theory must fit your data, not the reverse.

While there are certainly alternate, highly speculative theoretical explanations for many of the phenomena described herein, they do not lend themselves adequately to an operational definition of all the recorded events. The smoking gun regarding discarnate intelligence is a substantial body of circumstantial evidence that cannot be ignored due to its unique properties and recurring nature.

There are three basic categories of cases in this realm of paranormal research: ghosts & hauntings, apparitions and poltergeists. This chapter is dedicated to exploring the possibility of the first category that is more precisely referred to as discarnate intelligence, therefore the vast majority of poltergeist cases are excluded.

It should also be noted from the outset that cases where the occupants of the house or apartment displayed any overt or even subtly covert symptoms of psychopathology, alcoholism or drug abuse, were automatically discarded from my files and database.

The entity known as a haunting or ghost is generally associated with a particular location or residence, as opposed to an individual, and it can last anywhere from years to centuries, while poltergeist cases are extremely short lived; from days to months at best. In the majority of haunting cases there is usually a particular violent or traumatic event, whether recent or long ago, that precipitated the haunting.

In general, the simple ghost or haunt appears to be some sort of an audio-visual playback mechanism from a deceased person's former behavior patterns. They rarely display any overt signs of intelligence apart from their audio-visual reconstruction of past events. This type of phenomena rarely, if ever, appears cognizant of being observed and it gives no direct signs of recognition.

However, their playback occasionally displays characteristics suggesting that some type or form of crude interactive mechanism is at work (although this mechanism does not have to automatically conjure up a spirit or specter to account for this seeming relationship).

As an example, think about the new interactive systems frequently used in modern video games. You make one of several choices during the course of the game. Each different choice leads to different outcomes for the game. We graphically see how a change in human response (input) alters the playback of the video recording (output).

One theory speculates that perhaps a prior traumatic emotional event is somehow recorded on or within space-time in a localized environment. When a specifically sensitive person enters that environment, they act as the needle in an old fashion record player, the magnetic heads of a VCR, or the laser in a DVD/compact disc player -- they activate and facilitate a three-dimensional reconstruction and projection of what came before, i.e., the past.

What possibly makes a haunting interactive with its observer is that a living human being is unconsciously animating the pre-recorded information from nanosecond to nanosecond. Therefore, each phenomenon, in its own unique way, reacts to the particular individual's unconscious needs and desires. Such a mechanism might be labeled bioholographic animation, as a biological system triggers a seemingly holographic display of previously recorded information.

In fact, this particular theory might even explain why some apparitions are not collectively observed by everyone in a room in which they appear [only some people can perceive the event]. Does this theory sound plausible or reasonable? Remember, it is only a technical sounding theory at best, based on observed data.

It is also crucially important to understand that very few cases evolve into full investigations due to the scarcity, evasiveness and general transient nature of these phenomena, whether its source is bioholographic, psychokinetic or discarnate.

The following stories bear repeating because they demonstrate the objective differences between phenomena that is believed to be caused by a hypothetical discarnate intelligence rather than living psychokinetic agents.

Prophetically perhaps, the very first case I ever investigated in 1968 dealt with phenomena that blatantly smacked of survival, but unfortunately, not the human kind.

Aliens Above, Ghosts Below by Barry E. Taff

An elderly couple living in a quaint house in Pasadena, California called to discuss the fact that they had been seeing, hearing and actually feeling their recently deceased cat around the house. After a lengthy phone interview, I decided to pay them a visit to further pursue this intriguing case.

During the course of an exhaustive audio-taped interview, the couple spoke quite openly about frequent encounters with their dead cat; an orange tabby. To say the least, I was very skeptical.

According to their testimony, even several close friends experienced the phantom cat. Although I was quite impressed with all their stories, that's all they were, stories.

However, while sitting by myself on the couch, I suddenly felt a rather substantial weight descend into my lap. Mind you, this was not just any weight, this had all the particulars associated with a rather heavy, overfed cat, which I was familiar with as I owned one myself. I could feel the distinct paws and their occasionally distended claws tugging at my jeans. The entire, invisible weight was subtly vibrating or resonating, just the way a normal cat does when loudly purring.

When I attempted to reach out and touch the disembodied feline, my hand passed through empty air. Moving my legs in an attempt to dislodge the cat's stance upon me resulted in the cat apparently jumping off my lap onto the couch to my right. To my astonishment, the couch also responded as if a weighty cat were now resting on its soft cushions. Again, I reached out to touch what could not be seen and the phenomena vanished as abruptly as it "appeared."

This quite unnerving feline specter made very random visits that substantially waned over the next several months and so a detailed investigation of this case was not possible. What is to be made of the effects described here? Is this the result of a grief-stricken couple, who were unconsciously creating psychokinetic manifestations of their lost beloved pet? This couple had experienced far worse personal losses in their lives without such paranormal responses and so this hypothesis did not explain much.

In 1970, another case appeared while three college students were sharing a large house in the San Fernando Valley. One young man was tragically and violently killed in an auto accident. Within several days after the fateful event, loud, disembodied footsteps were heard by the two other roommates. The bathroom door opened and closed on its own, the lights went on and the toilet flushed. This all followed the refrigerator being opened and a large glass container of orange juice being removed and emptied.

Interestingly, while alive, the deceased roommate had a very small and apparently weak bladder that forced him to make frequent nightly trips to the bathroom, especially after drinking his favorite form of liquid refreshment -- orange juice. I guess some physical problems transcend even death -- when you gotta go, you gotta go.

As the case began to evolve, even more startling behavior patterns of the deceased man manifested to such a degree that the possibility of survival was strongly suggested to virtually any pragmatic mind.

The deceased young man was a "Trekkie" and enjoyed watching syndicated re-runs of the Star Trek television show weeknights from 6-7 p.m. His roommates did not share his interest in Star Trek and never watched the show. After his death, every weeknight at precisely 6 p.m., the television turned itself on, manually tuned itself to channel 13, the correct channel, and remained on that station until 7 p.m. when the set would abruptly turn itself off (the television had no remote control or automatic on-off capability). The two surviving roommates went so far as to unplug the TV.

However, the plug somehow always found its way back into the wall socket. Of all the events experienced in this case, it was this specific one that most disturbed the two remaining roommates. I wonder how Gene Roddenberry would have reacted to the knowledge that loyalty to his great creation knows no mortal bounds and extends beyond the grave? As Roddenberry is now also no longer with us in the proverbial sense, perhaps he already knows?

The final series of events following the Star Trek episodes were when the favorite tapes of the deceased man mysteriously found their way into and playing within the 8--track tape deck in the wee hours of the morning. The surviving roommates of the house were not particularly fond of his taste in music and therefore did not put the tapes in the player or even turn it on. As to why they never simply threw out the audiotapes, is another matter.

Following several months of such continuing phenomena, the activity abruptly stopped after the two remaining roommates tried talking to their deceased friend, literally pleading with him to leave them alone. Inasmuch as there was never any form of RSPK prior to their friend's death, or after this all-too-brief outbreak, it's highly unlikely that such was the result of sudden surge of mind-over-matter functions.

Another fascinating case from the late 1970's dealt with a house in the Silverlake area of Los Angeles that was also shared by several young men attending college. The house was quite old, having been built in the first decade of the twentieth century.

Late one evening, while on his way to the kitchen to get something to eat, one of the roommates was startled by the apparition of a young screaming girl wrapped in a sheath of flames. There, off to one side of the living room was the horrific, three dimensional image of a child being immolated.

Interestingly, there was no sensation of heat, even though the apparition was only ten feet away and fiercely burning. The girl's painful screams were heard but the crackling sounds normally associated with such a rapid consumption were absent.

The witness estimated that the sighting lasted no more than ten seconds. Totally disoriented and panicked, he bolted upstairs to tell his roommates what he had just seen. Their response was extremely skeptical, especially after going back down to the living room and finding no evidence of the sighting. They finally accused him of smoking too much pot. Later that week, the other roommates independently corroborated and verified their friend's sighting when they each observed the same apparition in the same place, but at different times.

Many months later, after an exhaustive background check of the house's history, the residents learned that more than fifteen years earlier, a young retarded girl's clothes caught fire on that very spot in the house and she was, in fact, consumed by immolation.

This discovery had two major effects. For one, it confirmed the source of the apparition and it clearly established that their house was haunted. Second, it caused the young men to abruptly move. Well, that's one way of solving their problem.

One of the most fascinating cases in my files turned up in the Hyde Park district near Inglewood during the summer of 1970. It was the first case where I encountered direct malevolent phenomena. The case actually began months earlier when the two elderly occupants of the house, a retired husband and wife, Dompu and Rafugio, were killed in an auto accident.

After their death, neighbors witnessed the deceased occupants doing various chores around the house. They called the grandson, Dwayne, who then contacted me to investigate the matter.

Aliens Above, Ghosts Below by Barry E. Taff

Phenomena began with Dompu and Rafugio's apparitional appearances in and around the house. Many of the neighbors who did not even know that the occupants had died, continued seeing them doing various work about the house as if nothing had changed. It was not uncommon for the neighbors to observe their ghostly next-door tenants taking out the garbage, cutting the shrubs or mowing the lawn!

On several occasions, individuals present in the house saw various objects being flung about or floating through the air. Doors and windows opened and closed, and the sounds of a man walking about the house, were heard.

There was one particular display case or breakfront, that for some unknown reason, remained dust free in a house unoccupied for more than nine months, as if it was being dusted and polished daily. Virtually every other piece of furniture in the house was heavily laden with a thick layer of dust, as the house had not been maintained during its vacancy.

A number of my associates and I gathered at the house in an attempt to observe and hopefully stimulate some events. In the hope of the latter, a seance was conducted. The results were quite startling and totally unexpected.

During the course of the seance, not much in the way of phenomena transpired. The only thing of note was that I heard some strange sounds emanating from a bathroom that did not have any running water or electricity as they had been turned off long ago. Once the seance was concluded, primarily from boredom, I decided to check out the bathroom in question. Although absolutely nothing out of the ordinary was discovered, it was an act I would later live to regret, barely.

Upon re-entering the central foyer where the seance had been held, I saw a strange, stocky, gray-haired man in the opposing doorway, someone who definitely was not part of our group. He was clothed in khaki colored slacks and a pastel colored shirt. Before I could ask who this unknown man was, he lunged in my direction and began strangling me as he yelled, "This is my house, get out!"

Initially thinking this was some type of sick joke, I simply tried to dislodge myself from his powerful grip. As this proved impossible, and his grasp tightened, I employed some of my martial arts training and attempted to break his arms off from around my neck.

To my astonishment, my arms were repelled as if hitting solid steel (and no, he did not have an "S" on his chest). I then kneed him in the groin, hard. There was absolutely no effect. Suddenly, this brawny man literally picked me up like a rag doll and threw me into the bathtub in the bathroom directly behind me. Temporarily stunned, I was unable to jump out of the tub.

My next recollection was of laying face up in the bathtub with this immense man on top of me continuing his attempt to choke the life out of me. As he maintained his death grip, with his large, bulging, blood-shot eyes fixated on me, he began tearing my jacket and shirt as he shouted, "Get out of this house, this is my house!"

I was fighting a losing battle as I was vastly overpowered by a seemingly supernormal force. The other participants in the seance all witnessed the attack. Not exactly expecting this sort of activity, they were shocked and momentarily taken aback not knowing what to think or how to respond.

Fortunately, it did not take much longer for the six other men witnessing the event to rush to my aid, as there was a clear and present danger to my life. It took several minutes for these six men to physically dislodge and drag the attacker from on top of me. A struggle ensued, and the assailant was eventually rendered unconscious by the blows received, at which

20

point he hit the floor with a loud thud. His huge body began convulsing in seizures resembling those of epilepsy.

As I was helped up from the tub, I looked down and beheld a sight that if not for the presence of more than ten witnesses, I would never feel comfortable repeating. The image of the large man who attacked me slowly dissolved and metamorphasized into that of a much younger and smaller stature individual.

What now lay before us on the bathroom floor was the prone form of a 29 year- old man with dark hair and of average build -- it was Dwayne, the grandson! We immediately attended to him, as he appeared all but dead. After he was roused, he had no recollection of how or why he came to be lying on the bathroom floor. He was in great pain from the bruises on his body that were the ones originally delivered to the elderly man everyone saw strangling me. The last thing Dwayne remembered was being in the kitchen and hearing a voice say, "Get out of my house."

When Dwayne was told what had just transpired, he could not believe it. After we described the appearance of the elderly man who attacked me, Dwayne finally got to his feet and went to the bedroom where he rummaged through a dresser drawer from which he withdrew a picture. The picture was of his deceased grandfather, presumably the same one haunting the house with his wife.

To our collective astonishment, the image of Dwayne's grandfather in the photograph was identical to the man who had just attacked and attempted to strangle me. Yet, other than Dwayne, no other person at the house knew what his grandfather looked like prior to this point in time.

Is this a simple case wherein the discarnate entity or consciousness of Dwayne's grandfather "possessed" his grandson to such a degree that we actually visually observed the image of that man, or was something even stranger occurring?

To make matters more difficult was the perception of some of the witnesses. All six male friends who came to my assistance agreed in their description of my assailant. However, the other seance attendees, all women, did not see the same apparition. Instead, they all saw Dwayne himself physically engage me in battle, not the larger apparitional image of the grandfather. No further comment here except that the subjectivity regarding this type of perception is always of concern and makes one wonder what is really going on here.

I vividly recall the attack as if it was yesterday and I do not remember seeing the face of Dwayne during the scuffle. For the most part, the attack broke up the evening, sending Dwayne and his friend home, along with several members of our group. However, a number of us decided to remain behind and attempt to once again catalyze something within this anything but dormant house.

During the course of attempting to conduct another seance, with only the light of a candle on an otherwise empty wooden bookshelf, my associate's brother began acting strangely. Suddenly, and for no apparent reason, he started ranting and raving before violently attacking me. While he did not physically change in appearance, he did appear to be in some kind of altered, trance-like state. Unlike the previous attack, this onslaught was immediately halted by a quick punch to the jaw that rendered the young man unconscious.

While attending to this man's condition, the burning candle moved itself down the shelf in several distinct bursts of motion and eventually landed on the floor where it caught the rug beneath it on fire. It was at this point that we all decided that perhaps discretion, in this case, was indeed the better part of valor. We abruptly left.

The following day I received a phone call from one of the neighbors to the house. He claimed to have heard loud smashing noises and observed strange lights emanating from the house after we left.

Upon our return to the house the next evening, we observed that all the furniture, except for the well-dusted breakfront, had been thrown down to the floor and partially destroyed. There was a great deal of broken glass throughout the house and almost every drawer was pulled out and thrown on the floor. Yet both the front and rear doors were still locked and there was no sign of forced entry or burglary. The house looked as is if a tornado had ripped through it. A paranormal tornado, that is. During our examination of the wrecked house I observed a large cuckoo clock jump off the wall.

Eventually, the house was put up for sale and our ability to further investigate the case ended because the realty company was not pleased with the possible adverse publicity resulting from our investigation.

Since the fall of 1971, numerous families have lived in this average looking house. In fact, almost every ethnicity has at one point occupied the residence. There have been Asian, Hispanic, African-American as well as white families, taking up residency. While none of the owners/renters knew of its sordid background, almost all of them experienced some form of paranormal phenomena, ranging from simple psychokinetic activity to full-blown apparitions.

I would learn of such continuing activity after I appeared on local TV news or talk shows. The then current occupants of the house saw or heard me, obtained my phone number and called. The last call from this house was in 1979. One can only wonder as to what has transpired there since that time.

As 1970 progressed, another case came to my attention that, perhaps more than any other, clearly demonstrated the presence of a discarnate entity. A woman in her late twenties, Blair, who lived at home with her parents in Pacific Palisades, approached me while I was teaching parapsychology at UCLA and asked if I would like to check out her family's house.

According to Blair and her family (they had no pubescent or adolescent children), the house was haunted by the apparition of a large man dressed in the armor of a Spanish conquistador. There were several intense cold spots in the house, and on numerous occasions, objects were apported from one room to another.

While visiting their home and interviewing the family, my pen was transported (apported) from the front living room to the rear bedroom, just seconds after I placed it on the coffee table directly in front of me. The walls of the house often provided the occupants with a concert of poundings and scratching,

As if these sounds were not disturbing enough, the family soon began hearing rather distinctive disembodied voices. The voice was sophisticated enough to address the various family members by their first names, but always in Spanish. To make matters even worst, these disembodied voices were heard only at night.

I personally felt the cold spots in the bedroom and heard the knocking. These phenomena occurring within a healthy emotional atmosphere added up to what appeared as a true haunting case. However, this was but the surface of a very substantial case.

The most significant event occurred many months after the initial sightings of the conquistador. While a number of rooms were being added to the rear of the house, workmen uncovered graves bearing bones and suits of armor similar to that of the conquistador. Such confirmation is extremely rare in these type of investigations. This was one of only two of such cases in my files. It was not long afterwards that the family moved, perhaps for good reason.

Aliens Above, Ghosts Below by Barry E. Taff

Moving to 1973 in Van Nuys, California, the manifestations at Wise home came to my attention. From all indications, the family appeared free of any psychopathology, even though there were several children. While I never observed any phenomena at this location, I took the accounts by the family at face value due to the extremely healthy psychodynamic environment combined with the high degree of convergence, multiple witnesses and independent corroboration.

According to Mrs. Wise, her three children and her husband, the house was figuratively alive at times. On one particular occasion, the family watched in amazement as a large drinking glass was wrenched from the hands of their 17 year-old son Skip, and thrown clear across the room.

In another incident, a group of large bath towels flew from on top of the dryer across the laundry room to hit Mrs. Wise in the face. This act was in full view of two other family members. On many separate occasions, Mrs. Wise actually felt something or someone pinch and caresses her while in the laundry room. From these acts, she assumed that the presence in their home was male. But then again, this is Los Angeles, and you never know.

At the very onset of the phenomena, the family began finding money in various denominations, ranging from $5 to $50, floating down from the ceiling. The sum total of the unaccountable money exceeded $5,000. The source of the money was never determined.

Jokingly, I asked Mrs. Wise if we could move in with them, as the entity might well be the answer to our funding needs. Well, one thing is for sure. I am positive the Wise family did not declare the money to the IRS. Although, I wonder if the IRS would really consider this type of money as income? But then again, knowing how the IRS tries to squeeze every last penny from us, they just might.

For weeks on end, the family heard heavy footsteps restlessly pacing back and forth in the hallway between the bedrooms and bathrooms in their one-story home. Early one morning, Skip was so terrified by the approaching footsteps that he ran and locked himself in the bathroom only to hear the ghostly footfalls approach the door of the bathroom and then stop. Skip, a hulking high school football player, peeked out of the bathroom door only to find an empty corridor. He spent the night sleeping in the bathtub.

On another occasion, after many months of these hectic ghostly nights, Mr. Wise suddenly awoke in the early morning hours to see a sparkling or glowing male apparition at the foot of their bed. He immediately grabbed a nearby flashlight and turned it on the figure. When the light hit the figure, it disappeared, but not before Mr. Wise caught a good glimpse of it. He claims that it was a tall male figure garbed in a flowing robe.

As time passed, this manifestation, whatever it was, took on more of a violent character. Its forceful nature was somewhat revealed when it ripped the Wise's forced-air heater off its steel foundations in the attic on three separate occasions.

Further activity in the house finally permitted several family members to actually see their unwanted tenant. The youngest child, John, initially supplied the most vivid details, as did several of the neighbors. The Wise's ghost was apparently a short, black man, who wore old tattered Levi's blue jeans and a light blue work shirt. He was seen wearing tennis shoes or something similar to them.

John described the apparition as a "short Bill Cosby, like on TV," only he was carrying a lit candle in some type of holder and kept jumping up and touching the ceiling. On several occasions, neighbors said they saw this figure leave through the front door of the Wise house recounting similar features. The neighbors said the figure gave them the impression of being from a different era. They felt that he was dressed as a cowboy or work hand from the late 1800's. We established that three previous owners of the house had moved because of this particular haunting disturbance, though they had no prior knowledge of the house's reputation.

One of the latter sightings occurred about seven months into our investigation. The youngest son, John, who was five years old at the time, was apparently chased through the house by the apparition. His description matched the other reported sightings, except that he claimed the figure did not always walk on the ground. Much of the chase, according to Mrs. Wise's interpretation of John's hysteria, sounded as if the figure materialized out of thin air, after which it pursued him by floating through the hallway.

In fact, at one point during the final chase, Mrs. Wise heard John screaming as he ran toward the front screen door. She turned just as John reached the door and pushed it open. To her amazement, hot on John's trail was the apparition they had all come to accept as living with them.

According to the Wise's, the phenomena tended to run in cycles, hot and cold, on and off, so-to-speak. Over the ensuing fifteen years, the haunting has significantly weakened, although every so often it kicks up its heels even though all their children have long since moved away from home.

In the spring of 1974, another case turned up from the home of Salvador Delgado in Monterey Park. Initially, it appeared to be haunted by the presence of the family's deceased daughter, Yolanda, who along with her expectant child, had died under mysterious circumstances during labor.

The family situation within the house was unique for two reasons. First, there appeared to be a very healthy psychological atmosphere. Second, all family members did not believe or have any interest whatsoever in the paranormal prior to the outbreak of phenomena.

This Monterey Park house appeared to manifest many typical poltergeist phenomena along with the more classic haunting displays; loud pounding and knocking on doors and walls coupled with the movement of various pieces of furniture. One evening, in full view of a small family gathering, their cat was lifted up into the air by its front legs as if by unseen hands. The cat remained stationary in the air for about five to ten seconds and was then gently lowered back to the floor. The cat panicked, ran from the house and was never seen again.

Another dramatic event occurred about three weeks after Yolanda's death. Early one morning, Mrs. Delgado was awakened by a strange scraping or scratching sound emanating from the living room. She immediately woke her husband and they both left their bedroom to investigate the unusual sounds. After walking through the hallway and turning into the living room, Mr. and Mrs. Delgado were shocked to see an apparition of Yolanda sitting before them on the floor of the living room playing with a cat they once owned (that cat was also deceased).

The Delgado's became quite stiff with fear as they continued to watch the faintly translucent image of their dead daughter as she stood up and turned towards them. They could not completely see through Yolanda's apparition, but she nevertheless appeared to glow at the edges of her spectral form. She was fully clothed in apparel they recognized.

Yolanda's apparition approached to within two to three feet of her parents and spoke, apparently attempting to console her parents, "Don't worry mommy and daddy, I'll never leave you. I'm really lonely and miss all the family."

Mrs. Delgado stood there in a dead (excuse the pun) stare, while Mr. Delgado simply passed out cold. This type of collective sighting is extremely rare, but nevertheless, I feel it was authentic.

Following this incident, Mr. Delgado wanted nothing more to do with our investigation of his house and he made it a point to be absent whenever we returned.

After these initial series of events, Yolanda was apparently seen on many other occasions, frequently in the mirrors around the house while various family members were washing their face or combing their hair.

One particular event that was of high strangeness occurred when the Delgado's came home one afternoon at approximately 3 p.m., to see Yolanda casually sitting on the living room couch with another girl whom they did not recognize. Yolanda was reading the copy of Redbook magazine that was already lying on the coffee table.

Suddenly, their daughter stood up and told them she had to go and open some doors. Yolanda and her phantom friend abruptly disappeared from sight after which numerous doors throughout the house began opening and closing, as if she was on some kind of compulsive spectral schedule.

The last known incident when Yolanda appeared was about three months later when she told her parents that her death was not due to medical complications during labor, but rather to negligence. Yolanda's parents finally summoned up enough nerve, strength and courage to confront the physician and nurse involved.

Interestingly, both the doctor and his nurse suddenly and mysteriously left town, never to be heard from again. This event, more precisely, a portion of it, hit the local newspapers, although the sudden disappearance of the doctor and nurse was not in any way whatsoever attributed to Yolanda's ghost.

Not surprisingly, after this seeming resolution of Yolanda's death, the haunting abruptly ceased, almost as if she had finally achieved a desired sense of closure and peace of mind.

When one of your cases finds its way into the National Enquirer or onto the front page of the View Section of the Los Angeles Times, you generally know that one or both of two things have occurred.

Either the case was unique enough to attract the attention of the press and tabloid media or, you've made a serious error in judgment by allowing yourself to be interviewed by them. In a case that began in the late spring of 1976, both of these reasons can be cited as true. In view of the manner in which the case was reported in both papers, I should have exercised better judgment and more caution as neither publication came close to accurately reporting what actually transpired.

Strangely enough, the greater of the two evils here was not the National Enquirer who, we were aware, grossly misrepresented their stories, especially about the paranormal. In this case the venerable Los Angeles Times did a much worse job.

Contrary to what most people believe, there really is not much difference in the sensationalistic style of journalism practiced by either publication. They both distort, slant, embellish, exaggerate and frequently misinform their readers about subjects they consider to be less than credible. The resulting campy, tongue-in-cheek article was not just unprofessional, it was downright rude and disrespectful.

Over the last forty years, most cases have come to my attention via conventional means, e.g., word-of-mouth, occasional appearances on local TV talk shows, teaching, lecturing, or random calls coming to UCLA's former parapsychology lab. However, this all changed in May of 1976 as a young undergraduate student came storming into the lab in shock over what had transpired at a party on the previous night.

Mark was quite excited to share all of the incredible events he had witnessed just hours earlier, especially since he found the entire matter difficult, if not impossible, to believe. Once I was able to slow down his rate of speech, he attempted to coherently discuss the barrage of paranormal events during the all-too-brief party.

As Mark's story initially was nothing more than the ramblings of a very frenetic young adult, I tried to get him to start from the very beginning so I would have some perspective in the matter, rather than attempt to sort and collate a series of divergent events. When Mark understood what I needed to actually begin investigating his experience, he started describing the location of a large, three-story house on Hollymont Drive in the Hollywood Hills.

While at the party, Mark and several of his friends witnessed some of the most amazing things they had ever seen. When the owner of the house, a banker named Don Jolly, first moved in, he immediately hired a houseboy to clean and do the cooking. Shortly thereafter, the houseboy began telling Jolly of strange events that really unnerved him.

Objects were rapidly moved from one room to another, and enigmatic shadows and apparitions were seen out of the corner of his eye. The frequency and magnitude of these events escalated to such a degree that the houseboy seriously considered quitting rather than putting up with any more of the bizarre phenomena.

According to Mark, during the party, many loose objects began flying about the house. At one point after a young woman entered the house, a large throne chair suddenly moved under its own power across the room pinning her against the wall of the living room directly in front of other guests. This was followed an instant later by a kettle flying in from the kitchen stove which quite deliberately dumped its water over the girl's head. Later that evening, the houseboy was chased around the house by a cabbage with a huge butcher knife stuck in it. It was this particular event that finally caused the houseboy to abruptly quit his job.

Needless to say, these stories were more than sufficient to arouse my interest and desire to attend yet another party to be held at the same house the next evening. I figured that the worst-case scenario would be one where I would speak to some interesting individuals who were first-hand witnesses to the previous party's events. It also presented the opportunity to personally observe, if not record, some astounding phenomena. Never in my wildest dreams did I ever imagine that this possibly embellished story would turn into one of the most incredible cases in my files suggesting discarnate intelligence.

The next evening, my colleague and I went to the house to attend the party. The area of Hollywood where the house is located was not exactly known for its beauty or safety. In fact, it was noted mostly for its high crime rate and drug trafficking. As such, I was far more concerned about the threat from burglars, muggers and flying lead than belligerent ghosts.

While at the house, we did have the opportunity to observe some of the most astounding psychokinetic displays we had ever seen. On several occasions, numerous books would take off from their resting place, fly madly about the house and abruptly drop to the floor. A telephone left its secure position on a stand and then flew over Don Jolly's shoulder in my direction, as did a large glass jar.

The most humorous event occurred while several of us stood in the foyer directly at the entrance to the house. In the middle of us was a large wrought-iron chandelier. As we continued to speak, I commented that I was very hungry. Within seconds, a large clump of bananas came flying across our path landing at my feet. I bent down to pick them up and noticed that they were rather cold to the touch.

Their exact source could not be determined even after checking out the kitchen where they supposedly originated. We eventually returned to the foyer to continue our conversation [that was about the only really vacant room in the house where a conversation could be heard given the party's boisterous nature].

Suddenly, the front doorbell began ringing relentlessly, as if some madman outside was seeking entrance. When we examined the doorbell, we were shocked to discover that it was disconnected from the house's power as its wires were completely frayed and rotted, incapable of carrying even the minimal household voltage or current. What then caused the doorbell to ring? Or more precisely, what allowed it to ring?

After some background research, we discovered that the Hollymont house had a rather sordid background. Two murders and one suicide had occurred there over the last fifty years. These historical tidbits combined with the fact that both Robert Taylor and Barbara Stanwyck once lived there, contributed to its celebrity atmosphere.

After talking at length with Don Jolly, we discovered that the apparition of a young female had repeatedly been seen by both workers in the house, as well as Jolly himself. We also learned that Jolly was a part-time minister and had a small chapel set up on the second floor. This seemed a little suspicious and made me wonder whether we might be dealing with a religious zealot. By about 11:30 P.M., the house finally settled down and we decided to leave.

We were not able to return until about ten days later on May 14, 1976, at which time we were accompanied by a news crew headed by Connie Fox from local Los Angeles television station, KTTV [which coincidentally became part of the Fox Network (no relation to Connie].

On this particular visit, we experienced more sustained phenomena in a finite period of time than in any case before or since. Due to the detailed nature of the recurring phenomena, it is easier to list them in an itemized manner.

- We arrived about 6:30 P.M. and at one point we all were in the dining room. Suddenly an ice tray came flying out of the kitchen and soared across the dining room into the west wall.
- Shortly thereafter, a large sack of cloth napkins flew out of the kitchen (which was empty) and struck silverware in the dining room directly in front of Connie Fox.
- A pewter goblet flew out of the kitchen storage area and impacted the west wall of the dining room.
- A religious vestment [metal cylinder] disappeared from the upstairs chapel and appeared outside in front of the house dropping in open air.
- A large world atlas suddenly appeared flying in front of the house and literally chased a screaming and terrified Connie Fox down the front Z-shaped stairway, making three distinct ninety degree turns (changes of direction) in doing so. All the while, the atlas was flapping its pages as though it was a bird in flight.
- When one of my friends laughingly commented on the above event, an old shoe flew around the outside of the house and struck him on the side of the head.
- While in the pantry area between the dining room and kitchen with Jolly, showers of coins, primarily pennies and dimes, fell from the ceiling, pelting us. These thousands of coins appeared to fall from the empty air.
- While several members of the crew and I stood in the foyer discussing these occurrences, a large black robe aported itself onto the massive wrought iron chandelier positioned immediately above and between all of us. One instant the chandelier was empty, in the next the robe appeared out of thin air. When examined, it was discovered that the robe was intricately wrapped around the workings of the light fixture requiring several minutes with a stepladder to remove.

- We learned that Jolly had invited a local Bishop over to the house to bless it. Shortly after the Bishop entered the house, his hat disappeared off the top of his head and was later found lying on an inaccessible part of the roof.
- A large shower head from the main upstairs bathroom came flying down into the living room under its own power. It somehow managed to miss the more than fifteen (15) individuals present in the room at the time.
- Several sharp and loud explosive sounds came from the hallway. Investigation could not determine their source.
- When the Bishop attempted to bless the house using his Holy Water scepter, the top explosively blew off its base and flew around the room.
- Coasters from the dining room table took off and flew into the living room.
- Several keys came flying down the stairway although no one was upstairs.
- Several chairs in the dining room changed locations.
- A thick chain and padlock suddenly appeared around the front door and gate, essentially locking everyone in the house.
- A fire broke out upstairs in one of the wastepaper baskets in the bathroom.
- A telephone, several large jars, and a large book were observed to fly across various rooms.
- Electrical power in the house was turned on and off repeatedly during our visit that evening. Checking out the fuse box provided no clue, as it had not been tampered with. Whatever force was accomplishing this feat could selectively negate the power along specific circuits whenever the TV news crew attempted to use the AC lines in the house. The power to those lines was cut off while other lines were left unaffected.
- Even the battery powered equipment refused to function while in the house. Also affected was the street lamp directly in front of the house that began blinking erratically. However, the rest of the block's street lamps were not affected.

So ended our first full night of investigating the house. All that remained was for us to return and continue our work on another day.

Due to very fortunate circumstances, we actually were able to temporarily live in this house----a parapsychologist's dream. What made this case even more interesting was that both my colleague and I lived less than ten minutes away, almost in our backyard.

We formally took up residence on August 2, 1976. What follows is a chronology of events that transpired over the next nine days.

August 3:11:58 P.M.

Stove turned itself off and pulled away from the wall. Library door unlocked itself. Master bedroom door locked and unlocked itself.

After putting down a glass of iced tea on the kitchen counter, I went to the refrigerator in search of more lemon. Returning to the counter, the glass of tea was gone and was later found in the library three rooms away behind a door that I had locked the evening before.

August 4: 12:20 A.M.

Library door unlocked itself again.

August 5: 10:40 P.M.

Bar door on dining room side locked itself from the inside by throwing dead bolt.

11:57 P.M.

Something approached the master bedroom door, grabbed and jiggled the knob, then turned it to the right. Opening door revealed nothing. Large chair was moved 5 feet and turned around while I was out of the bedroom for not more than 3 minutes.

August 6: 2:40 A.M.

I was awakened in the downstairs bedroom by sounds of someone walking around the kitchen and lower portion of house. Investigation revealed nothing.

9:45 A.M.

While sitting on couch in living room, I heard the sounds and sensation of someone walking down the stairway and up behind me accompanied by a strong, sweet perfumed smell. No one was there.

4:45 P.M.

While talking on a newly installed telephone, the jack pulled itself out of the wall and threw itself over a chair, pulling the 25 foot cord along with it.

August: 2:30 P.M.

While attempting to make repairs to the upstairs bathroom shower, a large tool box that I had just brought upstairs was aported from the floor next to me back downstairs kitchen drawer where it was originally located. My attention was taken off the tools box for not more than 15 seconds while removing old shower handles. Upon turning around, the tool box was gone.

The sound of someone walking around the house was heard throughout the entire day.

9:45 P.M.

While talking to a friend on the kitchen telephone, I observed a dark humanoid form cross my visual path in the dining room area. No salient features or characteristics were distinguishable, nor could gender be determined. The dark form was observed through the open pantry storage area separating the dining room and kitchen. Friends sitting in the living room at the time thought they heard the sounds of someone walking in the dinging room but assumed it was me.

August 10: 4:30 P.M.

Rear French doors opened by themselves

Thinking that the case was now in a waning mode, we were really shocked when approximately two months later, the neighbor to the immediate east, Dexter Grey, who was renovating that house for his sister, made an interesting discovery associated with the Jolly home.

He accidentally discovered that one of the built-in bookshelves pushed inward revealing a secret passageway leading beneath the basement of the house. Apparently, several of the homes on that particular hill were connected by a subterranean passageway dating back to the prohibition era. In all likelihood, liquor was run through it.

While Grey was exploring this tunnel with his girlfriend and a neighbor, they found the remains of an old, makeshift grave with an engraved headstone that read Regina. The inscribed date of death was 1922. However, to the best of our knowledge, the Coroner's Office was never contacted, nor were the remains, if any, exhumed. Interestingly, the Jolly house was built in 1924! Perhaps someone was using that plot of land as a cemetary plot?

The last occurrence in this case was one of high strangeness indeed. Just before we abandoned the house prior to the new tenants moving in, we left a note on NPI/UCLA stationary informing the new residents that their house was haunted and if they wanted us to continue our investigation (free of charge, of course), to contact us directly by telephone.

Several weeks later, I received a peculiar phone call from a young lady who lived several miles east of the Hollymont house. She asked if I was the author of a note she found stuck to the inside door of her bedroom closet at home. Somehow, the note I had left on the inside of the kitchen cupboard ended up in someone else's closet many miles away who had absolutely no relationship to the old or new owners of the house. I've heard of apports, but this was ridiculous.

On several occasions throughout the 1980's I was able to re-visit the Hollymont house, once in October of 1986 for the syndicated TV show Two On the Town. At that time the house was being shared by three gay men. Their experiences were consistent with those of Don Jolly, myself and others. However, there was one particular aspect regarding their encounters that was unique. Apparently, the ghost in the Hollymont house may have been homophobic. Phenomena only occurred when straight men or heterosexual couples were over, never when the three men were there which each other or their significant others.

Since 1986, after one of the men died of AIDS and the others moved, there have been many different occupants residing in the Hollymont house. Various rooms are frequently rented out to different people. From time to time we have had sporadic contact with individuals living within the house and learned that phenomena still occurs. Unfortunately, the new tenants would not give us permission to continue our investigation. Until now, that is.

I have had occasional contact with Dexter Grey in the last fifteen years and, if he is to be believed, his house is almost as haunted as Jolly's, although we never experienced any phenomena there. According to Grey, he has had numerous guests over the years that were so terrified by strange sounds and apparitions that they fled in the middle of the night.

However, I personally question Grey's credibility and memory because of his apparent obsession of promoting and publicizing his haunted house is a little too important to him. He'll apparently talk to anyone within earshot about events transpiring in his house and provides copies of "ancient" tabloid stories regarding paranormal events within his house to literal strangers walking in front of his home. Think about the fallout such random disclosure could have on your life. Would you want to tell the whole world about such occurrences in your home?

In the late summer of 2008 we (Jack Rourke and this author) trekked up to Hollymont to show the location to a producer friend, Mark Downie, visiting from New York. While we were all speaking in front of the property, Jack (a gifted Los Angeles psychic who had been working with us for several years) turned to this author and asked if there was a river running under the property. My reply was that I knew nothing of the subterranean features of this area.

Aliens Above, Ghosts Below by Barry E. Taff

Shortly thereafter, we were fortunate to meet one of the 6221 house's new tenants, who invited us in. While walking up the steeply inclined stairway, Jack started feeling dizzy and nauseous, unaware that this author was having the exact same reaction at precisely the same moment, walking just several steps ahead of him.

The house looked pretty much the same as it did in 1976, although now badly in need of restoration. There had been substantial remodeling of the kitchen though, which now extends into the area that was once the pantry, where pennies once fell from nothingness decades earlier.

In October of 2008, we (Barry Conrad, Paul Clemens, Todd and Annie Fariss, Laurie Jacobson, Alex Mistretta, Jack Rourke and this author) returned to 6221 Hollymont on an investigation for the first time in more than twenty-five years.

A local businessman by the name of Abdi Manavi, now owns this fascinating house and was very gracious in allowing us access to his residence given that he didn't know any of us. Mr. Manavi is what I call true gentleman.

Abdi (knowing a great deal of what transpired on his property three decades earlier) casually spoke of recent paranormal events such as books flying off shelves, disembodied voices, chandeliers swinging from no apparent cause, items disappearing and reappearing [apports], numerous light bulbs being removed from their sockets and left in a neatly formed triangular pile on the ground floor, and the very rare apparition of a young woman, whom Abdi believes to be Regina, whose body, allegedly, still remains buried beneath the house.

Perhaps the most intriguing information Abdi spoke of was his belief that the ghost or presence, seemed to be very reactive to skeptics, in that the more skeptical guests were regarding such phenomena, the more responsive the phenomenon was.

Abdi's belief is very interesting, in that it might help explain why this particular house was so very volatile during this author's initial investigation during the mid-seventies, as the Los Angeles Times' reporter and the KTTV news camera crew with their reporter, Connie Fox) were extremely skeptical, as was their nature.

The underground tunnel, within which Regina's remains allegedly still resides, has long since collapsed due to the frequent earthquake activity in Southern California area since 1976. The tunnel would have to be excavated and shored up before anyone could safely enter it again.

One major difference in this current investigational visit was that we brought our suite of instruments to measure the environment. Back in 1976, portable, handheld instrumentation to measure the Earth's geomagnetic field, electromagnetic (EM) fields, ion concentration and density, ULF/ELF EM spectrum analyzer, temperature and humidity, were only science-fiction pipe dreams in the minds of parapsychologists.

And by the way, if you want the best one-stop shopping experience for purchasing your high-end, engineering-based instruments as referenced above, there is only one place to go: The Less EMF Safety Superstore (lessemf@lessemf.com or www.lessemf.com. However, please do your research well before ordering your instrumentation, as not all sensors are applicable. The man in the know to speak with at Less EMF is Emil De Toffol. One last bit of advice here, the correct instrumentation for use in paranormal field investigations does not come cheap from any source, so be prepared to spend some real hard earned money.]

In spite of our strong expectations given the 1976 investigation, we were not prepared for what we were about to learn. By checking on the US Geological Survey (USGS) website, we discovered that several earthquake faults intersect almost directly under Abdi's home.

Adding even more fuel to our anticipation was additional USGS data indicating that a shallow river runs beneath the homes on this side of this particular hill, precisely as Jack Rourke had sensed. What a coincidence! I knew there was a reason I wanted to work with Jack, and I guess I was right.

Jack Rourke is the only psychic I've ever worked with due to his emotional grounding, intellect, healthy ego and comprehensive knowledge of clinical psychology, and the paranormal, coupled with an intense desire to learn. This man knows more about clinical psychology than thus author forgot over the decades. This psychically gifted young man is a steadfast seeker of truth and knowledge in his insatiable quest to understand and improve the quality of life.

Most, if not all, of the psychics I've met prior to Jack, and there has been thousands, had one disturbing traits in common (besides emotionally unstable with borderline personalities and frequently dissociative) which was very unnerving and a little frightening to this author.

That most disturbing characteristic was that everything they did (psychically, that is) was about them. Their continual reference to "I" was indicative of pretentious egomania, almost never about improving the human condition through acquired knowledge. About the only improving these "gifted" individuals were after, was that of their wallet or purse size as it swelled with cash as obtained from ignorant, gullible and naïve individuals.

What made and makes such a person intolerable to this author is their overt sense self-righteousness combined with incredible ignorance and arrogance. A dysfunctional combination of qualities, to be sure. Jack Rourke possesses not even a trace of these less than desirable behavioral qualities.

In true science, there is no such thing as "I", as it is not about the people; it is about the advancement of the human race through what we learn and how we apply it.

Decades earlier, thus author briefly worked with another psychic. However, there is one caveat here, she was my girlfriend at the time although truly gifted, that is, before her emotional meltdown due to a intense trauma she suffered, possibly related to our being together as a couple. You can read about her, in detail, in Chapter 10 (Abduction Central?).

Back in Hollywood Hills, perhaps it was the aforementioned geophysical forces underlying the Hollymont property that made Jack and this author mildly disoriented while ascending the stairway on our prior visit? Well, at least we now know where the energy comes that possibly feeds and sustains the paranormal activity in Abdi's house over the years, don't we?

But why did we not again feel ill during this most recent visit? Probably because these geophysical forces are in constant state of flux and therefore will not always exert the same physical effects every time one is present.

Given this, it was certainly unfortunate, that even in the face of such extraordinary accumulated evidence as cited above, every one of our instruments read the environment as "normal", as there did not appear to be anything unusual or anomalous about this location at that particular moment in time. However, we do know that such geophysical forces wax and wane over time due to numerous factors, none of which are predictable or controllable.

Laurie Jacobson, author of Hollywood Haunted, showed up about two hours after the rest of us. Only then, did anything seemingly paranormal begin to occur. Maybe it was the sheer presence of a particularly unique lady? Or, maybe it was the fact of Laurie's being a well-respected Hollywood historian who's been very interested in this particular case for decades. In point of fact, Laurie dedicated an entire chapter of her aforementioned book to this specific house and case. In the end, who knows?

When we ventured upstairs with Laurie, it felt as if we were in a hyperbaric oxygen chamber, where the atmospheric pressure would well above normal, that of 14.7 pounds per-square-inch.

It was actually quite painful to this author as well as to several others. This sense of overpressure is commonly associated with certain "haunted" environments and is frequently felt as pressure around the head, ears, mastoid region and neck. It felt like being at the bottom of a very deep swimming pool or scuba diving a little too deep for comfort

Suddenly, the chandelier in the small, front, southern bedroom began to swing on its own. While Paul Clemens was videotaping that action he captured a large luminous anomaly that was not visible to the naked eye.

There was no wind, and the anomaly looked very different than what people some commonly refer to as "orbs", which for the most part as explainable as tiny particulates or what's more commonly referred to as dust (which is everywhere) being illuminated by bright light sources at specific angles. This anomaly was definitely not dust.

While Barry Conrad was shooting with one of his cameras into Abdi's bedroom, a large, bright, red luminous anomaly was recorded that, once again was not visible to any of us. And still, the sense of overpressure lingered. Then, as suddenly as it began, the events ceased. Once again, things unfortunately returned to normal.

The hour was late and we decided to call it an evening, but not before thanking Abdi for his hospitality and asking him to keep a journal or log of events as best he could in the hope of discerning a pattern to the phenomena transpiring in his home.

As I was packing up our Pelican instrument case, I noticed what appeared to be an unusual marking on the bottom of it. Upon examination, it looked as if someone, or some thing, had carved a bizarre shape into the case.

Closer scrutiny of the carving depicted a large, backwards "R" (a lazy "R"?), as in Regina! What? There definitely was not any such physical damage of the case when we arrived at Abdi's, but there was when we were about to depart. Hmm.

If the carving didn't appear as a backwards "R", that in itself would still be very interesting, especially as these Pelican cases are very strong and durable, not prone to being easily damaged.

The only other time this case was damaged was in 2005 when something very sharp tore into the middle and backward underside of the case while on another investigation. Those marks were very distinctive and looked as if a wild animal had torn into the cases belly, which was all the while resting upon a soft sofa top where that type of damage could not have occurred.

Maybe what the Hollymont location requires to bring it back up to the frequency and magnitude of phenomena it displayed in 1976, is a collection of much younger people (with their concomitant high-energy nervous systems, glandular systems and emotions) attending such an investigation.

When the 6221 Hollymont house was under investigation in 1976, other than Don Jolly, the property's owner, who was thirty-three (33) at the time, I was perhaps the oldest person present, all of twenty-seven. This time around, this author was only ...well let's just say a lot older. You do the math this time, for when I think about the passage of years, it's somewhat depressing. I guess time really does fly when having fun?

The real question now is, did Regina's spirit cause the damage to our instrument which just happens to be in the shape of a backwards "R"? Many questions, but as yet, no real answers. Hopefully, we will return again to this fascinating Hollymont home when feasible.

What do all the aforementioned cases have in common? They all lack even the remotest possibility of being manifestations of psychokinesis as there were not any dysfunctional family environments to speak of, nor was there the presence of pubescent and/or adolescent children or young adults. While this, in and of itself, does not in any way prove the existence of discarnate intelligence through a process of elimination, it does reduce the number of probable hypotheses to explain the encountered phenomena.

However, just because the phenomenon does not conform to our criteria of poltergeists, does not automatically throw it into a discarnate domain (let's not forget the bioholographic animation theory discussed earlier). In all probability, there are numerous other alternative theories that have not, as yet, been proposed that might just as easily explain such phenomena.

What then constitutes evidence supporting the existence of discarnate intelligence or survival? For one, the phenomena displayed would have to occur in an environment free of any potential humanly generated RSPK and secondly, there would have to be some way of differentiating between what I've referred to as bioholographic animation from a past traumatic event and discarnate intelligence.

This is, of course, assuming that such is even possible given our current level of understanding of this phenomenon and virtually non-existent tools for measuring what we do not yet know.

The most compelling evidence, in lieu of hard scientific data, is the voluminous anecdotal literature existing within virtually every culture on earth from the last five thousand years. Such literature, once sanitized of all hallucinations, hysteria, illusion, misidentification, religious zeal and fraud, strongly speaks to the endurance of phenomena that can, at least for the moment, be most appropriately described as discarnate. In the end, perhaps all of these differential classifications boil down to a process of elimination and subjective interpretation.

In the end we are left in pretty much the same uncomfortable place we were when we started. We cannot totally prove or disprove any hypothesis. Nevertheless, we should remember that at the primitive stage parapsychology currently resides (due primarily to the paltry funding it has received over the last one hundred and twenty-five years), we are essentially left doing little more than measuring the effects of an unknown cause.

However, to conclude that this type of phenomenon is no more than the product of an emotionally disturbed mind, would indeed be a haunting thought.

END.

Chapter 2:
THE REAL LIFE ENTITY CASE

As Published In:

PSI Journal of Investigative Psychical Research
Vol. 4(1), 2008, pp. 9-26

Beginning in February 1983, when 20th Century Fox released The Entity, there has been considerable speculation, conjecture, rumor and misinformation regarding what factually transpired during the investigation of the real-life case as compared to the novel and motion picture. As dramatic license was exercised in both the book and the feature film, the result was a significantly fictionalized account of the actual events.

Making matters even worse is the fact that the original articles published on The Entity case were in scientific journals or periodicals that were not generally available to the public. Desiring to set matters straight on what really occurred thirty-four years ago in a Los Angeles suburb, I am reprinting the original article with only minor upgrades and adjustments to compensate for three decades of time and acquired knowledge regarding this type of research.

ABSTRACT

Beginning on August 22, 1974 (not 1976, as indicated in the scroll at the end of The Entity movie) a ten-week investigation of a reportedly haunted house located in Culver City, California, demonstrated evidence that it was infested with and frequented by occurrences of poltergeist activity in the form of object movements, collectively observed apparitions, as well as cold and stench spots. Investigative visits resulted in six consecutive encounters between the author/investigators, numerous assistants, and various forms of phenomena reported here.

Additionally, this particular case displayed a stereotypic, anxiety-ridden emotional environment generally associated with poltergeist incidents; teeming with pubescent and adolescent children with overt animosities existing between all family members.

The house demonstrated a heretofore unknown, or at least unreported manifestation in the form of dynamic 3-dimensional lights that behaved unpredictably in that they were not consistently photogenic in nature although appearing to the unaided eye as visible light for lengthy periods. With the limited resources, space and time available in this investigation, the subjective conclusions reached was that the observed phenomena were of a multiple and differential source origin, and cannot as yet be explained by any coherent theory involving RSPK or discarnate intelligence.

The enigmatic and inconsistent behavior of employed instrumentation further reinforces the fact that the causal element in this situation is an almost total unknown, which cannot even vaguely be operationally or functionally defined, and therefore remains as it always has been: a phenomenon.

****

It becomes dismayingly clear upon comprehensive review and examination of both research and anecdotal literature within parapsychology, specifically in the area of poltergeists, hauntings, apparitions and ghosts, that it is one enigma of nature that does not easily, if at all, lend itself to empirical evaluation due to its seeming randomness, scarcity, and general lack of consistently and predictability (or in some cases, believability). Additionally, it is quite obvious that no one has developed or provided a successful method or technique of physical documentation that has been able to substantiate the presence of these phenomena to the satisfaction of the scientific community.

Nevertheless, considerable research has been done in the collection of data over many years, and certain longitudinal patterns of trends have emerged regarding specific phenomena, especially in the case of poltergeists. There have been numerous theories put worth to account for the abundance of both physical and non-physical phenomena related to such occurrences, but as yet, no one hypothesis has proven viable.

As numerous academic investigators have pointed out, it is unlikely that these phenomena have changes in their nature throughout the centuries simply as a product of our investigations and formative beliefs about them. However, it is highly probable that our attitude towards these phenomena has been considerably altered from their original status; the belief that they stem from a discarnate source.

As hardened physical scientists, it is almost inconceivable to consider, let alone accept, the possibility of a non-corporeal intelligence influencing and directing the actions of physical matter and energy. These were the concepts of and early suspicions of our ancestors in psychical research, for what they suspected the poltergeist of being was a mischievous, prank-playing, ghost that derived some form of pleasure from tormenting individuals.

Modern, academic parapsychologists, however, strongly influenced by the success of our physically oriented, technological world, have conveniently provided a new theory (and only a theory) for poltergeist activity, which suggests that living human agents are providing the energy responsible for the phenomena occurring during poltergeist outbreaks.

This easier-to-accept theory for many, intimates that this "energy" given off by certain particular individuals is directly related to, and possibility that product of, the psychodynamic atmosphere and environment of the afflicted residence or that of a single individual.

Admittedly, the majority of work done in this area at least superficially appears to support and reinforce this belief of recurrent spontaneous psychokinesis (RSPK) from human beings. However, whatever "energy" is responsible for these paranormal phenomena, it cannot, at present, be detected, measured or quantified, which in fact, leaves us essentially where we began.

The investigation of Doris Bither's (not Carlotta Moran, that was the character's name in the book and movie) house came about as a result of her overhearing Kerry Gaynor's (my associate at the time) conversation with a friend about haunted houses while at the former Hunters Book store in Westwood Village. Doris approached Gaynor in a somewhat hesitant manner and informed him that her house was haunted. After a brief discussion with Doris, Gaynor informed her that he would contact his associate and get back to her as soon as possible.

On our first visit to Doris' tiny Culver City house on August 22, 1974, we spent the evening securing detailed information pertaining to the alleged phenomena that had been occurring over the past few months. The family consisted of Doris, a petite, mid-to-late thirty-year-old woman, a six year-old daughter, three sons, one ten, thirteen and sixteen. We questioned all members of the family with the exception of the six year-old daughters, whom we never saw.

Their accounts were fairly uniform in reference to a particular apparition whom they called "Mr. Whose-it." The alleged apparition would appear in semi-solid form and was well over six feet in height, according to their testimony. Both Doris and her eldest son claimed to have seen two dark, solid figures with Asian features appear from out of nowhere within their mother's bedroom, who at times appeared to be struggling with each other.

This particular event occurred several times, with one episode where Doris claimed to have physically bumped into the apparition in the hallway. Neither Doris nor her eldest son would accept the possibility that the apparitions might have been imagined or simply prowlers or intruders who forcibly entered the house.

Doris believed most adamantly that these "Asian beings" were evil and indeed was quite emotionally distraught at the prospect of her family's possible imminent danger. Considering what Doris was about to tell us, this belief on her part was well within the boundaries of rational thinking.

Undoubtedly, the most extraordinary occurrence, which Doris related to us, was that she had been sexually assaulted by three semi-visible beings. Two of the smaller beings or apparitions literally held her down by the wrists and ankles, while the remaining form entered her. According to Doris' testimony, this event took place on several separate occasions, each time leaving behind large and distinct black and blue wounds, especially around the ankles, wrists, breasts and groin area of the inner thighs.

Even more dramatic was Doris' claim that during one particular attack, her eldest son overheard the scuffle and entered the bedroom. According to Doris, he witnessed her being tossed around like a rag doll by the entities. She alleges that when her son came to her aid, an invisible force picked him up and threw him backwards into the wall. The son corroborated his mother's story, speaking of the sheer terror he experienced during that struggle.

Unfortunately, Doris' claim of "spectral rape" could not be substantiated due to her failing to report the incident to medical or other authorities. The fact that these alleged instances of paranormal rape occurred several weeks prior to our initial arrival, prevented us from observing her already healed bruises.

Understandably, the resulting household environment was one of extreme anxiety and Doris' relationship with her four children was anything but cordial, in fact, it was downright belligerent. I will refrain from going into all the bizarre stories that were related to us for we cannot substantiate them.

Needless to say, after hearing Doris' incredible story, Gaynor and I looked at each other, collectively both rolled our eyes back while shaking our heads. Our initial impression was to totally discount Doris' claims and simply refer her to one of the psychiatrists at the NPI.

However, as we ourselves would have been somewhat embarrassed to even reiterate her totally incredulous account to a medical professional back at UCLA, we decided to think about it for a while rather than act on it. In retrospect, this hesitation turned out to be a wise decision.

However, a few days hence, Doris called to inform us that five individuals outside her family had now seen the alleged apparitions. We immediately decided to return to the house armed with cameras and a tape recorder. Preceding this return, an investigation into the background of the house revealed two male deaths from natural causes since its construction, neither of which, in our opinion, was relevant to the study of the phenomena occurring within the residence.

Upon our second visit this house, we became increasingly aware of the broken-down, shabby nature of the wooden dwelling that had been twice condemned by the city. Nevertheless, the second visit to this house marked the beginning of what was to become our most extraordinary investigation to date.

An intriguing factor, which in our opinion is highly significant, was that from the very first occasion we entered Doris' bedroom, we both immediately noticed that the temperature was unusually low in comparison to the rest of the house, even though it was a hot August night and all the bedroom's windows were closed.

This peculiar and penetrating cold varied in intensity as we moved throughout the bedroom, again reminiscent of "cold spots" experienced in other investigations. Also noticed upon first entering Doris' bedroom was a strong olfactory sensation (smell) of rotting, decomposing flesh, such as might be experienced in a physiology lab or a morgue. Both the stench and cold spots faded in and out irregularly, sometimes completely disappearing. A thorough examination of the house and its immediate surround offered no explanation for these anomalistic effects.

Another particularly noteworthy physical sensation within the bedroom was a strong sense of overpressure, that is, the feeling within the inner ear of being at the bottom of a very deep pool. Interestingly, this particular effect is perhaps one of the most common subjectively experienced sensations in suspected haunted/poltergeist environments. Who knows what it represents.

The two cameras we arrived with on our second visit were a Polaroid SX-70 and a Honeywell Pentax 35 mm. SLR loaded with high-speed infrared film. The first of many to come, seemingly inexplicable happenings, occurred while Gaynor was talking to the elder son in the kitchen.

Gaynor was standing approximately one foot away from the lower cabinets when suddenly the cabinet door swung open. A frying pan flew out of the cabinet, following a curved path to the floor over 2.5 feet away, hitting with quite a thud. Now, of course, the immediate thing to surmise is that the pan was leaning against the cabinet door and finally pushed it open as it fell out. But we cannot accept this explanation for the trajectory of the pan as it came out of the cabinet was elliptical. It was seemingly propelled out of the cabinet by a substantial force.

After carefully examining the kitchen cabinet from which the pan was propelled we proceeded to Doris' bedroom. There were four of us in the bedroom, which appeared to be the focal point of the phenomena according to Doris. Her friend Candy, who had joined us on this evening, and whom we were told was psychic, concurred.

We took a preliminary shot of the bedroom with the Polaroid SX-70 that came out perfectly. After about fifteen minutes Candy shouted out that there was something in the corner of the bedroom. After hearing Candy's shouts I rapidly ran back into the bedroom from the kitchen where I was examining the developed first photograph and immediately aimed and fired the Polaroid camera.

The resulting photograph was completely bleached white, as though exposed to some powerful magnetic field and/or ionizing radiation, which if present, might have had strong adverse effects on our bodies, perhaps even to the degree of causing burns and extensively damaging cells.

About fifteen minutes later Candy again screamed out that there was something in the corner (not that she could see, but sense) and accordingly I fired off the Polaroid. Once again, the picture was badly bleached, although not as severely as the first one.

Inasmuch as we were both aware of my rather dubious distinction of being a "film fogger," we decided it best to trade off taking pictures with each camera. However, at no time did either of us see anything in this corner of the bedroom.

A few minutes later, I took another picture, but this time it was in another room of the

38

house, and oddly enough, the photograph came out near perfect except for lack of proper focusing adjustments. Following this, Gaynor used the Polaroid, as I did again, both within the bedroom, resulting in two perfectly normal photographs. It's interesting to note that on both of these last shots, Candy did not sense the presence within the room, as she did earlier.

The next picture I took facing the door to the bedroom. The motivation for shooting at that particular time and in that direction was the sudden onset of a cold current of air accompanied by a pervasive stench flowing in from the direction of the closed bedroom door. Curiously, this picture turned out to be the most interesting one of the night. On the floor just inches from the door were a small ball of light about one foot in diameter. The baffling thing was, that none of us saw it, but the camera certainly recorded something.

Standing there in amazement for several minutes discussing this phenomenal picture, I happened to glance over toward the bedroom's eastern window and suddenly observed several rapidly moving, electric-blue balls of light.

Immediately raising the Polaroid, aiming and firing in the direction of the curtains over the window, I produced a picture that was once again blurred and badly bleached in nature. It should be stated here that the only light within the bedroom during all the aforementioned shots was a single candle's illumination and the flashcubes of the camera.

The attempted photographs of the rapidly moving, glowing blue starbursts did not reveal the actual display that I observed. But within a short period of time, Candy told us that there was something standing directly in front of her. Once again, I fired the Polaroid and the resulting picture was most bizarre.

Her face was completely bleached out, yet her dress and the surrounding background of curtains and various objects within the bedroom were quite clear and distinct. The bleaching closely resembled that which is on the majority of pictures taken until that point.

A short while later Candy again informed us that there was something right in front of her. This time Gaynor took the picture with the Polaroid, developing similar to the previous one. Beautiful detail was picked up in the curtains in the background, her dress was clear to the point of recognizing detail on its buttons, yet her face was completely obliterated by the same type of bleaching or fogging which afflicted the earlier photographs.

It is important to emphasize, that without moving his position so much as a hair, Gaynor took another picture of Candy with the Polaroid as a control approximately two minutes later. Before Gaynor fired the shot, Candy said the presence was now gone, and the resulting photograph came out perfect; completely absent of any fogging or light diffusion. Gaynor took another control photograph of the bedroom and it too turned out quite normal, without any aberrations on the emulsion.

It is important to note that when Candy said there was something (whatever it was) in front of her, the picture was severely bleached, while minutes later when she said it was gone, the ensuing picture fired by Gaynor demonstrated high resolution and clarity, that is, no fogging.

At this point, Gaynor passed the Polaroid over to me. I was about to place it on the dresser across the room after checking the camera to determine how many pictures remained. After examining the camera's number window while walking towards the bureau, the Polaroid suddenly and inexplicably took the last photograph by itself. I was fully aware at all times that my hands were nowhere near the button that activates the camera.

My reaction was one of absolute amazement in conjunction with a little fear as I was positive that I did not cause the camera to fire. The resulting photograph, somehow occurring without the expected flash, showed utter blackness with nothing whatsoever discernible within it.

The infrared film in the 35-mm. camera on this evening was inadvertently exposed due to our own carelessness. This marked the end of our second visit to this most unusual house.

On the third night we visited the residence, which was approximately one week later, a young female photographer accompanied us from a Brentwood camera shop. Almost immediately upon entering Doris' bedroom, the young woman remarked quite emphatically that the horrible stench was making her nauseous.

Our third to Doris' house was most notable in that it was the first occasion where we both collectively witnessed identical visual phenomena. On more than twenty separate occasions, all of us present in the bedroom, including Doris and the female photographer, simultaneously observed what appeared to be small, pulsing flashes of light.

It was at this point that we decided to further darken the candle-lit room and hung several heavy quilts and bedspreads over the windows and curtains. Our attempt partially succeeded in that we significantly attenuated the outside light.

The change in light intensity within the bedroom did not affect our most unusual luminous "friend" that now appeared even more brilliant against the darkened surround. It should be noted that we both alternately watched the various window areas in the hope of determining if the source of light was originating from outside the house, perhaps from a passing vehicle or neighbor's flashlight.

After several such attempts, we were satisfied that whatever these moving, pulsing lights were, they were not originating from outside the house as the thick quilts draped over the window curtains would have easily told us of such an photonic intrusion. The sudden and rapid appearance and disappearance of the lights on this night made it virtually impossible to obtain any photographs, regardless of the fact that it appeared over ten times on the front of the bar area alone.

Overall, the third session at Doris' house netted us very little in the way of objective photographic evidence similar to that of the second encounter. Not one of the photographs taken by either the Polaroid SX-70 camera or the 35 mm. loaded with infrared film showed anything of interest.

Similarly, out attempt to record the luminous anomalies (radiation?) visually observed with X-ray dental tabs placed on the walls around the room and a sheet of 8" x 10" film sandwiched between radiation intensifying plates proved equally fruitless. Although the lights were photographically elusive, they nevertheless visually appeared both circular and triangular in their displays to all of us.

We learned the next day that our attractive female photographer, after being dropped off by us at her apartment, became so overpoweringly ill from the effects of the bedroom's malodorous environment that she regurgitated heavily before retiring.

Our fourth excursion to Doris' home further heightened our already peaking curiosity, for the light show witnessed on our last visit was in no way comparable to what was about to occur, exactly one week later.

The purpose of this evening was to conduct a séance (not generally advised) with the hope that it would bring forth whatever phenomenon was related to this locale or woman. The séance circle consisted of some eight individuals, including more than ten spectators, many of who came with cameras loaded with high-speed infrared film with IR flashes, and high-speed black and white film with deep-red filtered strobes.

On this night we all observed what appeared to be extremely intense lights, which were not stable either in size or luminosity. The lights were at times three- dimensional in nature, reaching out between various individuals within the circle. Judging from the rapidly changing size, dimensional characteristics and intensity of the lights observed, it is our opinion that these manifestations were not fraudulently created, nor the result of collective hallucinations.

In order for such unique lighting effects to have been artificially generated, large, high-powered laser equipment would have had to have been employed, requiring extremely sophisticated and technical skills.

The type of three-dimensional lights observed on this occasion are almost exclusively restricted to laser light shows, and from the conversations with Doris and her children, we were totally convinced that not one of these individuals would even understand the functional principles underlying lasers, let alone how to operate one within a light show.

The lights frequently displayed a sort of dimensional netting or grating effect, resembling Fourier convolutions observed in holography, undulating, expanding and contracting to encompass the entire corner of the bedroom at various times.

Another factor prohibiting any attempts at fraud with sophisticated laser equipment was the very lack of available power within this residence in that the electrical circuitry was installed shortly after the old house was constructed resulting in it being weak and faulty in nature.

It is our estimation that the power of a krypton or argon gas laser with peak power output somewhere between 1-3 watts (remember, this is 1974, not 2007 where tabletop petawatt lasers are not uncommon) with a coherence length of at least fifteen feet would be required to produce the optical effects observed on this evening.

Understanding that lasers (especially in 1974) operated at about 5% maximum efficiency, means that the input power must exceed approximately 55-60 watts at over 10 kilovolts. Where this amount of power could have been drawn from if fraud was attempted, is certainly beyond our knowledge. Such demands would have required a separate generator and transformer (power supply).

All of this cumbersome apparatus would have certainly necessitated a relatively large space to erect and operate, and considering the small size of the bedroom that was literally packed with people, such available space was, an impossibility. And of course, let's not forget the cost of renting or owning such equipment.

Doris' eldest son informed us, prior to the beginning of the séance, that there were certain record albums that appeared to, in his words, "infuriate it." Strangely enough, these albums were by Black Sabbath and Uriah Heep and both specific songs mentioned by the son dealt with devil worship. Both Doris and her sixteen year-old son were of the belief that the phenomena within their home had some connection with evil or the devil itself, given its belligerent propensities.

Much to our surprise, when the records were playing the songs indicated by Doris' son, the anomalous light activity dramatically increased, reaching a crescendo in conjunction with the music, in fact, with specific passages within each of the two songs.

Two distinct possibilities existed with regard to the music's effects; one was that the frequency and amplitude modulation of the mechanical compression waves generated by the music were somehow directly affecting the source producing the phenomena; or, the same elements of the music were alternatively affecting the people in the environment which caused the emission of an unknown biological energy (RSPK) that in turn reinforced the phenomena.

Aliens Above, Ghosts Below by Barry E. Taff

Since both albums contained very high-strung music, either hypothesis has equal merit in this situation.

With three 35 mm. cameras continuously firing at these oscillating greenish-white, three-dimensional lights, only one photograph depicted anything significant. The camera loaded with Kodak Tri-X black and white film with a deep-red filtered strobe captured what appears to be a small ball of light flying across the corner of the room. The sixth obtained photograph displayed an object bearing strong resemblance to a comet with a tail behind it.

However, due to the fact that we did not have any background reference against which this shot was taken, no estimate of its size, speed or distance from the wall could be made. Because these exposures were pushed in development past 6000 ASA, the available background was extremely grainy, which further hindered analysis (See photograph 1).

This photograph was the only meaningful one that was obtained that evening, for not one of the cameras captured the images we saw with our unaided eyes. The three-dimensional lights lasting more than ten minutes at-a-time, which was collectively observed, also failed to appear in any of the photographs.

However, several other pictures showed what appeared to be faces or figures outlined in light against a sliding closet door. But, as these images are highly subjective in nature, much like a Rorschach, we did not subject them to further analysis. Another photograph depicted an intense light against the south-facing wall in several separate frames.

The professional photographer who took these pictures was convinced that this exposure could not be explained away as irregularities in paint or a "hot spot" of reflection. The photographer was similarly convinced that the flying ball of light, discussed earlier, which he also caught, was not an artifact of overdeveloping or scratch marks on the negative.

The criticisms raised against the facial and figure outlines on the walls were, in most respects valid, in that the lack of uniformity of paint on the bedroom walls in conjunction with the slight penetrating power of the pushed Kodak Tri-X film could have conceivably accounted for these unidentifiable figures, which unfortunately were not recognizable by everyone examining the photographs.

Our fifth visit to Doris' house resulted in a large-scale magnification of all phenomena. We began by duct taping large black poster boards up on the walls and ceiling of the bedroom, all of which were numbered and identified with a magnetic orientation. White duct tape was placed between the dark panels that formed a grid network, like graph paper, therein providing us with a reference for further attempts at photographing the lights. Black poster boards were also used to seal off all the light entrances into the bedroom that rendered the environment almost pitch black.

With over 30 individuals, some of whom were volunteers from our UCLA Parapsychology laboratory, the lights returned and were even more brilliant than before, as well as demonstrating a direct responsiveness to our verbal suggestions. The three-dimensional lights seemingly reacted and responded to our jokes and various provoking remarks, especially those of Doris.

In fact, when Doris began to swear and curse at the lights, assuming that they were in some manner related to the entities that attacked her, the lights, always appearing bright lime green in color, intensified beyond all previous displays. The room being almost completely dark further enhanced the brightness of these excited luminous structures. It almost seemed as if the lights were a direct product of, or counterpart to Doris' psychic state, waxing and waning in accordance with her emotional fluctuations.

This evening marked the first occasion where we attempted to establish communication with whatever it was in the house. Communication with the lights consisted of our asking them (or it) to blink out coded (numbered) responses on different numbered black poster boards on the walls of the bedroom's corner where the phenomena seemed to emanate from; two blinks in panel three for "yes" and four flashes in panel six for "no."

To our mutual amazement and astonishment, the lights almost immediately responded to our request. The answers out our questions, coming as numbered flashes of light, were sharp and fast, illuminating the numbers on the selected panels, and thus indicating that we may have been dealing with some type of incorporeal or discarnate intelligence.

From the observed modulations in light activity, which displayed both vertical and horizontal parallax when seen from different angles, it is our collective opinion that we did indeed communicate with something, whether it being Doris' unconscious mind, who was always in the room, or the agency itself (conceding for a moment that it did separately exist).

The answers we received could not be confirmed, and never really made any sense. The most intense response was to the questions as to whether or not "it" feared extreme cold, such as with supercooling or absolute zero. To this, the light responded most dramatically, almost as if it knew exactly what we meant and was disturbed at the thought of it. It should be remembered however, that these are no more than our speculations based upon our observations.

One of the more interesting events of this night involved an extremely sensitive Geiger counter that we had brought along in the hope that it might reveal some significant information about the phenomena occurring within the house. The instrument, sensitive in the milliroengten region, behaved oddly in that when the lights were at peak intensity, the previously constant background radiation registering on the device suddenly dropped off to zero.

When the light activity began to dwindle, fade and finally abate, the Geiger counter's meter returned to its normal level of ambient background radiation, which is generally comprised of high-energy cosmic rays from solar events, deep space, as well as other stray sub-atomic particles which penetrate through to the Earth's atmosphere due to their speed and energy.

Although this peculiar reaction of our Geiger counter occurred only that one evening, we must take it into consideration for the possible implication is noteworthy.

There are three possible alternatives regarding the Geiger counter's behavior. The first, is that whatever energy was causing the various phenomena in Doris' house were somehow setting up its own field and therein scattering, deflecting, defusing or absorbing the background radiation, similar to that of an energy sink.

Perhaps this phenomena's power source is ambient background radiation or noise? The second choice is that the phenomena present, whatever it happens to be, generates a moderately high-strength electrostatic or magnetic field that is known to have adverse effects on the tubes within Geiger counters, sometimes to the point of nulling them out, as with our device.

The final possibility is that the Geiger counter itself was simply malfunctioning. This latter hypothesis is not valid in this situation because the unit accurately registered the emission of radiation from my tritium-dialed watch both prior to and following the evening's excursion.

The photographs resulting from this evening's encounter surprisingly did not reveal the incredibly detailed images of the corpuscular masses of light we observed with our naked eyes. Instead, were brilliant arcs of light, one essentially framing Doris. The others were floating in the middle of the bedroom when Doris was not even present in the room.

Aliens Above, Ghosts Below by Barry E. Taff

We believe that these arcs of light represent a time-dilated rendering of the rapidly moving, corpuscular masses of light that our camera's shutter speed was not fast enough to stop its rapid motion. Therefore, instead of balls of light, we captured what amounts to tracks or, more precisely, time-lapse photos. Similar to what you get if you photograph stars on long time exposures without a moving platform. As disappointing as these results were, in a strange sort of a way, they helped us rule out fraud. (See photos 2 & 3).

From a scientific point of view, what is absolutely fascinating about photograph one is the fact that the arc appears to be floating in free space? It is crucial to understand that behind the arc's image, two bedroom walls meet at a 90-degree angle. Therefore, if the image of the arc were projected against the wall, it would appear bent at a 90-degree angle in accordance with the wall.

The fact that it is not signifies that the arc or it's source, the corpuscular masses of light, were in fact, flying over and around Doris's head at the time. Exactly what we all observed. Equally compelling is the fact that the arc perfectly frames Doris, the subject or focus of the haunting. Certainly, this is not a coincidence!

In photograph two, there are depicted two separate, inverted arcs that give the appearance of being at a 90-degree angle to each other. However, the perpendicular walls described above are now far off center (to the left) and the wall behind the dual arcs is flat (opaque curtain covering a large bedroom window).

When Adrian Vance, the West Coast Editor of Popular Photography examined the negatives of these photos, he was as perplexed as we were. According to Vance, the very nature of optical glass in a 35 mm. SLR camera prohibits such inverted arcs from occurring. Yet here they are. Vance could not conceive of any known artifact or anomaly to account for such images.

These enigmatic physical effects, although remaining unexplained, brought our fifth encounter with Doris' house to a close, at least we assumed it did. The next evening we received a frantic phone call from Doris informing us that all the black poster boards that we so carefully taped up on the walls and ceiling had been torn down. That literally "all hell" had broken loose that afternoon, which apparently climaxed at one point with the poster boards.

Doris told us that while she was in the bathroom, which is directly adjacent to the bedroom, she suddenly heard (quite loudly) the boards being forcibly torn from the walls.

Upon entering the bedroom, Doris observed, as we did later that evening, every poster board lying down along the floor of the various walls, and the duct tape, which is utilized on occasion to fasten aircraft parts together, literally hanging from the walls and ceiling, as if pulled by some unseen hand.

This phone report prompted our return to the house that night, allowing us to observe that the tape and boards were pulled away from the walls with such force that large portions of paint and plaster beneath the tape were removed along with it.

It was suggested by several of our colleagues that a sudden, sharp rise is temperature and humidity could possibly account for such an occurrence, in that the tape's adhesive power would be significantly diminished to the point where it could no longer maintain the board's weight against gravity on the wall.

However, such a change in tape bonding strength would not result in it hanging from the ceiling and the plaster and paint being pulled from the wall beneath it. That is, even if we conceded for one moment that there was a significant increase in temperature and humidity to radically weaken the tape, which we do not.

It should also be pointed out that the duct tape used here is the same as that employed near high-temperature jet engines in supersonic fighter aircraft and thus would not be affected by any conceivable room temperature change.

Upon examining the fallen poster boards and the tape surrounding them, it was apparent that the tape was still quite sticky and fully capable of supporting the relatively light boards on the walls. Also apparent that evening was the intense presence of the penetrating cold, which in itself defeats the argument regarding the rise in temperature affecting the tape.

The foul stench was back with a vengeance as well. Doris told us of more activity on the part of the apparitions within her house, much of which was similar to what she had previously reported to us. After calming her down at some hour past midnight, we decided to leave.

Our sixth session at the house took place five days later and in most respects was a repeat performance of our fifth visit with the exception that the lights repeatedly began to take shape; forming the lime green, partially three-dimensional, apparitional image of a very large, muscular man whose shoulders, head and arms were readily discernible by the more than twenty individuals' present. However, no salient facial characteristics of this apparition were discernible.

Suddenly, we heard two loud thuds. Turning quickly in response I observed the unconscious bodies of Jeff and Craig that had hit the floor with a resounding noise. Apparently, observing the apparition was just too much for them and they simply passed out. Needless to say, they never worked with us again on any investigations.

On this evening we came armed with nine cameras loaded with very high-speed Tri-X and recording film, all of which was eventually pushed in development past 6400 ASA. On stationary tripods were a Hasselblad, a Bronica, and a Nikon FTN with a motor drive, all with wide-angle lenses.

In keeping with the previous séances in the house, the three-dimensional lights appeared almost immediately upon starting the session and were again seemingly reinforced by the record albums, Doris' verbalizations and the emotions of all present within the room.

The display of lights this evening was so intense that they easily illuminated the numbered poster boards covering the walls of the bedroom's corner. Even the clothes of the individuals observing the lights from outside the séance circle were brightly lit by the luminous activity. In fact, so piercing were the lights that they were seen to reflect off the camera's aluminum frame and lenses, all of which were aimed directly at the corner where the optical display was concentrated.

Consequently, we expected to obtain some reasonable representation of what our eyes were seeing, especially since the Hasselblad and Bronica were set at five-minute time exposures; being held open for the duration of several lengthy bursts of light activity. It should be emphasized that during the dramatic optical manifestations before us, all of the seven mobile cameras were continuously firing, the noises of which could be heard behind us. In other words, the cameras were simultaneously firing at the lights as we were observing them at their peak intensity.

Not surprising to us, considering the past two attempts at photographing the lights, all the negatives were perfectly clear, as if no light whatsoever was present to expose the film. Even the motor-driven, strobed, 35 mm. cameras with extremely fast black and white film pushed as far as possible in development, which on a previous occasion (4th) provided us with the flying ball of light, failed to capture anything.

The events that occurred during the sixth visit were seemingly paradoxical. Lights sufficiently intense to illuminate the darkened room should have extensively overexposed our fast film, especially with time exposures exceeding five minutes. What type or kind of light will reflect off solid objects, including lenses, cast shadows, be visible to the naked eye and yet not pass through the camera lens to expose the film? This of course, begs the question as to whether we were actually "seeing" anything at all. More on this aspect, later.

In the attempt to answer this most puzzling question, we speculated on the possibility that long-wave ultraviolet radiation, just above visible light, was in some manner generated by this phenomenon, which in an extremely dark environment such as the room we were in, is occasionally visible to the unaided eye of young persons (which we all were in those early years).

The presence of this form of light or radiation might conceivably explain the absence of photographs in that ultraviolet radiation is almost totally attenuated by conventional optical glass of which the camera lenses are constructed.

Such being the situation, theoretically, the lack of a spectrometer, or the use of specialized color film with the appropriate lenses and filters that are sensitive to ultraviolet radiation, allowed us only to visually experience the small amount of seemingly visible light reflection and refraction off the lenses. This, of course, prevented our validating the presence of long-wave ultraviolet radiation.

Another intriguing possibility arose with the suggestion that the greenish-white light collectively observed by more than twenty individuals (only with eyes open) was the result of localized atmospheric gases being ionized and emitting light. The prime candidate for this theory would logically be xenon or neon with representative ionization thresholds of 12.13 eV (electron volts) and 21.56 eV. Xenon might display its characteristic green spectral line at 4671Å, while 4912Å and 5401Å of neon might also be accountable for the greenish-white color of light observed.

Considering the relatively low ionization threshold of such atoms in these atmospheric gases, it is conceivable that the presence of some unknown energy source strong enough to affect the tube in a Geiger counter, could generate such luminous effects. However, lights as emitted from these ionized atmospheric gases, should be not only visible, but be very photogenic, especially at close range in a darkened environment. Yet this manner of light was not. This intriguing mystery was the end of our sixth night of investigation at Doris' house.

Given the nature of what was just described, there is a distinct possibility that what we had visually observed was actually not "seen" at all.

Normally, light is either emitted or reflected by objects around us. Those photons enter our eye to strike the retina, then the optic nerve. The related neurological signals are then sent to the occipital region of our brain for processing. This is the way we visually perceive our world. But what if we are able to perceive an event not through this conventional mechanism, but directly within the brain itself?

The best analogy of this mechanism is the incredibly detailed imagery we experience during dreaming when there is no photonic stimulation from the eyes, yet there is rapid eye movement (REM), which seemingly tracks internally generated imagery. What I would really like to know regarding REM, is on exactly what screen in our brain is this imagery displaying itself on? Perhaps there are situations where our brain is stimulated via environmental energy that emulates normal vision?

The pioneering work of Dr. Michael Persinger, a Canadian neurophysiologist who has placed electrodes within head-hugging helmets worn by subjects to study the mental effects and reactions to the applications of weak, low frequency, electromagnetic fields, simulating what might be experienced during the encounter with geophysical anomalies.

The results of Dr. Persinger research, clearly indicates that our brains are extremely pliable in terms of their susceptibility to subtle changes in the surrounding electromagnetic fields (EMF's). Such changes can induce both visual and auditory hallucinations. While this fascinating energetic effect has been clinically validated well beyond reasonable doubt, there are still some nagging questions that linger on this matter as related to what transpired during this case.

Unlike what is frequently voiced in movies and television, there is no such thing as a "mass hallucination", while there is mass hysteria. Apparently, while our brains are essentially the same, there are sufficient neurophysiological differences from person-to-person to prevent identical visual/auditory hallucinations from similar EMF's. More simply, the effects of such EMF's are very subjective in nature. These types of interactions with the environment might explain some haunting effects as well as UFO encounters.

The last, and perhaps the most significant aspect regarding potential psychophysiological effects of EMFs, is that if we are indeed this reactive to such low-amplitude environmental energies, then might not our perception, reasoning, judgment and behavior suffer as a direct consequence?

If our brains really are this incredibly pliable, are we not always at risk while driving, flying, fighting a war, conducting business, testifying as a witness in a trial or any human activity that requires a clear and focused mind that is unhindered by mind-altering influences? Then again, what is the probability of running into such "energetic anomalies" and being so sensitive to them?

But, how do we account for the high degree of convergence in what numerous individuals observed in this case? We cannot. It is also important to realize that just because something can be simulated or recreated by means other than the real event, does not preclude the actual event from occurring.

Moreover, just because Stanley Kubrick made a brilliant movie about our landing on the moon before we actually did (2001: A Space Odyssey, MGM, 1968), does not mean that the "real" event did not occur at Tranquility Base in July of 1969. This type of thinking is a good example of faulty logic.

Our seventh visit began with Doris informing us that on the previous night, which was exactly six days following our last stay, "all hell" had again broken loose in the house. Doris detailed her and her son's experience with a pair of candelabras which of their own accord literally took off from the kitchen sink to fly across the room (about 10-12 feet) and strike her in the arm.

Doris' twelve year-old son fully corroborated her story in that he witnessed the event, as the flying candelabras barely missed him in their attack on his mother. Doris and her son also related another incident to us which occurred the same day in which a large wooden board, firmly nailed to the wall beneath one of the bedroom windows, was literally torn from its secured position, again as if by some unseen hands, and with what seemed tremendous force, was propelled more than fifteen feet across the room, missing his head by mere inches. Fortunately, Doris dodged in time to avoid being struck herself.

We both observed the rather large red bruise on Doris' forearm sustained from the flying candelabras, which had already begun to raise a considerable welt. Upon entering the bedroom we were again greeted by barren walls as all the poster boards were, once again, on the floor with the tape surrounding them fully intact.

Aliens Above, Ghosts Below by Barry E. Taff

At numerous locations on the walls the tape was left hanging with large sections of dislodged paint and plaster beside them, while everything else within the bedroom, as on previous occasions, remained untouched.

Again, Doris claimed to have heard the boards being torn down. Needless to say, the thought did cross our minds that Doris was the one tearing the poster boards down and was simply lying about it. Unfortunately, history has indicated that it is not that uncommon for individuals within such volatile environments to occasionally fraudulently "create" additional events to maintain our attention.

Accompanying us on this evening was Dr. Thelma Moss, head of our laboratory at UCLA's Neuropsychiatric Institute, various assistants from the lab, several psychiatrists from the institute who professed an interest in such phenomena, and Frank De Felitta, a renowned writer, producer, and director of The Stately Ghosts of England (NBC, 1965).

De Felitta brought along one of his professional cameramen (Mort Zarkoff) with a 16-mm. motion picture camera mounting a zoom lens and loaded with packs of high-speed black and white as well as color film.

After the re-taping of the poster boards back onto the walls, we decided to begin another séance. There were some faint glimmerings of light, but they were in no way intense enough to cause any real excitement. Recalling how the earlier attempts with time-exposure photography had failed, we did not seriously expect to record anything substantial on film. Such indeed was the case. At first, even the playing of the record albums with their extreme emotional response of the observing crowd, failed to produce anything of value.

Sadly, those attending only on this evening did not witness the "magnificent" display of swirling, three-dimensional lights or the apparition that had occurred within the house. However, at one point during the séance, Gaynor suggested to the "presence" in the house, whatever it was, that it should demonstrate its strength by again tearing the poster boards off the walls, but this time, in our presence.

As if in immediate reply, within five seconds following Gaynor's request, several of the poster boards directly over Doris' head were suddenly torn loose from their position and sharply struck her in the face. Both Gaynor and I, as well as others in the room, could easily observe the bizarre sight of the duct tape being pulled, again as if by unseen hands, from the boards on the wall.

After quieting down Doris following her ordeal with the poster boards, Gaynor again requested the "presence" within the room to remove more poster boards from the walls. Once again, the request was honored as two more well secured boards were ripped from their position on the back wall and thrown across the bed to the floor, although this time missing Doris completely, to her great relief.

It should be stressed, that on this evening, which marked the first decline of luminous phenomena, Doris' emotional state was immensely improved as compared to earlier visits. She was considerably calmer, and for the first time in our series of visits to her home, was not even mildly intoxicated. However, we do not feel that Doris' fondness for alcohol in any way invalidates her testimony regarding the unusual occurrences within her house, as the phenomena were collectively observed on frequent occasions.

Needless to say, the opinions of some of those attending only for the seventh visit to Doris' house were anything but positive, as our claims were only marginally supported. As far as the activity surrounding the poster boards was concerned, many of those present felt that their sudden removal from the walls and ceiling was explainable under the heating and humidity hypothesis discussed earlier. Yeah, right. And pigs can fly too.

Needless to say, Frank and Mort were absolutely amazed by even this, less than expected, occurrence. Unfortunately, when they had their special films processed, it did not reveal anything significant as related to what we all had observed that night in Doris's bedroom.

The eighth and final visit to the house, ending a two-and-a-half month investigation, the labs longest (until that time), took place on October 31, 1974. What better night than Halloween, which coincidentally, happened to be a full moon? This last evening we came prepared in that we brought an image intensifier (low-light or starlight scope) video recording system that we believed was sensitive enough to capture the weak light and images that our cameras could not.

On this occasion, again without an intoxicated Doris, the event was a total failure, even worse than the seventh visit with the entire lab attending. There was a weak odor and sensation of cold, but the lights that had intrigued us for so long, were now absent from the residence.

Also missing was Doris' hostility, belligerence, and fear of the occurrences in her house. These emotions were replaced by almost total apathy and indifference towards the entire situation. Perhaps in Doris' mind, she felt that she had won the battle against the Entity. Or else, she had given up entirely. Who knows? Doris was not the greatest at communicating all of her feelings and thoughts to us. In point of fact, we never even knew her exact age.

After this visit, we temporarily lost contact with Doris as she finally moved from this location in Culver City and apparently was too preoccupied with her relocation to phone us, a situation that forced us to locate her. (Although, perhaps she just wanted to get away from all that was going on around her.) Not surprisingly, after re-establishing contact with her three months later, early in February 1975, we learned that the phenomena around her was continuing within her new environment, although at a considerably lower frequency and magnitude.

The question we are now faced with is just what the appropriate explanation is for the phenomena that over fifty individuals, some collectively, including ourselves, observed. The answer can be narrowed down to three distinct possibilities, while completely rejecting the hypothesis of hallucination or fraud.

One possibility suggests that living human agents, in this case Doris and her children were directly responsible for all the witnessed phenomena. This belief falling under the previously discussed category of poltergeists in which unconsciously released energy of an unknown variety affects surrounding matter and energy and is assumed to be associated with the psychophysical state of the occupants of the house (in many cases, one individual in particular) in which pubescent or adolescent children are present, which in this case was extreme.

The psychodynamic environment within Doris' household was extremely intense and anxiety ridden, with overtones of animosity and belligerence underlying its nature. From a psychoanalytic perspective, it is interesting to note that Doris' reported attacks and alleged rapes were by three male "beings," the same number of male children she has. Considering the strong antagonisms existing between Doris and her children, especially the three boys, the potential for subliminally projected hostilities are self-evident and require no further clarification at this point.

Understandably, it is within the realm of reason to suspect that the poltergeist hypothesis in this case is a viable one and therein taking responsibility for all of the paranormal activities, although not explaining their mechanics.

However, due to the frequency and consistency of phenomena experienced by us and numerous assistants during the short course of this investigation in conjunction with its responsive, directed nature, which is not in keeping with poltergeist cases, the possibility of something beyond a recurrent spontaneous psychokinetic effect must be considered.

Even if Doris could, through some presently unknown paranormal mechanism, direct energy to move objects and create visible lights that behaved unpredictably, how often would this ability or faculty operate in our presence? The probability in view of past-recorded cases of it operating six out of eight times consecutively is almost nil. Indeed, not one known poltergeist case involves collectively visible three-dimensional lights. Additionally, we must not forget the cold spots and the terrible odor that almost always preceded the onset of phenomena.

Taking all of the aforementioned effects into account, we are inclined to believe that the phenomena witnessed cannot as yet be explained by any coherent theory involving poltergeist activity (RSPK) or discarnate intelligence. While we recognize that a belief in discarnate intelligence is almost inconceivable, we nevertheless must align ourselves with the theory that best explains the experienced phenomena (remember, your theory must fit your data, not the reverse).

Perhaps what was demonstrated here was a unique combination of different types of phenomena acting in concert. The evidence in this particular case, in our opinion, leans slightly towards the hypothesis of discarnate intelligence, or at least one capable of acting independently and at-a-distance from its operator, agent or source.

To conclude that these phenomena are no more than the products of neuro-chemically and emotionally disturbed personalities would indeed be an insult to those individuals plagued with such phenomena. This single investigation seemingly appears to reinforce the findings of contemporary academic researchers in this field in that there is some abstract form of relationship between electro-chemically unstable individuals and paranormal phenomena.

Whether there really are such entities as ghosts or apparitions, whether these terms are really appropriate for such a state in view of reported incidents of RSPK, and where within space-time such non-physical energy exists, remain problems that we may solve only in the distant future.

Meanwhile, what we have here is a study which, in our opinion, and considering the limitations imposed, meets the requirements of a contribution to science in that once you eliminate and rule out all the known possible causes, you're left with something truly extraordinary, something that has been with us since the dawn of civilization. Something that may eventually tell us more about who and what we really are, whether we like it or not.

Furthermore, it illuminates an area of human experience that continues to occur in spite of our advanced technology, ignorance and lack of recognition, and appears to be relatively inaccessible to the scientific method. However, such might not be the case in view of current beliefs within the field, especially considering the analogies drawn between holographic processes and paranormal phenomena. Although this investigation shed no further light on the real source or true nature of the phenomena encountered, we believe that it constitutes a diligent effort in that direction, despite financial and technological handicaps.

The occurrences outlined within the body of this study, which were documented to the best of our ability, cannot be explained or accounted for by any conventional physical, scientific theory or model and therefore remains just as it began; a phenomenon.

ADDENDUM

50

Aliens Above, Ghosts Below by Barry E. Taff

As previously discussed, as is quite common within the entertainment industry when it comes to enhancing the intensity of non-fiction stories, dramatic license was extensively exercised with The Entity novel and feature film.

For example, we obviously never recreated Doris' house in a controlled laboratory environment. Nor did we attempt to restrain and capture the entity by supercooling it with liquid helium as discussed in the book and depicted in the motion picture.

The logic behind the attempted supercooling of The Entity, is based on very tried and true physical principles. Light is produced when electrons jump from higher to lower orbits in atoms that have been sufficiently excited. This is a mechanical process and thus will be affected by a rapid drop in temperature to near absolute zero. In fact, in modern electro-optics/physics labs, they have been able to literally slow photons down to rest through the application of supercooling.

Such efforts, while scientifically feasible, would have been prohibitively expensive given the non-existent funding of our lab. However, what was visually observed by more than 50 eyewitnesses between August 22nd and October 31st. of 1974, was far more incredible and astounding than what was shown on the screen. If you wish to blame anyone for the major diminution of the movie as compared to the book, blame the producer and director.

Unfortunately, the producer of The Entity, the late Harold Schneider, was vehemently opposed to Frank De Felitta directing the film, as was originally planned. Given Frank's extraordinary credentials within the entertainment industry, this was a real shock. An even greater shock was the director Schneider hired to replace Frank (as if such was really possible). From the Ipcress Files and Lady Sings the Blues fame came Sidney J. Furie.

As is all too common in this business, the first thing Furie and Schneider did was to substantially re-write Frank's screenplay, significantly diminishing the magnitude and sometimes the nature of phenomena experienced along with my methods of how to document it, i.e., holographic laser cameras, thermal imaging, etc.

The most significant changes made by the Schneider/Furie team involved the climax where The Entity is literally frozen by liquid helium. What was described in the book was quite compelling and thought provoking. What ended up on the screen was, in my opinion, a hack's attempt at controlling and devaluing De Felitta's brilliant labor of love. Think I'm a bit biased here? You'd be right.

The special effects depicting the luminous anomalies within the film were not even close to what was actually observed within Doris' bedroom during the summer and early fall of 1974.

The fast-moving lights in the movie were more reminiscent of tracer rounds from an automatic rifle. What we visually observed were more graphic, following very circular paths and moved at a significantly lower speed.

Another significant change from reality to the silver screen was the scene where Carla's (Doris') boyfriend observes her naked body being fondled by the invisible hands, picks up a chair in an attempt to get The Entity off her. The result of this event lands Carla in the hospital.

What really transpired was for more impressive from both the paranormal and entertainment perspective. Doris' boyfriend came out of the bathroom ready for a good romp in the sack. What he discovered, however, was a large, luminous, male apparition on top of Doris, having its way with her sexually.

51

Aliens Above, Ghosts Below by Barry E. Taff

Momentarily shocked by what he observed as anyone in that situation might be, he froze. Without much further hesitation, the boyfriend picked up his guitar intensely hammering it into the apparition on top of Doris, hoping to force it off her. The guitar went right through the apparition and struck Doris.

Thankfully, this real-life incident did not require Doris going to the emergency room for treatment (as Carla did in the film). Unfortunately for us, this particular event occurred long before our investigation of the case, making it difficult, if not impossible to verify.

If you really want to see an accurate recreation of what as collectively observed by more than twenty people, you must go out and purchase one of two DVD's that display these images. You have a choice between Barry Conrad's California's Most Haunted, in which one segment is dedicated to The Entity case, or you can purchase or rent The Entity DVD which has this author in the special features section discussing the case as well as showing clips from Conrad's DVD.

Fortunately, when Conrad was making California's Most Haunted, he hired a very gifted and talented effects artist named Rodd Matsui. As Rodd is a consummate professional, he interviewed me for several hours while taking detailed notes.

The result of Rodd's dedication to the facts was a very accurate, almost perfect, recreation of what many of us witnessed in the summer of 1974 in Doris Bither's dilapidated house in Culver City. It's a real pity that Rodd wasn't around when The Entity was being made. Unfortunately, in 1981, Rodd was a teenager. That certainly was our loss.

It should be understood that Frank's script was rewritten not simply as a matter of dramatic license or putting their own two cents in, but more due to the fact that Furie and Schneider were total skeptics, verging on debunkers. They basically believed that we were all "a couple fries short of a happy meal" and essentially fabricated the entire case. This prevailing attitude was the primary reason for their altering Frank's exceptional screenplay.

During one conversation with Furie prior to the start of production, I straight out asked him why he took on the direction of The Entity if he felt it was nothing more than a cheap hoax. His reply was equally straightforward; "money!" My only retort was, "Well, given that you are essentially little more than a mercenary, if we give you even more money, will you leave the production and let Frank direct it, as was originally intended?"

By the look on Furie's face, he was not amused. The exact words I used here are not worthy of being repeated as they would cheapen this article. I never even attempted a conversation on this matter with Schneider, as intellectual communication with him was all but impossible.

On one of the many occasions when Schneider was lambasting this author, he was somewhat perplexed by my lack of reaction to his ranting and raving. At a later date, he finally got around to asking me why I didn't appear to be upset over what he had said. My response was short and concise: "I've already been paid. So, I really don't give a damn as to what you and Sid decide to do with this film. If you want to ruin this film by cheapening it at every turn, thereby diminishing its box office, then be my guest, it's your problem, not mine. Like I said, I've already made my money."

While my retort sounds equally mercenary to Sid Furies', I just felt that once the script was sold, the director is at liberty to do pretty much anything they want with it, depending of course upon the contract existing between them and the screenwriter.

I know that one should not speak ill of the dead, as they cannot defend themselves. In this case however, Schneider was such an angry, bitter, rage-filled, argumentative and confrontational man (get the point?), it's of little or no concern.

Lest you think I am simply slamming The Entity movie for some ulterior motive, rest assured that my comments reflect the fact that I read Frank De Felitta's superb script long before production began. Therefore, I knew what was originally intended to be put on the screen and the way it was to be directed.

Personally, I did not, at all care for the resultant, Sid Furie/Harold Schneider re-write for reasons far too detailed to be discussed here. If one put a gun to my head, I might be willing to consider some of Furie's camera angles as homage to the original Twilight Zone episodes (circa.1959-1964), but that's it.

The passage of time can have dramatic and sobering effects on one's interpretation of reality, especially when it pertains to an area of science that lacks voluminous amounts of hard, replicable data, like parapsychology.

More than thirty-eight years of investigative research into more than 4,000 cases of ghosts, hauntings, apparitions and poltergeists has significantly altered my attitudes, perspective and belief system. Very distinctive longitudinal data patterns have emerged, reinforcing existing theories regarding this type of phenomenon.

While revisionist history does not generally lend further credence or substantiation to any event, in this particular case, time-acquired knowledge and experience has provided a unique perspective that would otherwise be unobtainable. The result is a reinterpretation of events from thirty-three years ago.

In the simplest terms and contrary to the popular media hype, The Entity case was not, in my opinion, an instance of haunting or discarnate intelligence, but one of extreme RSPK, that is, a poltergeist manifestation which make up well over ninety-five percent (95%) the my case files.

In this regard, it was apparent from the outset that Doris was a deeply troubled woman, whose claims of spectral rape were due in large part to extreme emotional distress coupled with an overactive imagination and libidinous fantasies.

The fact that the phenomena moved with Doris as she moved, first from Culver City to Carson, then to San Bernardino, then all the way to Texas, and then back to San Bernardino, strongly suggests that the phenomena was a direct product of her tortured unconscious mind and not of her environment. In fact, once she moved from her original residence in Culver City at the end of 1974, the house was forevermore free of phenomena as far as we knew.

Another relevant question at this juncture is as to whether the property in Culver City had a unique or uncommon geophysical, i.e., electro/geomagnetic signature associated with it that might have contributed to the initiation of paranormal events that were to plague Doris for years to come?

We did not yet suspect the now acknowledged correlation between electromagnetic/geomagnetic fields and poltergeist outbreaks. Nor did we possess the portable instrumentation for such environmental field monitoring, as they did not yet exist. Therefore, I guess we'll never really know the answer to this question.

In an even stranger twist to an already mind-boggling case, while in San Bernardino, Doris claimed that she had gotten pregnant from The Entity. However, medical results were more consistent with an ectopic or hysterical pregnancy (no fetus). Once again, leaving us scratching our heads for answers. Understandably, given the circumstances, Doris believed that The Entity would eventually kill her.

Now back to what we believe to be reality. Lending further support to the poltergeist hypothesis was the fact when Doris moved into her new residence in Carson in late 1974, the tenants of the houses flanking her immediately began experiencing outbreaks of intense and varied poltergeist activity.

It's important to understand that the neighbors had no knowledge of Doris' identity or experiences as we kept her away from what little media then existed. The continuing events around Doris suggested that this phenomenon was perhaps radiant in nature along with a proximity effect.

After investigating thousands of poltergeist cases over the subsequent decades, data has clearly indicated that this type of phenomena moves with the agent over time and does not appear to have any lasting or residual effects on the house or apartment once the agent leaves. When the suspected poltergeist agent takes up residence in a new abode, psychokinetic storms shortly follow after the PGAs are acclimated to their new environment.

It appears that these highly energetic environments may act as irritants or triggers to individuals with sensitive and highly reactive central nervous systems. In the same manner that bacteria or virus infects a susceptible individual, perhaps this energy infects such a person who then carries it beyond the physical boundaries of their original residence and continue to propagate its enduring effects. Is it possible that this type of phenomenon has quasi-biologic properties?

By analogy, imagine you go to visit a friend whose family is sick with the flu. You spend a short time there doing your best not to touch anything, which of course is impossible, and return home where everyone is healthy. Several days later, you and your family come down with the same flu. It's not beyond reason that certain aspects of poltergeist activity may operate in a similar, although not identical manner. I've labeled such contagious episodes as related to the poltergeists as a "psycho-virus", for lack of a better term.

However, what constitutes or determines ones susceptibility in such matters? It could be as simple as being seizure prone or epileptic. Such a distinctive electrochemical brain may dramatically increase one's vulnerability to such a hypothesized psycho-virus. The evidence accumulated in my own files, as well those of many other researchers over the past four decades, certainly implicates this nexus between poltergeist outbreaks and their human locus of temporal lobe lability as manifested through epilepsy.

Unfortunately, back in 1974 the questions we asked of the experiencers of such phenomena, did not include queries into their specific neurophysiological constitution and as to whether they've ever experienced seizures or epilepsy. If we only knew then what we know now, the database on this matter would truly be overwhelming and beyond reasonable doubt. But then again, hindsight is always 20/20.

However, even accepting the substantial evidence in favor of the psychokinetic nature of The Entity case, does not account for the inexplicable 35 mm. photographs recorded during the course of the investigation. After a detailed analysis by Adrian Vance, the West Coast Editor of Popular Photography (May 1976, pp. 102 & 115) and others, we were still left wanting for answers.

The last and perhaps most compelling psychodynamic indicator of the case's RSPK underpinnings is Doris' claim of being repeatedly attacked by three male entities, where two allegedly held her down while the third raped her.

It is no coincidence that at the time she was living in a highly volatile relationship with three male children. It does not take a great leap of logic to understand the obvious conflict ridden environment that spawned this incestuous hallucinatory projection, especially given Doris' incredibly abusive past at the hands of both her parents and numerous men.

In this case, the circumstantial evidence appears to speak for itself. But, what if we are wrong? What if there really are discarnate entities that prey on weak, emotionally troubled or chemically imbalanced individuals? What if ancient mythology regarding the incubus and succubus are more than just legend, superstition and religious hysteria? Are we so absolutely sure of ourselves, and our neonatal paranormal science that such a definitive statement is possible? I think not.

Given that the discipline of parapsychology (or more precisely, psychical research) is but an embryonic science (albeit after 125 years), we are all in the position of the three blind men touching different parts of an elephant trying to determine the nature of the beast. One touches the tail and thinks it's a rope. The other touches a leg and believes it to be a tree trunk, while the third blind man touches the elephant's trunk and is positive it's a hose.

Might we be in exactly the same situation here? At this time, due to the lack of any developed paranormal instrumentality, all we are able to do is speculate, conjecture and theorize about the true nature of the phenomena based on fleeting encounters with its multi-faceted components.

It is very important to understand that one cannot measure what they do not know. The instrumentation we currently utilize in the course of our work (which has been portable for just the last fifteen years or so), only measures those forces of nature we are currently aware of, i.e., electromagnetism, gravitation and the strong and weak nuclear forces, although the last three seem unlikely candidates regarding the paranormal.

There are only a limited number of options open to us here. One is that these phenomena are the result of known energies working in, as yet, unknown ways. The other, more likely choice, is that these phenomena are the result of unknown forces working in, as yet, unknown ways.

The best analogy of this idea is measuring a wake that disturbs the surrounding water while never being aware of the boat producing it. In all likelihood, were are detecting and measuring little more than the way this unknown form of energy interacts with the types of energy and matter we already know. At this point in time, we do not possess the level of sophisticated technology to do otherwise. Though I'm sure there are some who will say that EVP's and the like are opening doors to this domain. Only time will tell.

In reality there is little, if any, hard evidence pointing to a credible, objective description of this phenomenon. In science, a theory must conform to the data supporting it. To look only for data that supports your theory, is quackery and pseudoscience.

Coming back to the human part of the equation, the last this author heard from Doris was in February of 1983, when The Entity motion picture was released. She said that to her great relief, the phenomena had ended quite some time ago. Not long afterwards, I again lost contact with her. The last Frank De Felitta heard from her was in 1990. So, at present, we do not know where she is, or even, if she is?

There has been a substantial quantity of misinformation regarding The Entity case in general, more so to the whereabouts and condition of Doris Bither. Recently, several websites erroneously reported that Doris died in 2006 of Multiple Myeloma, an insidious and highly lethal form of bone cancer. To make matters even worse, these websites reported that while I was on A.M. Coast to Coast with George Noory in November of 2006, I made such an assertion.

The truth of the matter is that I did, in fact, speak about The Entity case during the opening segments of the show. However, during a later segment of the show I discussed an extraordinary poltergeist case that had surrounded my associate Barry Conrad's girlfriend, Lisa McIntosh. The woman who unfortunately died in July of 2006 of Multiple Myeloma was NOT Doris Bither, but Lisa McIntosh, who had absolutely no connection whatsoever with Doris Bither other than knowing me through Barry Conrad and being aware of the case. So much for the accurate reporting of facts on the Internet!

After thirty-eight years and thousands of field investigations, The Entity case still stands as one of the most remarkable encounters with such an extraordinary level of psychokinetic and luminous phenomena that was collectively observed by dozens of individuals.

However, even with all our newly acquired sensors, theories and quasi-scientific nomenclature, The Entity case is just as unfathomably enigmatic today in the early 21st century as it was in the 7th decade of the 20th.

So much for real progress in a field of unfunded scientific research.

Chapter 3:
A HAZARDOUS HAUNTING

Many things can be said about investigating cases of alleged hauntings, ghosts, poltergeists and apparitions. However, saying that this avocation is dangerous to one's health is not one of them.

Since the dawn of psychical research in Great Britain in 1882, there have been only a handful of documented cases where the phenomena demonstrated discrete, malevolent or belligerent behavior, or more precisely, where it actually harmed someone.

In point of fact, to the best of my knowledge, there has never been a reported case where the phenomena directly attacked the investigators. Until now, that is. I won't even touch the Bell Witch case, as I believe that the poisoning was, most likely, done by a very corporeal being who tried to conceal their heinous act by blaming it on a ghost.

One of the few contemporary instances that demonstrated such violent activity was The Entity case. The focus of The Entity case, Doris Bither a mid-to-late thirty year-old woman on welfare living in a two-time condemned house with four children, claimed to have been repeatedly sexually assaulted by three male ghosts: two held her down and one raped her.

The Entity case demonstrated a high degree of psychokinetic (PK) activity along with the materialization of visible, three-dimensional balls of light that were captured on film. On one eventful evening, the apparition of the upper torso of a large man appeared in a lime green light in the corner of the bedroom while numerous witnesses watched in stunned amazement. Two friends assisting in the investigation felt their knees buckle and lost consciousness after observing the apparition. That was the last time they accompanied us on any cases.

Somewhat substantiating the psychokinetic hypothesis in this case was Doris' psychological profile, which was a perfect match for the emotionally volatile, self-destructive stereotype researchers have come to recognize over the decades. However, in all fairness, a retroactive assessment of The Entity case cannot account for the appearance of apparitions anymore now than it could then? Like many other cases from my files, there is a very fine line differentiating true hauntings from poltergeists.

Since most cases never evolve into a full investigation due of the lack of observed and/or recorded phenomena, it was the furthest thought from our minds that we would run into another case that, for the most part, paralleled The Entity in almost every way.

This case began in early 1989 when I received a phone call from Susan Castenada, a woman who claimed that her close friend, Jackie Hernandez (whose maiden name was appropriately, Hazard), was being troubled by ghosts.

However, at this early stage, Jackie was very concerned about the possibility that we would automatically assume she was emotionally disturbed and so she would not allow us to meet or speak with her. Adding to the emotional turmoil and frenzy was the fact that Jackie was pregnant with her second child from her estranged husband in a made-in-hell marriage.

We did not hear from Susan again until August of that year when Jackie herself finally gathered up the courage to call me and allowed us to pay her a visit. As we approached Jackie's little, turn-of-the century bungalow in a seedy, gang-infested, run-down area of San Pedro, we had no way of knowing that this case would alter all of our lives in ways we could never imagine.

Accompanying me on the evening of August 8, 1989 was writer, producer, director and cameraman, Barry Conrad who had been working with me for about eighteen months, Jeff Wheatcraft, a highly skeptical still-photographer and long-time friend and associate of Conrad's, Beth Shatsky, a local photo-journalist, and Larry Brooks, a close friend.

Upon meeting and finally interviewing Jackie at length, it was apparent that she had endured a very intense, hectic life. In fact, in many ways her background and psychological profile were almost identical to that of Doris in The Entity case; a quintessential poltergeist agent (PGA), if, there ever was one.

In other words, Jackie was depressed and anxiety ridden. She had intense generalized anger, distress, pent-up hostilities, massive unresolved emotional conflicts, and a history of emotional abuse in a dysfunctional family environment wherein Jackie was the black sheep. If Jackie had been wound any tighter and more distressed, she would surely have been under a psychiatrist's care. I believe that Mr. Spock from Star Trek fame would have summed up Jackie's personality as "A mass of conflicting impulses."

Immediately upon entering Jackie's house, we were overwhelmed by an intense putrid stench of decomposing organic matter and a strong sense of over-pressure, like being at the bottom of a very deep pool at several atmospheres of pressure. Interestingly, both of these sensations were present at the onset of The Entity investigation.

While taking a tour of her small, disheveled home and talking with several other witnesses, we kept hearing what sounded like a 200-pound rat running around the attic.

Several months earlier Jackie had allegedly seen the disembodied apparitional head of an old man and heard muffled voices some months earlier. We checked out the rather large attic, but found nothing that could account for the loud, recurring noises. We were also told of several incidents where large quantities of water spewed from a two-by-four in the corner of the dinning room as if a garden hose were somehow attached.

We observed a peculiar, viscous liquid dripping down from the inside of the dining room cupboards and we put some in a plastic sample bag. Analysis by a local forensic lab determined it was male, human blood plasma with a heavy iodine and copper content that was heavily oxidized. Jackie related how various pieces of furniture--lamps, children's toys, chairs, framed paintings, etc.--were violently thrown about the house.

Additionally, cans of Pepsi were thrown about and were frequently hurled directly at her. There were numerous instances where electrical appliances behaved as if they had a mind of their own -- for instance, the TV would turn itself on but would be unable to obtain reception.

Jackie's most dramatic claim was the observation of male apparitions. One night while she was pregnant and on her way to the bathroom, she saw a gnarled old man. On several other occasions, she saw another old man sitting at her dining room table. This was not the same man whose head she had earlier seen in the attic.

According to Jackie, this apparition was an elderly man in his late fifties or early sixties, wearing a plaid shirt and 1950's-style gasoline station attendant high-water pants. He had a sunken, emaciated look with large peering eyes. Considering an artist's rendering that was drawn from Jackie's description, the image bore a striking resemblance to a very gaunt Ernest Borgnine.

Shortly after this last apparitional sighting, Jackie came close to losing her life while sleeping on the living room floor with Susan Castenada. They slept in the living room to avoid the continual onslaught of phenomena in the bedrooms. A strange, dense, brightly luminous cloud appeared over Jackie's head and began suffocating her. As she started choking in her sleep, the sound awoke Susan who observed the hovering cloud and pulled Jackie out from under it to safety.

After completing the initial interview we began wrapping up and were about ready to go when Larry Brooks casually suggested to Wheatcraft that he go back up into the attic and shoot a few more photographs, just in case anything showed up. Although still very skeptical about the entire situation, Wheatcraft agreed and went to climb back through the tiny crawl space located above the laundry room at the back of the house.

After a few minutes, we heard a loud thud and Wheatcraft flew down out of the attic as if the devil himself were on his tail. When Wheatcraft came into the living room where the rest of us were talking, he was literally drained of all color and shaking intensely.

He told us that something had forcefully grabbed his 35-mm. SLR camera and wrenched it from his hands while he was shooting. Considering that this statement came from Wheatcraft, an ardent disbeliever was rather impressive, even though the rest of us did not witness the event.

Immediately we again went up into the attic and found Wheatcraft's expensive camera. We discovered that whatever agency pulled the camera from his hands had neatly detached the lens from its body and placed both pieces down on opposite ends of the attic, some fifteen feet apart, all without damaging them. The camera's body lay in a fruit box and the lens on the floor.

While examining the attic in even greater detail and finding nothing to account for what happened to Wheatcraft and his camera, Wheatcraft was suddenly and violently pushed across the attic by an unseen force. Conrad, who was right in front of Wheatcraft with his video camera, witnessed the event and described it as if a very large, invisible hand had shoved Wheatcraft in his back, vaulting him forward. Wheatcraft suffered actual injuries that required medical attention.

At this point we decided to call it a night as the phenomena began to settle down. Needless to say, we certainly did not expect anything to occur during our visit, so the loud pounding noises and Wheatcraft's experiences were a welcome change from the boring tedium experienced while investigating most cases. Except, of course for Wheatcraft.

On September 4th, Jackie called Conrad at midnight complaining of intense activity. Conrad, Wheatcraft and photographer/assistant Gary Boehm arrived shortly together. (Due to a massive heart attack suffered by my father, I was temporarily sidelined for several months during the course of this investigation and as such could not attend several visits to Jackie's original house).

During this particular visit, small and sometimes large corpuscular masses of light were seen in the laundry room and later in the attic. These luminous anomalies were preceded by strange snapping noises and the sounds of heavy breathing, which eventually led Gary to the area below the attic crawl space. While Wheatcraft was again examining the attic in a desperate effort to determine what happened to him on August 8th, something unseen violently attacked him.

According to Wheatcraft, he was walking towards the crawl space where Gary was about to descend, when suddenly he felt a restriction around his neck pulling him up and to his left. As the force tightened its grasp around Wheatcraft's neck, he let out a loud yell or moan, that alerted Gary as to his plight. Being a trained photographer, Gary turned toward the direction of Wheatcraft's voice and fired off several shots of his 35mm. camera while rushing to his aid. The only light available to Gary was the camera's flash.

Aliens Above, Ghosts Below by Barry E. Taff

Apparently, something had wrapped a plastic clothesline around Wheatcraft's neck, severely tightened it and pulled him up over a large nail extending away from a rafter in the attic's ceiling.

The force behind the attempted hanging threw Wheatcraft's glasses off, sent him into momentary shock and rendered him unconscious. As Gary eventually got Wheatcraft down off the nail, he discovered that Jeff's eyes were glazed over and suffering from deep rope burns in his neck. We later determined that the knot tied in the clothesline was a bowline or "seaman's knot" which none of us knew anything about prior to this event. (See Photo 1)

One thing we did know was that if it had not been for Gary, in all likelihood, Wheatcraft could have died from strangulation or a broken neck. After attempting to bring Wheatcraft back down to reality and calm his nerves, Conrad and Gary went back up into the attic to search for what almost hung Wheatcraft. Nothing unusual was discovered.

Following this terrifying event, Wheatcraft had to face the disturbing contradiction generated by his otherworldly ordeal. He previously had absolutely no belief whatsoever in paranormal phenomena, and now he had to deal with the fact that a direct encounter with it almost took his life.

Wheatcraft's behavior did not demonstrate any immediate changes, apart from the stress resulting from the encounter. However, for good reason he never again returned to Jackie's San Pedro home.

During one of the numerous visits that followed without Wheatcraft, an immense ball of light appeared behind Conrad after which he suddenly lost consciousness for no apparent reason. In fact, Conrad himself did not directly observe the light as it appeared behind his back. Susan, Jackie and others witnessed it.

Another peculiar aspect of this investigation was the fact that our equipment, whether high-quality video cameras, tape decks, thermal imaging devices, 35 mm. SLR cameras or audio recording equipment, would mysteriously malfunction as if the internal electronics were neutralized. Even though we always arrived with freshly charged or new battery packs, most of our systems would inevitably shut down. This type of effect is actually quite common in our investigations.

One noteworthy event in particular was when Beth Shatsky's mini-35 mm. Nikon camera began shaking for no apparent reason while in my hands. I put the camera down on the kitchen table on top of an overturned glass and watched it rapidly rock back and forth while Conrad captured the event on video.

What was not seen by the naked eye, but caught by Conrad's video camera, was the appearance of a small yellow-orange mass of light speeding through the LCD readout window of the Nikon from no apparent source. Later analysis revealed that the diminutive ball of light was the image of a middle-aged man's head, displaying a receding hairline and large dark eyes.

On another evening, while leaving Jackie's house, both Shatsky and Conrad observed what appeared to be balls of light shooting skyward from Jackie's little bungalow. For the most part, it resembled roman candles used on the 4th of July or fast moving ball lightning. Investigation revealed no apparent source for these luminous anomalies. As usual, the phenomena happened too quickly to be caught on film or video.

Over the course of the next several months, Conrad captured many more orbs of light with his video camera. For the most part, these resembled tracer bullets, emitting their own source of bright light and traveling at speeds in excess of 60 mph. The majority of these lights occurred just prior to the manifestation of other, more disturbing phenomena.

When we first spotted these corpuscular masses of light (which were only caught by the camera and never observed by the naked eye) we thought they might be insects reflecting the cameras light. However, when we were able to slow down the frame rate and enhance the image, it was quite clear to us, as well as a professional entomologist, that these enigmatic light sources were not insects.

This type of ghost light is actually more common than believed, as they were observed quite frequently by the naked eye and captured on standard photographic film during The Entity case. Ironically, however, what was visually perceived during The Entity case could not be photographed and what was photographed could not be seen...a paradox.

In Jackie's case, Conrad was able to videotape what the eye could not see, and considering that he was not using the highest quality video camera incorporating low light capability, obtaining these images is even more intriguing and inexplicable.

During yet another visit, the smoke detectors kept activating and squawking in response to our yes or no questions -- even though we later found the electrical wiring and subsequently the power was disconnected! If this was an unconscious psychokinetic act on Jackie's part, it's almost unprecedented in parapsychological research.

After enduring several more months of intense paranormal bombardment, Jackie finally moved to a new environment in October of that year (1989). With the belief that substantial physical distance between her and her San Pedro home would put an end to the phenomena, Jackie moved to Weldon, a small trailer-park community in Kern County, California, some 380 miles north of Los Angeles.

However, it was not long before Jackie's worst fears were realized. The phenomena appeared to have moved with her, which again, is not that uncommon in these types of cases. Shortly after moving into the trailer park, she began hearing strange scratching sounds emanating from the shed behind the house. Shortly thereafter, the psychokinetic storms around her began anew, but with even greater fury.

One day, while moving an old projection television from a shed to her trailer house, Jackie and her new neighbors saw the apparitional image of an old man's head appear on the TV's screen even though it was not plugged in. Within hours, Jackie put in a call to Conrad asking for help.

On April 13, 1990, Conrad and Wheatcraft traveled north to the desolate area of Weldon to assist Jackie. Jeff mistakenly, and logically, thought that nothing significant would happen to him since this was a new residence for Jackie.

Upon their arrival, they almost immediately began observing numerous psychokinetic events as well as the same masses of light that surrounded Jackie in San Pedro. Since much of the activity seemed to be focused in the shed behind Jackie's house, Wheatcraft set up his video camera pointing directly into the shed from an outside perspective.

After returning to Jackie's house, Conrad and Wheatcraft soon noticed that the tripod-mounted and locked-in-place video camera had mysteriously turned itself around so it was no longer facing the shed, but was now aimed toward the house. When later reviewing the taped footage of the time just prior to the camera being turned around, an enigmatic light source was detected moving from behind the camera into the shed at approximately 122 mph.

At first, they again suspected that it might be an insect. However, the velocity of the lights combined with its luminosity and shape suggested otherwise. We even considered the possibility of fireflies, except that they do not exist on the west coast of the U.S. and then, of course, they do not accelerate to velocities of 122 mph, at least not according to entomologists we spoke with.

When this enigmatic light was slowed down and enhanced as the earlier ones were, it revealed a peculiar configuration. We showed this footage to more than 20 individuals who had no idea or suggestion as to what they were observing. The unanimous response was that the light looked like a very small, disc-shaped object with a hemispheric structure resting upon its upper section. Sort of a micro-miniature UFO.

I know. I know. We are not trying to mix our metaphors here by even suggesting that we are dealing with UFO-related phenomena as opposed to paranormal events, or even an indirect correlation between the two as there is no evidence for that nexus in this particular case. It's just that this particular image is quite distinct in its shape and therefore bears mention, if for no other reason. God only knows what it means.

As the level of phenomena began to dwindle, Conrad, Wheatcraft, Jackie and two of her neighbors, went back into her trailer house to relax. As they sat there talking, subtle psychokinetic events began to occur. This eventually motivated the group to bring out a Ouija board and try their hand at it, figuring that they had nothing to lose. In retrospect, their judgment in this matter could not have been more in error.

Sitting around a small card table used for eating in the dinning area, they began playing with the Ouija board. Almost immediately, the dining area grew extremely cold (while the outside temperature was quite warm). Suddenly, the chairs and table began to intensely vibrate then, violently shake.

In the next instant, Wheatcraft was physically levitated along with his chair and hurled backwards up into the air in a parabolic arc, striking the wall where it met the ceiling behind him. The resulting impact knocked Wheatcraft unconscious. The stunned group watched in horror as the event, lasting all of one second, resulted in Wheatcraft lying motionless on the floor, like a broken rag doll.

Given the amount of force demonstrated, Conrad was actually concerned that Wheatcraft might be dead. Fortunately, he was not. Wheatcraft related what he experienced during the levitation.

He first had the sensation of a large boxing glove compressing his diaphragm. He then felt himself lift upwards along with the chair he was seated in. He was aware of the chair falling out from beneath him as his body was forcefully slammed into the wall behind him. He then lost consciousness and awoke on the floor surrounded by the others in the room.

The emotional scars resulting from first, the camera being yanked out of his hands, then being shoved across the attic by an intangible force, the unforgettable hanging encounter in combination with this most recent experience, pushed Wheatcraft into a deep depression, from which he may still suffer.

After this event, Wheatcraft was never quite the same. His moods became very unstable, his temper grew volatile and intense, and his general temperament indicated extreme irritability. High levels of anxiety combined with a generalized anger, resentment and unresolved conflicts resulted in an irascible personality. More precisely, Wheatcraft manifested all the symptoms of Post Traumatic Stress Disorder (PTSD), for which he has never sought or received treatment.

As is quite common in such traumatizing events, Wheatcraft needed some form of closure to this matter. In the pursuit of such, he found it necessary to place blame for what happened to him on something or someone.

He obviously could not directly blame the unknown agency that repeatedly attacked him. That was far too intangible for closure and emotional grounding. Unfortunately, the only source available for blame was Barry Conrad, as he was the one who brought Wheatcraft into this event. Wheatcraft began behaving in a sarcastic, malicious and vindictive manner towards Conrad, that totally ended their friendship and working relationship.

While conducting video interviews on what had just occurred, Conrad captured another anomalous light that hovered just outside the kitchen window and seemingly peered in, pulsing at a very slow rate. Since Jackie then lived literally in the middle of nowhere, Conrad felt confident that this light could not have been explained by any conventionally prosaic source, such as a passing car or a flashlight.

On a number of occasions, Jackie came back down to San Pedro with her kids to visit family and friends. While staying at a local motel, Jackie had yet another indicator that these phenomena were far from being exhausted.

After leaving the motel to get some dinner, she returned to find bright red writing all over the walls of her room. The words "mad" and "angry" were scrawled all over the walls of the room in broad marker pen. Jackie immediately called the manager who was angered by what he believed was little more than the product of a disturbed mind and promptly asked Jackie to leave the motel.

This specific poltergeist event, the wall writing, is eerily similar to a scene in the Robert Wise' The Haunting (Fox, 1963) which was based on Shirley Jackson's book, The Haunting of Hill House. I wonder how much research Jackson did before writing her novel? Or, is it a case of life imitating art?

Isn't it fascinating how various aspects of Jackie's unconscious keeps manifesting itself in a physical manner? How would anyone feel whose life was turned upside down and left homeless due to conditions and events they had absolutely no control over whatsoever? I think the words "mad" and "angry" certainly represented a large part of the way Jackie was currently feeling about her life? More on Jackie's unconscious projections later.

Following continually escalating paranormal episodes [especially anomalous light formations], Jackie returned to San Pedro in July of 1990, and moved into an apartment about a mile from where she originally lived. Her new apartment was very small and had to be shared with her two young children and, of course, the ever-present phenomena.

Almost immediately, the psychokinetic movement of books, furniture, appliances, etc., began and continued for many months.

While entering her bedroom early one morning, Jackie spotted several large glowing masses of light hovering over the carpet close to the floor. Immediately grabbing a 35 mm. camera (which Conrad had given her for such occasions), she was able to capture some of the most incredible photographs of luminous anomalies ever documented.

One photo clearly displays three brightly illuminated "masses" of light. Each appears to be a point source of light, with defined edges. These brilliant luminous anomalies were clearly overlapping while simultaneously casting shadows over each other. The lights depicted true, three-dimensional properties that could not be achieved without the use of sophisticated optical printing technology. Jackie had absolutely no access to such advanced computerized graphic imaging and over-the-counter computer graphic imagery (CGI) was not even available at that time

Aliens Above, Ghosts Below by Barry E. Taff

These luminous anomalies looked exactly like solid objects (perhaps plasma), occupying three-dimensional space as opposed to a two dimensionally projected light source. It looked as though you could literally reach out your hand and touch them.

It is very apparent that these light sources are self-luminous and were sufficiently bright to clearly illuminate the carpet beneath them. Oddly, the light emitted by these objects appeared to only be directed downward onto the carpet and towards Jackie and the camera, but not backward toward the wall behind them. In fact, they were so luminous that the camera's flash was not used to photograph them. These lights are indeed of high strangeness. (See Photo 2)

Not long after this incident, Jackie again spotted strange lights, this time hovering just beneath the ceiling of her kitchen. She was again fast enough to capture these with her camera. The photographs reveal what looks like a plasma, convoluting and twisting, eventually separating into several different elemental components, then diffusing and dissipating into nothingness. (See Photo 3)

At this time, the case took on an even stranger turn, in that not only was frightfully disturbing but also contradicted almost everything we appeared to know about these type of phenomena.

On several occasions, after Jackie had visited Conrad at his apartment in Studio City, violent poltergeist phenomena erupted after her departure. The stove's gas burners repeatedly turned themselves on (in fact, during one outbreak, a film crew from Fox TV's A Current Affair were present interviewing us (Conard, Wheatcraft and this author) about the case.

Later, on another date, a box of bullets, which Conrad normally kept safely hidden in the closet, found its way to the stove where the burners spontaneously turned erupted. Various pieces of furniture began moving around. At one point, Conrad found his cordless phone handset on top of a lampshade, and a bottle of liquid paper was seen floating through the kitchen.

The manual and electronic controls of Conrad's video editing bay began reacting to the touch of unseen hands: levers being pulled and buttons being pushed (this was recorded on video tape). Various items in the refrigerator were turned upside down. Windows exploded, sending shards of glass flying inward and outward. A large pair of scissors began apporting around the apartment and repeatedly ended up under Conrad's pillow, just before or after sleeping. Not exactly a comforting thought, and not a point you want to get, if you will excuse the pun.

On another occasion, the scissors actually ripped through Conrad's pillow while he slept, waking him instantly. On another afternoon, while attempting to capture some of this activity on videotape, Wheatcraft, whose camera was rolling, was again attacked. Something struck him hard on his back sending him flying forward in a somersault. Fortunately, the bed in front of him broke his fall.

Examining Wheatcraft's back immediately after the incident revealed a large, deep scratch or welt, resembling that of an animal's claw scratch. Whatever this phenomenon was, it certainly did not like Wheatcraft.

When Conrad tried to videotape these outbreaks, his camera would frequently have strange, unaccountable smears or smudges over the lens, as if from a grease pencil. As with many of the other phenomena, we were never able to determine the cause. These psychokinetic outbreaks resulted in frantic phone calls from Conrad to me at about 1 A.M. It's one thing to go out to someone else's home to investigate these strange occurrences, it's another to come back home, to a supposedly safe and secure environment, and discover that you have brought the phenomena home with you.

I do not believe for one second that a ghost or discarnate intelligence followed Conrad back to his apartment to wreak havoc. It is far more likely that these occurrences were the result of some aspect of psychokinetic activity. Remember, that these outbreaks occurred only after Jackie visited Conrad's apartment. Two different theories might account for such phenomena.

One possibility is that the psychokinesis might have capacitor-like properties associated with it. That when a poltergeist agent (Jackie, in this case) visited the proper environment, the localized geomagnetic and/or electromagnetic environment literally charges up that "special occupant" which is then later discharged somehow by the same person in a secondary environment, which is when phenomena occurrs.

The other theory is that psychokinesis has a quasi-biological nature associated with it, sort of like when you have a bad cold or the flu. When you go over to a friend's house you unwantingly and unwillingly deposit a considerable amount of your airborne/sweat-based bacteria or virus into your friend's environment, and even though you eventually leave, your friend can get ill from what you have left behind.

Lending some degree of support to this particular hypothesis is the fact that on the last occasion when phenomena broke out in Conrad's apartment, Jackie, while present, did not even enter it. She simply picked up a camera from Conrad that he delivered to her outside in her car.

As Conrad did have physical contact with Jackie, which might account for the "paranormal contagion." Might not such a unique infective psychokinetic agent be labeled a "psycho-virus?" As odd as this sounds, remember, your theory must fit your data! And this is what the data strongly suggests.

As the operant mechanism underlying psychokinesis is not known, neither of these two theories can be tested, proven nor disproven. However, one thing that is known is that Conrad had never before experienced any form of psychokinesis in his own environment, and when Jackie stopped visiting him and/or his apartment, the outbreaks totally ceased.

Thus, on the surface, it seems that we might have a causal connection here, even though phenomena did not erupt following every one of Jackie's visit (given the transient nature of this phenomenon, that's expected).

There is yet another, even more intriguing aspect to the psychokinetic attacks on Wheatcraft and the outbreaks of phenomena at Conrad's apartment. During the course of this investigation, Conrad developed into far more than a paranormal investigator in relation to Jackie Hernandez, at least as far as Jackie was concerned.

In his efforts to console Jackie and assist her in overcoming her terrible situation(s), he rapidly became a close personal friend. However, Jackie grossly misinterpreted Conrad's affable, magnanimous nature. She developed a strong romantic interest in him (well, he does bear a striking resemblance to a youthful Elvis Presley).

So strong in fact was her attraction to him that she repeatedly attempted to seduce him, going so far as to break into his apartment through his open bedroom window at 2 A.M. on more than one occasion. To Conrad's astonishment, he awoke the next morning to find a naked Jackie next to him in bed. Given Jackie's appearance and condition at the time, that's a really scary thought. Yes, be afraid, be very afraid.

Later, Jackie's current boyfriend threatened Conrad and this author under the delusion that we were making money off this investigation that we were not sharing with Jackie and him. Jackie's boyfriend was very jealous of Conrad, as he was aware of Jackie's strong attraction to him.

Shortly after the telephonic threats, there were two subsequent break-ins at Conrad's apartment that was strongly suspected to be the work of Jackie's boyfriend. Conrad and I came to the realization that given Jackie's erratically distraught nature and the company she kept, nothing was beyond the realm of possibility.

For the aforementioned reasons, Jackie might have unconsciously viewed Wheatcraft, Conrad's best friend at the time and associate videographer/photographer, as a threat to her desired closeness to Conrad. As such, her psychokinesis might have repeatedly lashed out at Wheatcraft in an effort to remove him from Conrad's environment.

It's as if in her own unconscious mind, Jackie was trying to get rid of her competition, which in her distorted thought process, she believed to be Wheatcraft. Down deep, Jackie probably thought that if Wheatcraft were no longer around, she would not have to vie as hard for Conrad's attention. Remember, most of the time that Conrad came to Jackie's aid, Wheatcraft was with him.

There is another, more disturbing possibility as to why Wheatcraft was repeatedly attacked throughout the investigation of this case. If one gives any credence to the information emanating from the Ouija Board session up in Weldon, the one where Jeff was levitated and almost killed, there may be a very simple answer. During this Ouija Board session, the question was posed to whatever entity was present as to whether it hated anyone.

The board immediately, although not surprisingly, spelled out the name "Jeff." When asked why the entity hated Jeff, the board responded by "saying" that Jeff had the likeness of his murderer. Further questioning asked whether it was a ghost. And if so, how many of them existed.

The reply was anything but simplistic. In fact, it was quite melodramatic; "Phantoms fill the skies around you!" Certainly direct, but a little over the top, wouldn't you say? Or maybe, this was the only cryptic manner in which the psychokinetic projection from Jackie's unconscious could communicate through primary process?

Interestingly, when I discussed this theory with Jackie during the taping of the tabloid TV show Hard Copy, she openly agreed with virtually every aspect of it. However, even if the experienced phenomena were and are in some manner an extension of her libidinous psyche projected against Wheatcraft, this is almost unheard of in terms of its specificity and focus. Or is it? Remember The Entity case?

Needless to say, this banter never made it through editing of the show as the segment producer hadn't the foggiest notion of what I was talking about. If memory serves me correct, the producer said something to the effect of: "So you think Jackie's somehow telling the ghost what to do and he does it?" Yeah, right?

Even if we accept this psychological hypothesis, it does not answer any questions regarding the real nature of the phenomena encountered here. Again citing the most extraordinary example: The last time Jackie came by Conrad's apartment, she never even entered it. Conrad ran out to her waiting car to deliver a camcorder he lent her to videotape phenomena if it appeared.

She certainly could not have capacitively charged Conrad's apartment all the way from the street corner (although she could have affected Conrad himself with a psycho-virus) unless our fundamental concepts regarding the proximity effect of psychokinesis are totally wrong.

Making this case even more convoluted is the belief by Jackie and others that the phenomena are, in fact, the direct result of a literal haunting by men named Herman

Hendrickson and John Damon, the latter who allegedly once resided in Jackie's 11th Street, San Pedro house.

Apparently, Jackie believed that during several Ouija board sessions the ghost revealed that he was born in 1912 and was murdered in 1930 at the hands of a friend who was supposedly attempting to steal his wife away. With that information, old newspaper reports were discovered in the hall of records chronicling the death of a wandering merchant marine, Herman Hendrickson, whose body was found floating under a pier in San Pedro on March 25, 1930.

Further reinforcing this belief was Jackie's claim that on one evening she followed another enigmatic, although seemingly benign, ghost light to the grave of John Damon in a local cemetery, only half a mile from where she lived.

Now if we assume that in reality, she did not simply locate the burial site of Damon on her own and lie about it in the attempt to obtain closure on this case, then this event takes on a very significance.

However, by this point in time, Jackie was so confused that she literally blamed and explained anything and everything she did not understand on the "ghosts," a typical overreaction common in these types of cases.

Meanwhile, back in reality, it turns out that Hendrickson was 10 years older than Jackie's Ouija board revealed. He had a jagged wound on the top of his head, and the coroner ruled that he had drowned. Authorities determined that the seaman had not been murdered but had sustained the wound when he fell off the dock while intoxicated. Unfortunately, these discrepancies did not dissuade Jackie from believing that Hendrickson was one of the two ghosts that had latched onto her.

To make matters worse, the second ghost's identity is even more problematic. Jackie and her friends said they learned from talking to old-time San Pedro residents that her bungalow was built by a man named John Damon. They assumed he was the old man who appeared to Jackie on her trip to the bathroom and at the dining room table, although there was no hard evidence that he, in fact, died in the house or even lived there.

As a parapsychologist, my attitude on this matter is very simple and straightforward. If there were photographs available of Herman Hendrickson and John Damon that happened to a bear striking resemblance to the observed apparitions, that might lend some credence to this line of imaginative thinking.

To lock the entire matter down would require clear, distinct photographs of the apparitions seen by Jackie (don't we wish), that when compared to photos of Hendrickson and Damon were objectively determined to be the same physical appearance. That, and only that, would serve as semi-hard evidence. Short of that, the precise nature of the phenomena afflicting Jackie Hernandez remains in question.

Another fascinating tale arising out of this case happened when Conrad, Wheatcraft, Jackie and I appeared on The Joan River's Show in the spring of 1993. Nothing significant occurred during the actual taping of our segments of the show (it never does in these types of programs). However, when Jackie initially entered the New York production studio, various psychokinetic events began.

Initially, the show's computers were supposed to print out several hard copies of the transcribed interviews with Jackie and the rest of us for Joan to refer to while on the air. When the computers started printing, all that appeared on the paper was unintelligible gibberish.

During the course of the taping [which in itself was quite difficult to endure because

Aliens Above, Ghosts Below by Barry E. Taff

Joan Rivers refused to deal with any of us without cracking one of her feeble attempts at humor] the facilities which control the introduction of slides and videotapes during the show suddenly, were unable to do anything, as many of the systems inexplicably shut down. Therefore, none of the slides or tapes supplied to the show by us ever aired. This problem became so annoying that Rivers even referred to it momentarily during the taping.

Another similar incident, that may be psycho-kinetically related, was when Conrad, Jackie and I were leaving Los Angeles International Airport the day before the River's show. For reasons that the airline never quite determined, the initial aircraft we were going to fly to New York refused to function properly.

The subsequent delays pushed our departure time from 8:30 A.M. to 12:47 P.M. This event may or may not be directly related to the others cited herewith, but it certainly cannot be ignored.

An interesting sidebar to this particular case emerged approximately twelve years ago when Conrad was talking to the woman who cleans his house. The conversation eventually led around to his interest in ghosts. The cleaning lady related a story to Conrad that tentatively supports the haunting angle of this case as opposed to the poltergeist one.

Back in the first few weeks of 1989, the cleaning lady lived only a couple of blocks away from Jackie's 11th Street bungalow in San Pedro. While residing there, she claims to have been harassed by the apparition of an elderly man wearing the same clothes Jackie described during her numerous apparitional encounters.

In fact, point-for-point, the physical description of the two apparitions was identical in virtually every detail. The cleaning woman's experience occurred just several weeks prior to those of Jackie's. Is there a connection?

Inasmuch as the cleaning lady's experience occurred long before there was any media exposure on this case, it's safe to assume that she was not fabricating or simply lying, especially since those apparitional encounters forced her to move from San Pedro to Playa Del Rey.

From an anthropomorphic perspective, it almost sounds as if something akin to a "paranormal predator" was canvassing the San Pedro area for a victim around the beginning of 1989. Assuming for one moment that this belief or scenario is anything other than an intriguing fantasy, the phenomena might have first attempted to "infect" the cleaning lady in question, but was unsuccessful. It then may have moved on to Jackie Hernandez, or should I say, Hazard (which certainly describes her life for the last nineteen years), where its effects speak for themselves.

The above sidebar strongly smacks of a virus or bacteria/virus-like life form that seeks out an intended prey, attaches itself to them and then proceeds to use the host's biological energy for its own needs.

As discussed earlier, this might also account for the instances where psychokinetic storms broke out at Conrad's house after Jackie visited, even though on one occasion she had not even entered his apartment.

This would also take into account the mini-psychokinetic maelstroms that broke out at both Wheatcraft's and Gary Boehm's homes (although Jackie had never visited either location) after they spent the better part of an evening at Jackie's house. The possibility that certain types of phenomena have a contagious nature cannot be ignored.

The only researcher who did not have any phenomena occur in his home environment was this author. Now admittedly, I did not spend anywhere near as much time around Jackie as

68

Aliens Above, Ghosts Below by Barry E. Taff

Conrad and/or Wheatcraft, nor was there the emotional association between this writer and Conrad as there was with Wheatcraft for Jackie to fixate upon. I believe that Jackie knew from the outset that I viewed her as little more than white trash and as such ignored me, which was a good thing.

However, there may be a more simple explanation for the phenomena avoiding me. Of all the individuals investigating this "hazardous" case, I was the only one who did not display any form of fear regarding the phenomena.

As skeptical as Wheatcraft was, and as incredibly curious as Conrad was, they both had very low "fight or flight" thresholds. Perhaps, this quasi-biological energy could sense fear (much as an animal can) and was drawn to those individuals generating prodigious amounts of adrenalin and who were thus reacting more intensely. Could it be that such terrified individuals offer more binding receptors for such a quasi-biologic energy to react with?

Further complicating matters in this incredibly convoluted case is yet another twist, one that forces us to give even more serious consideration to a haunting being responsible for these events.

In August of 1996, a video crew from the United Paramount (television) Network series Strange Universe visited Jackie's original house in San Pedro after interviewing Hernandez, Conrad and myself to obtain some B-role footage to accompany the segment on air.

Upon arriving at Jackie's original San Pedro home they discovered that the house was again vacant which allowed them access to its interior rather than relying only on exterior shots. While initially touring the house, they heard strange pounding noises emanating from the attic, just as our group did the first night of the investigation back in August of '89. As they began taping, their Betacam suddenly and inexplicably shut down. Apparently, all their freshly charged batteries had failed, just as ours did during many early visits to the house.

As they were unable to continue shooting in the house, they went outside. Once away from the bungalow, their Betacam and audio equipment came back to life. Intrigued, they again entered the house in an effort to continue taping. To the crew's astonishment and growing anxiety, their recording instruments once again failed.

When they finally exited the little bungalow and were talking in the front yard, their equipment again sprang back to life. Needless to say, the crew was somewhat perplexed and unnerved by this experience, as they knew their equipment to be very dependable and reliable.

Adding more fuel to the belief that the property is haunted (as opposed to nothing other than Jackie's psychokinesis) was the fact that we spoke with the relatively new property owners (a husband and wife) residing in the front house. They told us that in the years since they have been there, the longest anyone had resided in Jackie's old house was approximately six months. What a surprise?

This could more readily be explained by the fact that this area of San Pedro is a very low rent district attracting a lot of transients, thus having a high rate of turnover as many residents simply cannot afford rent and skip out.

However, when the owners spoke of loose objects being hurled at them while in the house and items that initially sat on the countertop in the kitchen frequently ending up on the floor many feet away, strongly suggested that there continues to be considerable phenomena associated with this property.

After we spent a small amount of time in the house around the middle of September 1996, nothing in the way of phenomena was experienced, although every member of our investigative group experienced a strong sense of overpressure that appeared to build in intensity.

This follow-up investigation strongly suggested that this case might be a haunting as opposed to a poltergeist. Still, how does one account for Jackie's continuing to manifest phenomena around herself long after she abandoned the 11th street house in conjunction with the fact that she claims to have never experienced any type of phenomena whatsoever prior to living in this particular house? It's always been assumed that phenomena were of one type or the other. Could it be that there is another possibility?

Postulate that there are certain environments that have experienced violent traumatic events in their past and somehow become charged with the energy of human consciousness, and that this residual consciousness is in some form intelligent, not random psychokinetic force. That this charge of consciousness is composed of energy that has properties akin to bacteria and viruses in that it can "infect" certain individuals who are susceptible to its influence.

Enter the unsuspecting individual into this unique energetic environment. If this person is highly susceptible to the energetic charge they might become infected. Such an infection would subtly alter the neuro-chemical and electrochemical composition of the person's physiology.

One of the results of this "infection" might be to generate various forms psychokinetic phenomena mediated by the host's unconscious mind. And of course, once infected, they might carry this force within them to other locations where they continue to propagate phenomena.

Simply put in biophysical/electronic terms, the psychokinetic agent acts as an inductively coupled trigger for the charged environment. Such an environment would likely be composed of a geomagnetic anomaly and/or high amplitude 60 Hz. electromagnetic noise. This then conveys the impression that the phenomenon is non-localized, as it appears to follow the individual from house to house; when in reality all that's occurring is the outward manifestation of a unique psychic infection or "psycho-virus".

The type of individual who is susceptible to this charge is perhaps that person we now define as a poltergeist or psychokinetic agent. Perhaps their unstable nature both at the neuro-chemical and emotional level may allow the earth's charge to easily couple with them?

In point of fact, there is more than ample evidence supporting the theory that the majority of these poltergeist agents are either seizure prone or epileptic. Adding more weight to this theory comes from numerous individuals this author has interviewed who suffer from temporal lobe epilepsy. Most, if not all of such uniquely wired individuals said that when they correctly take medication to inhibit their seizures, the psychokinetic events cease as well. What a coincidence.

In parpsychological research there are two known types of psychokinesis. At one end of the spectrum is the microscopic form that is somewhat volitional and has been documented as affecting random event and random number generators. When this level of PK is demonstrated there is fatigue observed in those triggering it.

At the other end of the scale is the macroscopic form of PK that appears to be at the root of poltergeist cases and is frequently referred to as recurrent spontaneous psychokinesis, more simply, RSPK. Surprisingly, macroscopic PK is not volitional and the suspected agents of such show absolutely no signs whatsoever of fatigue after such occurrences.

The majority of individuals who suffer from epilepsy do not experience poltergeist outbreaks while almost all macroscopic psychokinetic agents do. Therefore, somewhere in the middle is a missing or unknown variable. Could that variable be as simple as one's chemically imbalanced emotions?

We will never know as to whether Jackie suffered from such neurological problems as she was extremely reluctant to pursue this type of inquiry, probably due to the fact that she was a substance abuser and felt that such intense medical scrutiny would further complicate her already dysfunctional life.

That being said, it is important to emphasize that the forces at work regarding psychokinetic/poltergeist outbreaks are almost certainly not electromagnetic in nature as they affect matter that is both diamagnetic and dielectric. Well if not electromagnetic, then what?

Gravity as we understand it, requires a substantial mass, as do black holes and their less destructive cousin, wormholes, so we can rule them out. The strong and weak nuclear forces would not generate sufficient force other than through heat to be of any use in psychokinesis.

Oh, and let's not forget the fact that all of the aforementioned forces would be self-injurious to the extreme if humanly generated. Where then does that leave us in search of a power source? The answer to this question may be hidden within the nature of what repeatedly happened to Wheatcraft.

When he was physically thrown around like a rag doll, his immediate surround should have dramatically heated up due to the liberated heat generated as a byproduct of the work being done. It's the old $F = MA$, or more simply; force equals mass times acceleration. The result of which is the simple, straightforward, second law of thermodynamics at its best, and there's no way around it. Or is there?

Long before Jeff's 6'2", 215 lb. frame could be tossed across a room, the generated heat would set his clothing, the carpet and every piece of furniture ablaze. And of course, he would be instantly immolated by such an intense exothermic reaction. But again, this is how the forces we know of function.

There is but one candidate remaining that could theoretically fill the bill. We now must address something called Zero Point energy. That ubiquitous form of energy that may be related to dark energy and dark matter and that may generate cold as opposed to heat when doing work and could possibly neutralize inertia and gravity.

Given the potentially deadly consequences of biologically generating such power, it's far more logical to assume that PGA's are not producing such force, but rather tapping into what's already present. If this theory is correct, then such PGA's would be little more than biological operational amplifiers and waveguides.

However, the ways in which such energies couple with PGA's, most assuredly are electromagnetic, at least the portion of it we can currently detect and measure. It goes without saying that we cannot measure what we do not know. All we are able to detect and analyze at this relatively primitive stage of paranormal research is how such unknown paranormal forces affect the matter and energy we currently are aware of.

As intriguing as this theory may appear, parts of it generically resembles a pseudo-scientific definition of possession, which of course, is an untestable hypothesis and conjures up the notion where spirits of deceased individuals are controlling and directing actions of living persons. Right, and I can fly without a plane?

There is no suggestion here that a discarnate intelligence has entered into and taken control of an individual. What is being proposed here bears only the crudest generic similarity to it. Moreover, there is absolutely no suggestion here that the dead are in any way influencing the living. Unless, of course, you wish to consider politicians and lawyers, who in my humble opinion, have been dead from the neck up for decades, if not centuries?

Sorry about that. I do, occasionally, get carried away regarding my intrinsic hatred of lawyers and politicians who I believe to be self-serving, emotionally dead beings possessing absolutely no soul, redeeming qualities or conscience whatsoever. Such individuals drain people and society of money, hope and dreams while returning nothing other than misery, despair and financial destitution. Oops, there I go again.

However, it must be reiterated at this point that these descriptions (other than those of lawyers and politicians) are artful speculation based on observation, collection and analysis of data and analogy. While some of these theories may make sense to us rationally, they cannot be proved or disproved.

This disclaimer is made for those who question whether this investigation was a serious scientific inquiry. It's been twenty years since our involvement in this case began and, for the most part, we are just as much in the dark as to the exact nature of these phenomena as we were when it started. Although, a PGA inductively coupling with the environment seems to theoretically provide us with a testable working hypothesis.

If this theoretical inductive coupling between PGA's and the electromagnetic environments is correct, then it should be possible to artificially "drive" such coupling by modifying said environments within which PGA's are enclosed.

However, there are several major concerns regarding this specific approach. The most crucial of which is the problem of modifying said environments might prove to be very dangerous to the occupants both physically and emotionally, making such a venture immoral and unethical.

Secondly, each electromagnetic variable (frequency, amplitude, pulse duration, pulse interval, pulse repetition rate, ion concentration/density, etc.) would have to be individually manipulated in order to determine which specific independent variable, if any, produces a given result.

In a peculiar sort of way, this whole scenario is somewhat reminiscent of "Monsters From The Id" as depicted in the 1956 motion picture Forbidden Planet, a loose adaptation of Shakespeare's "The Tempest", wherein the indigenous alien residents (the Krell) of a planet within a distant star system developed technology that could translate their thoughts and whims into energy and matter that they then could project anywhere on the planet. Only later, did the Krell discover that their unconscious whims, wants, needs and fears were guiding the process, which eventually led to their own destruction. Does this science fiction plot seem strangely familiar?

What's being theoretically postulated here regarding humanly mediated psychokinesis is pretty much the same as in Forbidden Planet with one glaring exception; we don't have the technology to create such incredible effects. Although in the real world, it appears as if the interrelationship between certain individuals and their physical environment may serve as a poor man's substitute. Then again, maybe it's a good thing that we do not possess such advanced psychotronic technology given our predilection for violence? What do you think?

The final question that needs to be answered is as to whether there indeed is some form of human consciousness that survives corporeal death, and if so, does it play any role whatsoever in such paranormal events, or are we just anthropomorphizing occurrences that we cannot explain? Many questions, but as yet, no definitive answers.

Sure, we successfully recorded a significant amount of phenomena on videotape and

35mm. film, and personally experienced even more activity (including the near-death of an acquaintance that resulted in a severe personality breakdown). But in the end, Jackie's life is still in shambles much as it was before we met her and began our investigation. Although admittedly, the twenty-six years preceding our involvement, was not exactly a walk in the park, either.

The Hernandez case will certainly go down in parapsychological history as a unique one, perhaps even more so than The Entity, if for no other reason than the sheer magnitude of phenomena captured on film and videotape.

There is one last bit of high strangeness regarding Wheatcraft and the continuing onslaught of psychokinetic attacks plaguing him.

By the spring of 1993, Wheatcraft's behavior became demonstrably odd as discussed earlier. This resulted in both Conrad and I breaking off any and all contact with Wheatcraft. We did not have contact with Wheatcraft again until the early summer of 2007 when we all worked on a DVD at Warner Bros. In March of 2008, Conrad and I were invited to Wheatcraft's 60th birthday party at his sister's house here in West Los Angeles.

While at the party, both Conrad and I met one of Wheatcraft's ex-girlfriends that he met with us on a case during the summer of 1992 just following the San Pedro case.

Sandra Ramirez told us of an incredible account of Wheatcraft being attacked once again, but this time within her home in San Gabriel. It was summer of 1995, and Wheatcraft was at Sandra's house. There had just been a rather heated, emotional exchange between Sandra and her kids, which was quite common.

Moments later, Wheatcraft was walking towards Sandra in the living room when suddenly he was violently pulled backward, arcing up to meet the ceiling and finally impacting the wall and landing on the floor.

Sandra immediately let out a loud scream and momentarily froze. Unfortunately, this type of psychokinetic belligerence was all too familiar to Jeff had he remained conscious. Sandra ran over to find Wheatcraft lying unconscious on the floor. When he came to he described feeling the same bodily sensation during this attack as that of the one up in Weldon years earlier.

As this last psychokinetic attack on Wheatcraft came at least three or four years after the last time he was around Jackie, what was it that lashed out at him? Certainly not Jackie.

In search of answers to these continuing belligerent episodes, I had Wheatcraft take the Personality Assessment Inventory psychological test provided by my colleague and friend, parapsychologist Dr. Andrew Nichols. This specific test looks for indicators of self-loathing which some academic researchers suspect might help explain these types of recurring psychokinetic hostilities.

Unfortunately, Wheatcraft's answers to this comprehensive test failed to indicate any aspects of low self-esteem and self-loathing. Now what? Where does this leave us in terms of trying to understand the nature of this phenomenon? Absolutely nowhere!

However, the question of whether we were dealing with a complex situation of intense, biologically mediated psychokinesis or potential discarnate intelligence is better left to future academic interpretation, at a time perhaps when those conducting such research possess tools that are designed to measure what we do not as yet know.

Just because we, in the modern age of electronic wonders, as scientifically trained and oriented academic researchers, find the notion of survival and discarnate intelligence intolerable, does not preclude or prevent its occurrence.

In closing, there is but one salient point to remember; in all forms of scientific research your theory must fit the data you've collected. To only seek out data that conforms to your predetermined beliefs is not science, it's quackery and pseudoscience, which is what we see practiced on the majority, if not all, of the paranormally themed reality shows of today.

Unfortunately, this is one of the fundamental reasons why mainstream science tends to ignore much of what they hear and see within the paranormal research community (especially if its on TV), as the majority of it is conducted by un-credentialed individuals who have absolutely no training whatsoever in the methods by which such research needs to be conducted.

If one does not know how the physical world around them works, how then can they know what lies beyond its boundaries? That's entertainment and nothing more.

Even though Jackie Hernandez's psychological profile fits precisely what we have come to expect in poltergeist agents, it still does not fully explain or account for a substantial portion of the experienced phenomena.

Unless we begin to open up our all-but-made-up minds and let ourselves not be confused by what we think this phenomena might be, and at least accept (without necessarily conceding) the possibility of the improbable, our ability to properly evaluate and learn from these encounters will significantly diminish, if not totally cease.

END

Chapter 4:
AN ALL TOO HUMAN HAUNTING

Even the most devoted parapsychologist eventually desires to just layback and take a break or vacation from his research. I was presented with just such an opportunity in the summer of 1987 when an old friend made me an offer I could not refuse.

It had been a long time since I last heard from my friend Roger, a writer/producer living in Studio City, California with his new wife Robbie. I was quite startled getting an out-of-the-blue call from him asking if I would care to house sit as he and Robbie were going on a honeymoon to Europe for several weeks.

Visiting Roger at his new home for the first time I had little difficulty in deciding whether to accept his offer. His luxurious home was situated in a rustic neighborhood within the San Fernando Valley and had a large, heated pool for swimming away the hot summer days and nights, a large built-in barbecue, a master bedroom most people would slave years for, and an immense screening room with a large projection TV with a surround sound system most people only dream about.

My responsibilities were to feed Roger's two dogs, Cognac and Jennifer, and to keep the house clean and safe. The latter two requirements were a piece of cake as they had a house cleaner who came once a week and a sophisticated security system.

Little did I know the real reason Roger wanted me to house stay at his house. A reason that would drive any normal person running from the residence in fear. The house was haunted. A fact, I only learned later, that Robbie would not even discuss with Roger, as just the thought was disturbing to her.

Equally unknown to me was that just several weeks earlier, a huge magnum of champagne that was resting upon the kitchen table was mysteriously propelled across the kitchen's expanse into the area just below the sinks over ten feet away. The resulting impact shattered the magnum into tiny pieces, showering the entire kitchen with glass shards and bubbly liquid.

If I had prior knowledge as to the fact that this beautiful house was haunted, I wonder if I would have been so quick to take Roger up on his offer? Remember, I was there to simply relax and enjoy, not to continue my never-ending search for phenomena. But then again, most, if not all of my adult life, has been dedicated to such investigations and given the unique opportunity of actually getting to live in a haunted house which in research in very rare, could I have turned it down in all good faith? But then again, you know what they say. Be careful what you ask for!

I arrived at the house on the evening of August 28, 1987, and put my duffel bag on the bed. After leaving the room and returning sometime later, I found my duffel to be sitting on the floor.

Scratching my head, I tried to remember just how far onto the middle of the bed I placed my duffel. I was certain that I did not leave it close to the edge. Even if I did, the duffel was several feet away from the bed, not right next to it as it would be if it simply fell off.

Later that first night at around 10 P.M., I noticed that small items of furniture also seemed to have a mind of their own and moved about spontaneously.

One of the nightstands in the master bedroom found its way into the center of the hallway connecting the rear living room to the master bath and bedroom. I returned it to its correct location only to later (about an hour) discover that it was again moved back into the center of the hallway.

As I was alone in the house and the security system was on, I really did not know what to think. Not for one moment did I even consider the possibility that the house was haunted. I incorrectly assumed that my unfamiliarity with the house had tricked my memory and I had forgotten to place the nightstand in its proper location or that I was somehow distracted.

However, when another piece of furniture, the portable mini-music system in the bedroom, moved itself to the hallway from across the room, I became very suspicious that perhaps someone had broken into the house unnoticed and was attempting to terrorize me. And, truth be known, I have to admit it was doing a damn good job, especially given my multi-decade background in this field.

This was certainly a possibility. Perhaps I did not correctly activate the security system, as it was my first day in the house. A quick search of the house and the garage combined with a check of the security system proved me wrong on both counts.

The rest of that first night was quite peaceful and I went to bed at about 1 A.M. to what I thought would be an extremely restful night's sleep due to the remote location of the house. Again, I was wrong. Dead wrong to be exact.

At exactly 6:08 A.M. of the next morning, August 29th, something suddenly woke me from a sound sleep. To this day I swear that I was pinched on my side. Upon awakening in an already well-lit room and looking at the large digital clock to my left, I attempted to return to sleep.

However, before I could do so I felt and saw the bedspread and covers to my left rise up and the bed beneath them depress as if an invisible person was actually entering the bed.

Whatever was entering the bed, it casually approached and actually cuddled against my body. The phantom form appeared to be breathing and was lukewarm. It had a definite fragrance or odor to it, one that was immediately recognizable as floral and clearly feminine.

The ghostly form now pushed up tight against my body and was unquestionably female as I could feel its large breasts pressing firmly against my left side, its long hair falling on my left cheek and its head resting on my chest.

Whatever this thing was, its motions resembled that of someone taking their clothes off for lack of a better explanation. The bedspread lifted in seeming response to each apparent movement of this invisible presence. Finally, I decided to "reach out and touch" what I could not see. As I extended my arm to make contact with it, the presence rapidly departed the bed, throwing the bed sheets and covers into the air and the mattress rebounding.

The only quasi-sensory impression I had other than the tactile and olfactory ones was the thought the female entity had long, thick, black hair. Even after more than thirty years and more than 3,500 investigated cases of hauntings, poltergeists and the like, this experience was quite unsettling.

Over the twenty-one years since my encounter with this particular entity, I have often wondered why I was not the least bit terrified, or even startled somewhat by this experience. Perhaps my being acclimated to this type of phenomena in general may have had something to do with it.

However, as the phenomena did not represent any form of threat or clear and present danger to me, my fight or flight reaction never kicked in, in fact, from my perspective, the entire event was quite intriguing. And, if you now think that I'm just a little strange, given what I just said, I wouldn't blame you.

Another particularly interesting aspect of the phenomena, which was present from the moment I first set foot in the house, was the feeling of being at around 2.5 atmospheres of pressure--like being underwater in a deep pool or scuba diving.

The subtle pain accompanying this sensation of overpressure is primarily in the sinuses as well as the frontal and temporal lobes of the head. However, one's reaction to this condition is very subjective. Oddly, there is no correlation between this sensation and barometric pressure. Go figure.

This unusual feeling persisted without interruption through the end of my second housesitting episode, although the intensity of overpressure did vary over time and seemingly correlated with the onset of phenomena. Interestingly, virtually everyone entering the house felt the same type of physical sensation without ever knowing of the phenomena transpiring within.

As I settled in the house, so did the phenomena. On numerous occasions, the electrical power would go into a brownout mode, causing the digital clocks and other appliances to blink the all-too-common "12:00." Similarly, the houses sophisticated security system was repeatedly triggered (mostly late at night or early in the morning) for no apparent reason.

While it's possible that these transient electrical upsets could be the result of faulty wiring or power transmission problems, that likelihood was eliminated by professional examination of the houses wiring and a call to the local power company. The high repetition rates associated with the electrical malfunction combined with the fact that such events supposedly never happened before, lead me to speculate that the cause may have been paranormal in nature. Further reinforcing this belief was the security system's diagnostic mode, which indicated that there were no problems with it or its current feed.

The next weekend, I invited several close friends over for a dinner party; Frank, Larry, Marshall, Barbara and Laurie to name a few. We enjoyed a delicious barbecue that balmy summer night. After the main course was consumed, Frank brought out a fantastic ice cream cake he had brought for dessert.

Pieces were cut for everyone, but I found myself too full from the main coarse to ingest that much sugar. I told Laurie, who cut the cake, that I would hold off temporarily on the cake, and eat a slice later.

Laurie left what remained of the cake on the kitchen table while all of us retired to the rear living room, which is in full view of the kitchen. The dogs, as usual, were locked outside the house in the yard. However, their behavior was peculiar (even considering the presence of strangers unfamiliar to them in the house) as they were extremely nervous and restless given their normal laid-back nature.

As all of us sat in the glass-walled living room talking, both Jennifer and Cognac continuously walked around the outside of the glass walls as if they were watching and stalking something other than the people inside, quite intensely.

About ninety minutes later, Laurie asked if I would now care for a piece of cake. I nodded "yes" and she went to bring it bring it out to me from the kitchen. Suddenly, we all heard Laurie scream from the kitchen and ran to see what happened.

Aliens Above, Ghosts Below by Barry E. Taff

The remainder of the ice cream cake had completely disappeared from the plate it was on (yes, the air conditioning in the house was on). As none of us had left the living room and the dogs were still outside, there was no explanation for the cake's vanishing. This was the first incident of apport phenomena within the house, but far from the last.

Later that evening the security system again began acting up as it kept triggering then resetting itself. When its loud sirens began to howl at 2 A.M., it sounded like the diving klaxon of a Trident nuclear missile submarine. It was sufficiently loud to wake the neighbors across the street, who came out yelling for me to shut it off. You could say that it was literally loud enough to wake the dead, which in this case was probably an accurate assessment.

If that were not enough, the numerous smoke detectors within the house would intermittently go off throughout the night and early morning. Eventually, I was forced to dismantle them, either by pulling out their wires and/or batteries. Finally, I was able to sleep for an extended duration.

Several days later, my girlfriend, Jodi, came over to the house. She arrived with enough clothes and luggage to spend several weeks as opposed to a couple of days. After placing her prescription pill bottle on the master bedroom nightstand, it somehow found its way to the rear bathroom. As we had both observed the bottle on the now infamous nightstand, then its absence, I was positive that neither of us accidentally or unconsciously moved it.

Shortly after this incident, the pill bottle again moved. This time from the bathroom back onto the bedroom nightstand. Jodi was becoming a little concerned. It was one thing to talk about such events in the second or third person, quite another to be right in the middle of them. After numerous other apports, Jodi's hypersensitivity to the ever-constant overpressure, her stay at the house lasted less that one full day.

Whatever was present in the house now seemed to take a definite upward surge in its activity. A Los Angeles TV Times magazine moved from the bedroom to the kitchen. Almost every time I attempted to watch TV in the bedroom, the TV magazine would apport itself into the kitchen or den.

This was followed by the appearance of a foul odor, reminiscent of something musty that was accompanied by the sounds of barely audible conversations and heavy footsteps. Most of the odors and sounds appeared to emanate from the region of the hardwood floors in the front and rear living rooms. Both dogs reacted to these particular events with fear and intense howling and frequently seemed to be tracking the presence within the living room through their glass walls.

One evening, after returning home with a Numero Uno's pizza, for one of the few times in my professional career I was really startled and almost frightened. While cutting the pizza within its cardboard box and placing it on a plate in the kitchen, I suddenly became aware of someone standing to my immediate left.

I saw the reflected image of a large man in the glass wall panes to my immediate left. As I knew that I was absolutely alone in the house and was now quite experienced with the security system's operation, I was really caught by surprise and jumped over the table to my right, taking the pizza with me to the floor. Needless to say, there was no physical person standing next to me reflecting his image in the glass. Well, so much for my dinner. I wondered if Numero Uno would have replaced the pizza free of charge if I told them what happened?

It definitely seemed as if the presence in the house had a fondness for food. One afternoon, I bought a large submarine sandwich and brought it back to the house to eat for lunch. After taking the macaroni salad out of its container and pouring the Pepsi into a glass, I returned to the table to begin eating.

78

To my astonishment, half of the sub sandwich was nowhere to be found. In fact, the remaining half of the sub showed marks indicating that it was not cleanly cut in half. There were marks on the roll akin to human teeth, suggesting that the sandwich was bitten in half.

Teeth belonging to a ghost? Huh? Bitten in half? Bitten by what? Where in the hell did teeth marks come from? I guess you could say that the sandwich really had a bite to it? I know, another bad pun. Hey, friends don't say I suffer from paronomasia (compulsion to pun) for nothing.

My reaction to all of this was not fear, but amazement and a little anger as I just lost half my lunch and was very hungry. But where did half of the sub sandwich go? Was this loss of food getting to be a habit, or what?

Other unusual occurrences included the pool lights, TV, VCR and stereo system turning themselves on repeatedly, even though the batteries had been removed from their remotes. Between the audio/visual system and the many smoke detector's behavior, late night was not a time I looked forward to in terms of relaxing. To make matters worse, the rear door exiting the kitchen kept unlocking and opening itself, thereby activating the security system again.

On several occasions I had friends stay overnight to serve as witnesses to various phenomena. Both Larry and Dana stayed over in the guest bedroom on different nights with the intent of hearing and possibly observing what were causing the strange noises coming from the living rooms.

As expected, we all independently heard muffled conversations and loud footsteps throughout the night. Both Larry and Dana were so unnerved by what they heard that their fear kept them from investigating the matter further. Whenever I placed my voice-activated micro-cassette recorder in the rooms where noises were coming from they would immediately cease, only to reoccur once the recorder was turned off or removed. How typical.

The phenomenon was equally evasive when I feverishly ran out of the master bedroom in the dead of night in numerous attempts to observe their cause. Whatever this thing was, it appeared to be demonstrating a high degree of intelligence and evasiveness.

One morning while alone in the house, I was again awakened by something lifting the bedcovers off my feet and attempting to tickle me in the arch of my foot (fortunately, I am not ticklish). I looked down and saw that the covers had indeed been moved by nothing visually present.

As my stay in the house continued, I found it increasingly difficult to achieve or maintain sleep. There came a loud knocking and then pounding at the large glass-paned bedroom walls. Then came the sounds of bells or gongs, accompanied by more enigmatic noises. This was eventually joined by more disembodied voices and footsteps erupting from the front of the house. In concert, my senses were being assailed.

The dogs were ferociously barking at something through the glass walls in the living room and within the front bathroom. On several occasions I had to wake up and feed the dogs small amounts of tranquilizers in their food in order for either of us to get some badly needed sleep.

Several days later, Frank, Barbara and Laurie returned armed with more audiocassette recorders and a Nikon 4004 35 mm. camera. With all the lights in the house off, we wandered around looking for some visual element or component of the phenomena.

Aliens Above, Ghosts Below by Barry E. Taff

We heard some inexplicable sounds coming from the front bathroom that made us open its door to be greeted by two, large, glowing balls of light. They looked for the most part like ball lightning, which is very rare and supposedly does not occur on the west coast of the U.S.

The balls of light were blue-white in color and about one-third to one-half the size of an adult male head. We all jumped back and I instinctively raised and fired the camera. Shooting Kodak Tri-X film at 1,2000th/sec. at 6,000 ASA, I caught almost exactly what we saw with our eyes. The photographs of these large, luminous orbs are first horizontal in formation, then in the very next frame taken less than one second later, they are vertical. (See Photos 7 & 8)

The lights suddenly and quickly moved towards us and over our heads forcing us to hit the deck, as the thought of being struck by ball lightning is not enticing. The lights disappeared far too rapidly for us to follow them. Interestingly, we did not observe the horizontal/vertical positional shift captured by the camera.

Of particular interest in these photographs is the fact that one of the balls of lights appears to be "sputtering" or ejecting a plasma-like substance from its lower left edge. This effect appears in both photographs and strongly suggests that whatever this phenomenon is, it is not light, as photons do not behave in such a manner or possess such corpuscular properties.

Plasma, however, which is precisely what ball lightning is supposedly composed of, does behave in such a manner. Although, if we consider the possibility that these images are the result of plasma, a.k.a., ball lightning, we have to contend with their source, which is exceedingly difficult to explain, as St. Elmo's Fire is not supposed to occur in this geographical area.

Later that evening, we observed some additional anomalistic arcs of light within a diffused cloud moving across the eastern wall of the dinning room. These lights had no apparent source. The Nikon, now accidentally loaded with Kodacolor 400 film, caught only a small portion of what was seen by our unaided eyes. Fortunately, a large clock is within the frame and provided a straightforward time reference.

Towards the end of my first house sitting experience, I found that sleep became increasingly difficult to achieve regardless of my physical or mental state. My dreams became heavily anxiety laden, many of which dealt with a relatively recent emotional scar that had not yet completely healed.

In my own subjective opinion, the presence in the house was, in all likelihood, inducing these dreams so as to generate arousal within me, thereby feeding on it. At no other point in my life have I experienced recurring dreams even vaguely similar to these, either in nature of intensity. But then again, maybe there was a geomagnetic anomaly present which could readily induce such psycho-physiological effects. However, we did not have the portable EM instrumentation we have today.

One of the last incidents to occur during my first stay at Roger's house happened during an afternoon while talking with a friend on the kitchen phone. As I sat talking, the large wrought iron and glass kitchen table flew across the floor and firmly struck the right side of my ribcage. Just before the table hit me, I heard the sound of it moving and turned my head just in time to see it in motion. There was not enough time for me to move out of its way. The resulting injury raised a black and blue welt that was quite painful and lasted for a considerable time. Fortunately, no ribs were broken.

Shortly thereafter, Roger and his wife returned from Europe. For reasons of control, I did not discuss my experiences with either of them to see if they were going to say anything to me. Remember, at this point in time, I was not aware that Roger knew his house was haunted,

80

which is why he wanted me to housesit during his absence; to learn what I might experience to consensually validate the phenomena in his own mind. What a friend!

The day Roger returned, he called asking if I took his bathrobe home with me. My response was "of course not!". First, I do not steal and furthermore, I had a bathrobe of my own. On top of that, Roger is at least 6 inches taller and seventy-five pounds heavier. What was I going to do with his bathrobe? Sleep in it, or make 2-3 additional robes out of it.

Roger still did not discuss anything unusual about his house. Nor did I bring it up. It was not until about five days later, after another disturbing personal experience that Roger finally opened up to me.

One morning, Roger called me at home, his voice trembling, barely able to speak. After vergiberating for about a minute or so, I calmed him down and asked what the problem was. Roger said that while he was brushing his hair in the main bathroom, he casually placed the brush down on the countertop next to the sink. As he watched, the hairbrush actually disappeared from sight. Not dematerialize, per se, more like optically "wink-out." Roger stood there transfixed to the spot, not knowing what to do.

To say that Roger was frightened and disturbed by these events would indeed be an understatement. In the many years I had known Roger, I never heard him like this before. Finally, he began talking about the fact that his house was haunted and asked if I had any experiences while staying there.

Following my lengthy story, I asked if Robbie had ever had any run-ins with the ghost and Roger answered "yes," but that she was very frightened by such events and did not really believe in such things. Being a psychologist further heightened her inherent skepticism in such matters, as they are, by nature, a very disbelieving lot. Therefore, she did not want to discuss the matter, actually getting angry when the subject was brought up. I respected Roger's wishes and did not query her on the matter.

However, I did learn that Robbie actually grew up within this house, which she inherited from her family and eventually added to with an extra bedroom and bathroom. Interestingly, I also discovered that the house had manifested phenomena from the time it was originally built in the 1940's, when her parents described numerous encounters with phenomena they really did not want to deal with, so they tried their best to ignore it, hoping it would simply go away.

Several days later, Roger again called asking if I had left a very old book in his bedroom. My response was negative. He proceeded to tell me about finding a 150 year-old book sitting on his nightstand, which he could not account for.

Since my first stay at Roger's house, I was able to sit on three more occasions, ending in the later summer of 1988. Each stay was accompanied by similar phenomena, although at a lower frequency and magnitude.

During one of the last stays, I met with their housekeeper and asked her if she had ever experienced anything unusual. Her response was one of puzzlement in asking "what do you mean, unusual?" Without suggesting the nature of what I had been experiencing, I just said "anything that seemed a little odd that you could not explain." After thinking for a moment, she finally said that there was something that reoccurred which actually disturbed her.

After cleaning the front den, which Robbie used as a household office for her business, she would find the entire room in disarray, as if some powerful wind had blown through it. I asked her if the dogs might be responsible for this and she shook her head "no." "The dogs are always kept outside, except at night when they sleep in the front bathroom" she said.

It was now late November of 1988 and Roger again asked if I would stay at the house. When it relates to this matter, my motto is: "never say never". I therefore agreed. But unfortunately, this stay never occurred as Roger and Robbie had a major falling out, separated and filed for divorce.

Since their separation and subsequent divorce, I no longer had access to the house and have been unable to continue my investigation. When talking with Roger from time to time, he rarely, if ever, speaks of the house or with Robbie, who still resides there. Similarly, he would not dare ask her about the ghost knowing his ex-wife's attitude and response to such.

Though circumstances prevented a more thorough study of the phenomena related to this house, it seems to have clearly demonstrated qualities and characteristics indicative of a haunting opposed to a poltergeist.

However, as there was a substantial background at this location related to Robbie, there's a good chance that this is little more than another case of a PGA. Although, it would be very interesting to take instrumented measurements of this environment to see what's really going on here.

Further reinforcing the haunting hypothesis is the fact that no one of pubescent or adolescent age had lived in the residence for more than thirty years and phenomena were experienced immediately after a family that had absolutely no history of psychokinetic outbreaks built the house.

Lastly, the phenomena have persisted for more than forty years, which in itself, is highly suggestive of something other than poltergeist activity.

END

Chapter 5:
LIFE WITH POLTERGEIST AGENTS

These agents do not report to a station chief in some foreign country. Nor do they participate in spying and covert activity to further the CIA's hidden agendas. They are not Hollywood-type agents either, responsible for bringing in millions of dollars in revenue per year to the big talent agencies like the International Creative Management (ICM), the William Morris Agency or Creative Artists Agency (CAA) in Beverly Hills.

These particular agents do not work for anyone special or further anyone's aims except perhaps nature's and their own. In fact, these unique agents are never compensated for their abilities, over which they have absolutely no control whatsoever.

These agents are so utterly extraordinary that most people do not even believe they exist. They even have a peculiar prefix associated with their startling proclivities. They are called poltergeist agents.

Poltergeist agents (PGA's), also referred to on occasion as psychokinetic agents (PKA's) are known for allegedly creating, albeit unconsciously, pandemonium and mayhem by unleashing recurrent spontaneous psychokinesis (RSPK) around themselves, their environments and unsuspecting strangers. It might be said that PGA's give more than one hundred percent of themselves as their seemingly inexplicable manifestations, which cannot be instrumented or directly measured, produce results that today, even after more than 126 years of formal psychical research, still leave investigators perplexed.

Although it is generally believed that the majority of PGA's are youngsters in the transition to pubescence and/or adolescence, there is an ample body of evidence that strongly suggests that whatever mechanism is at work here can persist within an individual well into adulthood. While the chronological age of a PGA may grow in years, their internal physiology as related to neuro and electrochemical, endocrine/hormonal functions may lag behind or remain in stasis.

Describing the generic personality of a "typical" PGA is anything but difficult. It was most concisely defined by the late paranormal investigator D. Scott Rogo, as an emotionally volatile, depressed, anxiety-ridden individual with excessive amounts of pent-up hostilities and unresolved, deep emotional conflicts. A more succinct way of characterizing a PGA's emotional makeup might simply be "A mass of conflicting impulses," as described in Chapter 3.

At the physical level, PGA's are anything but ordinary either. In point of fact, a most unexpected and extraordinary correlational component to poltergeist phenomena has arisen through my own research as well as others in the field. A significantly high percentage of these individuals (PGA's) appear to be either seizure prone or suffer from epilepsy, either at a focal, petite or grand mal level.

Even more interesting is the fact that when these individuals take medication to quell their seizures, it appears to abruptly stop the psychokinetic outbreaks as well. This strongly suggests that the region or loci of the brain responsible for producing seizures/epilepsy in these individuals may, neuro-chemically mediate psychokinesis as well.

If this were true, it would be the first direct physiological link to any paranormal function. At the same time however, it should be understood that the vast majority of epileptics do not manifest RSPK. This unilateral aspect, suggests that there is a hidden or unknown variable here that, cannot at present even be guessed at.

The interrelationship between RSPK and neuro-chemistry (seizures & epilepsy) also presents some tantalizing possibilities for future paranormal research at the medical level. For instance, in order to determine if a specific locus in the brain is actually responsible for controlling both seizures and RSPK, various medical imaging techniques might be brought into play.

In a single blind longitudinal study, PGA's who are either seizure prone or epileptic would be examined and compared to normal patients without RSPK or epilepsy. A functional MRI (magnetic resonance imaging) would be employed to determine any specific anatomical and/or physiological characteristics unique to individuals epileptic PGAs. Even more detailed information would be obtained through the use PET (positron emission tomography) that would provide real-time data to determine if those specific regions within the brain are indeed hyper or hypo-metabolic.

Last, but not least, digital ambulatory EEG's of these most interesting individuals would be conducted. The resulting data would be quite interesting to say the least. Remember, this is the first time in history that we have what we believe to be the appropriate tools for scientifically investigating this phenomenon.

This distinct medical approach does not end at this point, however. Given what we now suspect might be going on, it is theoretically possible to artificially stimulate or "drive" the hypothetical physiological mechanism behind RSPK. Through the controlled application of photic driving (strobe lights) and/or 60 Hz. magnetic field induction, the possibility exists that macroscopic RSPK might be created under controlled laboratory conditions.

The one drawback to this approach is that the potential side effects are substantial in that such subjects could be driven into intense seizures. So, data might be obtained, but at what cost? Would not this type of high-risk human research be considered unethical given its potentially destructive biological side effects?

What is so particularly tantalizing about discovering the mechanism underlying psychokinesis is that this force is capable of moving massive objects and even inducing dramatic and sometime even violent electromechanical changes without any apparent thermodynamic effects.

This is unprecedented in the conventional physical world. Whether we are talking about electromagnetism, strong or weak nuclear forces or gravitation, they all behave according to the laws of thermodynamics. Moreover, in order for the known physical forces to do "work" as in F=MA (force equals mass times acceleration) for example, they as a consequence generate prodigious amounts of heat.

If we were to discover a non-polluting, potentially inexhaustible energy source that can do enormous amounts of work without the generation of heat, it would forever change virtually every aspect of the way we live on earth. Does the term zero point energy ring a bell here? Life would be easier and far more efficient in that most of our machines would not experience heat-related entropy, fatigue and failure. Can you begin to imagine the significance of a "breakthrough" at this level? Imagine a world without the need for oil, nuclear power, coal, hydroelectric power, solar or wind power?

The odds against anyone meeting a true PGA are literally astronomical. Even most parapsychologists rarely encounter such people or have the opportunity to directly experience them and their concomitant phenomena. Over the last thirty plus years, I have had the fortune (or perhaps misfortune, depending on one's perspective) to personally meet and get closely acquainted with six PGA's, five women and one man.

Aliens Above, Ghosts Below by Barry E. Taff

While working as a research associate at UCLA's former parapsychology laboratory located in the Neuropsychiatric Institute (NPI), I met Jim in late 1971 when he first visited our research facility. Jim was a 27-year old ex-police officer who was wounded in the line of duty, resulting in an early retirement. A husky, handsome individual who looked more like a model or actor than a cop. Jim was a man all wound up with nowhere to go.

With his hyper-accelerated voice, Jim frequently spoke of intense outbursts of RSPK since childhood, everything from loud banging and scratching noises on the walls of his family's home to furniture moving around on its own. He also reported common experiences with telepathy, clairvoyance and precognition, which is what initially had gotten him involved with our lab.

The first incident I witnessed occurred in 1972 when William Freidkin and William Peter Blatty, visited the lab.

Freidken took out an ancient, ankh he brought back from their location-scouting trip to Iraq earlier that year. As Blatty held it before the lab staff for closer inspection, Jim reached forward to touch it. Suddenly, the jeweled encrusted artifact powerfully exploded, sending fragments flying in all directions.

Surprise and fear sent Freidkin and Blatty running from the lab, never to return. As The Exorcist dealt exactly with this type of phenomenon, albeit with a religious spin, I'll never quite understand their reaction. But then again, they were involved with the making of entertainment, not investigating real-life paranormal events. Oddly, several years ago, one of my old friends bumped into Freidken who did not even remember visiting our lab in the early seventies.

Another incident took place when Jim and I had to make a stop at my apartment one afternoon in order to pick up some papers. While waiting for me to gather up my material, coins came flying at us from my bedroom, although neither of us had entered that area of the flat, nor did I have large quantities of pennies stored anywhere, The pennies were moving relatively slow and were seemingly directed at Jim. He excitedly smiled in response.

The last and perhaps most blatant episode of RSPK I observed around Jim took place many months later at an International House of Pancakes restaurant in Santa Monica where we were having lunch.

The waitress finally came over to take our order and it was obvious that Jim was very attracted to the shapely blonde. When she returned with our food Jim attempted to engage her in conversation. Because the waitress was not responsive to his advances, Jim simply smiled and casually told her to look at the massive chandelier hanging overhead.

Wondering what Jim could possibly be referring to, both the waitress and I looked up. The large wooden, metal and glass chandelier was hanging absolutely still. Suddenly, it began to turn on its own volition, starting to slowly rotate counterclockwise.

I immediately took notice of the numerous other chandeliers in the dinning room, all of which were stationary. There was no wind and the earth was not quaking. The waitress stood there transfixed as the light fixture began to wind around its tether and cord as if being turned by some giant unseen hand.

As the chandelier wound to the end of its turn, the waitress looked back at Jim who had a childlike grin on his face. Jim asked "Did you like that?" The waitress did not hang around long enough to answer.

This was the last RSPK incident that occurred around Jim when I was present, although he continued to display many other paranormal gifts during the work in our psi development group.

Over time, Jim found it hard to land or keep any type of employment. He also became obsessed with the need to know why he was always having such unusual experiences, while others around him were not.

This obsessive behavior greatly intensified over time to the point where Jim lost interest in most everyday events and retreated into a reclusive lifestyle, adopting a born-again Christian philosophy. He moved out of Los Angeles in 1975 and has not been heard from since.

My next encounter with a PGA began through a referral from Dr. Annis, a psychiatrist on the staff at the NPI. One of his therapy patients had a close friend who was reportedly barraged with a myriad of paranormal experiences and wanted to speak with someone working in the field.

In the spring of 1972, I first called 28-year old Sandra who, at the time, lived in an apartment in Hollywood. When we spoke, she too sounded like an old 45-rpm single-play record turned up to 78 rpm. She was excited about finally talking with a real parapsychologist. However, prior to meeting with her for the first time, I was able to interview her ex-boyfriend who was one of Dr. A's patient.

Don was a successful Hollywood screenwriter who was uncomfortable discussing his experiences with Sandra for a number of reasons. The foremost of which was that he was an ardent skeptic and always believed that all paranormal phenomena were the result of some type of psychopathology.

After assuring Don that I just wanted to hear his stories and that I was not going to in any way judge him, he opened up to me. Initially, he talked about events that were easily explained as simple General Extra-Sensory Perception (GESP). It did not get interesting until he reached the mind-over-matter part of his story.

He spoke of strange knockings and poundings from the walls of first Sandra's and then his apartment. This only happened when she was present. He had occasionally put objects down in specific locations only to discover shortly thereafter that they had somehow moved under their own power, or, were, nowhere to be found. This was followed by various appliances turning themselves on and off, doors opening and closing on their own. But, only when Sandra was around. He thought he was going to lose his mind.

The straw that broke the camel's back occurred just two months earlier when Don and Sandra were in bed at her apartment, something Don did not relish. As they were relaxing after making love, the bed started shaking as if a strong quake hit, although nothing else in the room was affected.

After the bed's motion finally ceased, a rocking chair several feet away began to move back and forth and the apparition of an old woman appeared within it. Don's heart almost came out of his chest as he became paralyzed with fear. Sandra just laid there watching the spectacle before her, as if in some altered state of consciousness.

Unable to restrain himself, Don bolted from the bed, ran from the room and found his way in the darkness to the living room where he grabbed a New Testament Bible and began praying for his life. The fact that he was Jewish made this reaction particularly fascinating.

This experience was more than sufficient to cause Don to immediately end his relationship with Sandra. Yet, Don hinted that there was yet another experience they shared that would make the ones he has already told me seem pale in comparison. However, he was too embarrassed to give me the details.

When I finally met with Sandra for the first time I was certainly prepared for anything, considering what Don had told me. And it was obvious upon first talking with Sandra that she was a walking bundle of exposed nerve fibers. She talked a mile-a-minute and had that same frenetic manner of body language and eye movements I had seen all too many times before.

Physically, she was quite striking, in the mold of Brooke Adams with lighter hair. Her eyes were the size of silver dollars, and although she possessed an incredible figure, her self-esteem was poor in that she was almost totally unaware of her outward appearance. She immediately and openly talked of unintentionally frightening away several boyfriends in a row.

There was a subtle, yet disturbing sense of satisfaction in her voice as she spoke of these incidents. She literally believed that she was haunted, although her childhood displays of RSPK would indicate quite the contrary.

During our second interview, while having lunch at the same restaurant where Jim somehow caused the chandelier to turn, Sandra unconsciously put on a little performance of her own. As my questions regarding her background, which was teeming with childhood episodes of exploding chinaware, emptying garbage cans, pounding walls and flying objects grew more personal and invasive, Sandra psychically lashed out.

Suddenly, the coffee cup in front of her started dancing around in its saucer, spilling liquid from its sides. We both watched in utter silence and amazement as the spoon laying on the side of the saucer rose up to a near vertical position and was propelled upwards across the expansive dinning room in a ballistic trajectory. Sandra's only comment was a near hysterical, "See, I am haunted!"

Even though Sandra was very much aware of the fact that this type of phenomena was commonplace in her past, she was reluctant to accept the notion that she was a PGA. In fact, this is a very common attitude demonstrated by such individuals.

They can readily accept the idea of some discarnate entity haunting them but utterly refuse to concede the possibility that they may be unconsciously causing the phenomena. This fact did not diminish the intensity of Sandra's reaction to such psychokinetic displays. Apparently, continued exposure did not serve to reduce her level of apprehension or anxiety.

On another occasion while we were driving to meet with some of my friends, the doors of my car began opening and closing by themselves against the wind at 65 mph on the freeway. The Santa Monica (10) Freeway at 2 P.M. on a Saturday afternoon will never quite be the same again to me or another person who watched a car behave in direct violation to everything we believe we know about reality. I do not know what concerned me more at the time, my initial shock of the doors "flapping" in the wind, almost losing control of my car or the other driver's reaction to it?

While the next incident was not one that I directly experienced, the story told to me, independently by both Sandra and Don, made it quite clear as to why their relationship ended so abruptly. As this particular event involved intimate aspects of their love life, Don was at first hesitant to even discuss it. Sandra, on the other hand, eagerly volunteered the information.

Their combined story, which converged on virtually every point, began one evening while laying in bed together, facing each other. As casual foreplay began with Don and Sandra locked in the building passion of kissing and groping, a blinding sheet of blue-white electricity formed between their cuddled bodies.

Aliens Above, Ghosts Below by Barry E. Taff

There was a sudden, loud snap of electrical discharge as the otherwise darkened room was brilliantly illuminated by the purple-white glow of lightning. Instantly, a powerful force violently threw Sandra and Don's bodies apart, each landing on opposite sides of the bed. This was accompanied by what sounded like a loud clap of thunder.

In their opinion, they both lay unconscious on the floor for several minutes. Don regained consciousness first, and although still somewhat dazed, went to Sandra's aid. As he reached out to touch Sandra's senseless form, his outstretched hand pulled a spark two to three feet long off her.

The streamer fiercely crackled and shocked and jolting Don. Considering that it takes approximately 10 kilovolts (10,000 volts) to bridge an air gap of 0.333 inches, this would roughly translate to as much as 990,000 volts. High voltage electrostatic buildup is well known, but close to 1 million volts of static far exceed our normal understanding of this process.

Lending ever more validation to their incredible story was testimony from other tenants in Sandra's apartment building. Many of them heard what sounded like a thunderous explosion that shook the entire building at the approximate time this event occurred. So much for privacy, but thank god for low amperage static.

As with Jim, Sandra also displayed strong GESP abilities throughout her life and in our psi development group. However, over time, she too became preoccupied and obsessed with her uniqueness and developed an attitude wherein she truly thought that she was a legend in her own mind, having messianic qualities. She eventually gave up the notion of being haunted and accepted her role in the RSPK events, even though they substantially diminished over time.

On several occasions, Sandra and Jim met. Their huge, fragile and overblown egos kept them from ever developing even a casual friendship, as they were always competing with each other on almost every level.

In November of 1978 I received a phone call from a young woman who was referred to me from the NPI's switchboard, as our lab was already disbanded. She told me that she was haunted by the ghost of her dead ex-husband and detailed some of the phenomena she had encountered. Her story was sufficiently intriguing to warrant an interview. Later that week, I and one of my colleagues went out to her apartment in North Hollywood.

At twenty-eight years of age, standing approximately 5'1" tall, Paula looked very much like a diminutive clone of Suzanne Somers, but with a much smaller mouth. Her eyes were large and robin-egg blue. Paula had much in common with the other PGAs discussed here in that she was extremely hyper, anxious and very confused and conflicted about her life in general, although she was divorced with a ten year old daughter who lived with Paula's aunt.

A chain smoker with nails bitten to the quick, Paula was an emotional basket case, frequently not knowing what to do with herself and her life. Her hands were almost constantly in motion, whether when talking, smoking or just sitting and listening.

It was quite apparent even during the initial portion of Paula's interview that she as a strong PGA, as her history was riddled with frequent accounts of glasses and dishes exploding when she was angry, malfunctioning electro-mechanical appliances and strange, inexplicable noises when she was agitated, which was quite often.

When I attempted to inform Paula that she was not the subject of a haunting by her dead ex-husband, she became angry and frustrated, since she thought that this automatically meant she was emotionally disturbed (the most common response to being told you're generating the RSPK). As I tried explaining what a PGA was, Paula resisted the notion entirely, and as her frustration peaked, numerous paperback books shot out in our direction from their resting place within a nearby bookcase.

During the next eighteen months there were frequent occasions where I would be greeted by sharp surges of psychokinetic activity around Paula. The next incident occurred when I was again talking with her in her apartment. We both heard a noise. Turning to look, both Paula and I saw my attaché case in mid-flight across the room, its contents being spewed across the floor. Yet, no one was even near it, and Rae (her sister, who also lived there) was still at work.

On another occasion, while driving with Paula in her car, the manual door locks began opening and closing on their own. The radio then started to tune itself, even though it was on old-style push button design rather than an electronically tuned system. As usual, Paula was distressed about something in her life. Upon witnessing the activity within the car, Paula kindly asked if I would drive as her anxiety level was too high for her to continue behind the wheel.

Besides being a PGA, Paula had considerable similarities to Sandra and Jim. Like the inability to hold down a job for any lengthy duration, several failed marriages, and a trait that would be best described as; Interested in everything, held by nothing, Jack- of all-trades, master of none, moreover, an unrelenting restlessness. These similarities aside, Paula provided what could be considered to be one of the most spectacular and uncommon manifestations of a PGA; disembodied externalization of voices.

While with Paula in her apartment one evening, a voice started addressing the two of us. It was quite apparent that it was not a radio or recording we were hearing as it was cognizant of our presence and actions. Upon searching the apartment for its source, we were further frustrated by its evasiveness and mobility. After as much as 20 minutes of the unexplained voice, it stopped. It is interesting to note that every time I managed to get a small audiocassette tape recorder ready, the voice would abruptly fade.

One particular evening when I spent the night on the sofa hoping to experience more activity (as that day had been filled with much) Paula awakened me in the wee hours of the morning to discarnate voices asking us to listen carefully. The voices then went on to utter nonsense. Again, as I prepared a tape recorder, the voices ceased their communication.

On another evening when I was recording yet another interview with Paula and decided to play it back, I was shocked to hear a third voice. Not belonging to either of us, the falsetto voice would continuously mock me as I spoke. Its frequency, pitch and tone was totally different than either my voice or Paula's,

One of the last events surrounding Paula occurred one evening when she attended our psi development group at UCLA. Seated within a pitch-black sensory deprivation room where participants in the study freely verbalized their responses to a given targets,

Paula was seen to emit a large ball of red light that raced to the other side of the room and vanished. All of the fifteen participants in the research group witnessed the event as I did. This was the first and last time Paula visited our group.

Since 1980, Paula has been married and divorced numerous times and has had countless different jobs. At the age of 47, it was believed that Paula's RSPK had all but waned, and her emotions had settled into a more restful state. The last I heard from Paula was in 1995, at which time she was living somewhere in Long Beach, California, managing a large apartment complex that just happens to be haunted. Haunted by Paula, that is! What a surprise.

While teaching an adult education class in parapsychology in Granada Hills in the San Fernando Valley during 1986, several friends in attendance brought a young woman up to the lectern to meet me. They thought I would find her story interesting.

Kym was a statuesque brunette with oversize blue eyes, who bore a striking resemblance to a very young Shirley MacLaine. At 21, Kym was in her final year of college. One of the friends who introduced her to me was her ex-boyfriend, Robert, whose mother I knew from graduate school.

During a break in my class, they told me about a series of Doppelganger effects that happened around Kym. They also said that Kym suffered from focal epileptic seizures.

To say that I was interested in pursuing Kym as a possible poltergeist agent was an understatement. While I did not personally experience the Doppelganger outbreaks, testimony provided by friends and family members supported what was told to me by Kym and Robert.

About six months earlier, when friends would call Kym at home, where she lived with her parents, they occasionally were greeted by a strange voice similar to Kym's but sounding somewhat younger. The voice was very well informed regarding Kym, and spoke of her in detail to her friends that called.

Since Kym did not own a telephone answering machine, this vocal double initially was thought to be a crossed or tapped line. However, after the phone company checked out that possibility and determined that neither was the case, calls continued to be greeted by this unknown voice.

The peak of these series of events occurred one day when Kym and Robert were both at her house and the phone rang. Kym picked it up to hear her own "other" voice answer the line and speak to the caller. Kym quickly summoned Robert and her mother to the phone to listen. They all heard the Doppelganger speak to the caller as if it were Kym. Robert ran to see if any of the other phones in the house was in use. They were not

After several tense and anxious weeks of such enigmatic phone calls, the mysterious voice fell silent.

I first got to interview Kym at length in November of 1986. I set up my cassette tape recorder, and after Kym finally sat down long enough to speak, I began with some simple questions about her past. Not surprisingly, Kym first talked about the focal epileptic seizures and how the phenomena seemed to occur more frequently during such times. Gee, tell me something I didn't already know?

Kym's childhood was filled with situations wherein she would arrive home to discover that her entire bedroom had been re-arranged. Even her stuffed animals were all turned around. She described her room as looking like a madman had redecorated it. This type of occurrence was quite common and would transpire in mere seconds.

At other times, Kym, her younger sister and parents would hear loud footsteps moving around upstairs accompanied by the sounds of doors and windows being opened and closed, although everyone was downstairs. All too frequent were footsteps coming down the stairway, moving to the front door----and the door actually opening as if someone was going out.

Then would come the knocking on the front door, rear door and sliding glass doors. Then the clock radio in her bedroom would turn itself on and randomly move around the stations, and the digital clock readout would wildly start running forwards or backwards at tremendous speed.

Young Kym's reaction to this was intrigue coupled with fear, especially as her parents demonstrated the denial all too common in these situations. Interestingly, these poltergeist outbreaks would usually correlate to her epileptic seizures. Even more troubling, however, was the fact that Kym was chronically depressed, suffering from very low self-esteem. Her depression became so severe at times that she repeatedly mutilated herself with knives and attempted suicide on more than one occasion.

As the interview progressed, Kym was continuing to answer my very probing questions into her background as my tape recorder continued to run as well as my taking extensive notes on my standard investigation form.

Suddenly, the cap of my pen, which was securely fastened over the back end while writing, was pulled off with a resounding "pop." It then flew across the dinning room. We watched it land some 8-10 feet away from its launching point.

As Kym leaned over to pick up the cap and return it to me I could feel a very strong electrostatic field emanating from her, perhaps as much as 200 kilovolts. Since it was raining outside with very high humidity, this was quite peculiar and unusual. But Kym was used to this sort of phenomena, and it did not really affect her as much as it did me.

At home the next day I started to review the audio recording I made of my interview with Kym. I was shocked when after only a couple of minutes, the tape went blank for several seconds and suddenly the sounds of our voices were replaced by that of an elderly woman complaining about her problematic life. Neither Kym's nor my voice was heard again for the remainder of the tape.

Inasmuch as I used my Sony recorder and a freshly purchased cassette tape, there was no possibility that I accidentally mistook one tape for another. I checked the other tapes in the pack I had bought the previous day and they were all in perfect working condition.

This event reminded me of what happened with Paula years earlier, except that the voice was addressing either of us and of course, that it was only heard as opposed to being recorded.

My last encounter with Kym's RSPK was when we met for dinner at a restaurant near her home. As we walked from the parking lot to the restaurant, we passed many cars. As Kym walked by each car, its alarm system would activate and its siren would blare. This happened to six cars in a row.

Knowing that the most sophisticated alarms have motion sensors that can be triggered by the proximity of objects or people, I alone walked by the cars after their alarms recycled and shut down.

Nothing happened. When I sent Kym back by each car to test my theory, they each again sounded off in succession. So much for Kym ever having a job as a security officers or a burglar.

However, she did have several jobs working with computers and the results were all too predictable. Each computer she worked with had the recurring and inexplicable predilection of crashing or locking up. Once Kym left the environment, things invariably returned to normal.

Could Kym's powerful electrostatic field be responsible for this effect? It's a well-established fact that computers do not react well to high-voltage electrostatic fields. However, as humanly generated, super-powerful electrostatic fields are not acknowledged in science, the answer here is not that simple and straightforward.

On several other visits to her house, I heard strange footsteps upstairs and walking in the hallway. I also heard and saw the front door opening on its own and heard other doors in the house slam shut.

Aliens Above, Ghosts Below by Barry E. Taff

The last time I heard from Kym was in 1996 and the majority of psychokinetic outbreaks had waned. The one exception was a series of events following Kym being violently raped. During the post traumatic stress that followed, the doorbell in her apartment began madly ringing accompanied by loud poundings and banging on the front door. There never was a plausible explanation provided for these last events. To her delight, these were the final occurrences around a now 31 year-old Kym.

In the summer of 1988, a close friend of mine, who previously worked for NASA training shuttle pilots, introduced me to a beautiful young woman named Beth. He thought that we might have a lot in common and that I would be attracted to her.

Beth was indeed quite physically attractive; 5'4" with streaked light brown hair and immense green eyes. Inasmuch as I have described all the other PGA women in terms of the celebrities they resembled, I will do the same here. Beth looked like a cross between a young Katherine Harrold and Kirsty Alley.

When I first went to meet Beth at her Mar Vista apartment, I simply expected to meet an interesting woman of 31 years of age who had been married and divorced once. When I walked into her apartment, there immediately was a strange electronic squealing sound followed by a peculiar hum that persisted for the entire length of my visit. Neither of us knew, until quite some time later, that all the phones, clocks, telephones and numerous other electronic equipment had all, simultaneously, stopped functioning.

While speaking with Beth, she demonstrated the same type of frenetic personality the other poltergeist agents had, one that easily loses track of everything, is never on time, and initiates dozens of efforts at the same time without successfully accomplishing even one.

As we sat talking on the couch, I began to notice that she seemed to be generating a substantial electrostatic field, much like Kym, although at a considerably lower amplitude. Needless to say, most of the behavioral characteristics Beth displayed alerted me to fact that any attempt at becoming better acquainted with her would be an act of utter futility and frustration. Thus, my interest was purely professional.

Spurred by numerous phones calls over the next several weeks, I revisited Beth's apartment to learn of continuing RSPK outbreaks such as electro-mechanical interference, doors opening and closing, repeated telephone calls without callers at the other end, sounds of footsteps and sudden unexplained power outages in Beth's apartment.

I went upstairs toward the bedrooms and felt a sensation of being at about 2.5 atmospheres, like being at the bottom of a very deep pool. Other tenants in Beth's building reported unusual episodes whenever she visited, pretty much similar to the psychokinetic events in her place.

In getting to know Beth over time as difficult as that was, my initial feelings about her unstable, angry, confused and frustrated persona was more than vindicated. Currently (as of 1998) Beth works as an assistant for a photo-journalist and is trying to secure a more lucrative job and hopefully get married again.

Over the last ten years, Beth seems to have slowed down somewhat and the phenomenon is more or less dormant, unless she becomes extremely anxious about something.

The last I hear from Beth was around 2005 when she moved to San Diego and got married. Hopefully, her marriage may have helped ground her a bit and bring a semblance of order to other chaotic life.

Aliens Above, Ghosts Below by Barry E. Taff

My most incredible run-in with what might be defined as a quasi-poltergeist agent took place in the summer of 1975, and while out-of-sequence temporally, I reserved it for the last because it was the only occasion where something physical materialized that I could hold on to.

A friend set me up on a blind date with a 23-year-old girl named Dotti who lived in North Hollywood. I arrived at her apartment for a dinner she had prepared. Upon meeting her I was amazed was to how much she resembled the actress Diana Mulduar (what can I say, other than I keep meeting women who resemble actresses)?

While eating, we were casually talking about this and that when suddenly an aluminum flashlight appeared virtually out-of-nowhere. Right in front of our eyes a flashlight aported onto the dinner table. We were both speechless as we looked toward each other with startled expressions on our faces. Even though I had already seen some truly incredible things in my career as a parapsychologist, eye-witnessing the materialization of a solid object is something one usually reads about, but never personally experiences.

I was elated. Dotti, on the other hand was frozen with fear and confusion. Her face was drained of color and looked as though she were about to lose consciousness from shock. Fortunately, she did not.

My first action was to reach out and touch the flashlight. It was an unremarkable unit, with numerous scratches on the body and lens. Its temperature was not out of the ordinary either. The flashlight was loaded with batteries that worked. As I continued to study the flashlight, Dotti finally found the strength to speak. "How can you just sit there and hold that thing?" she asked. My response was simple, "It's easy, do you want to look at it?"

Dotti did not know quite how to react; fear, anger or both. Sensing that her feelings about the apport were not even close to paralleling my own, I tried to defuse the tense situation somewhat with humor. When Dotti commented that she doesn't even own a flashlight, my retort was "Well, guess what? You do now. You could say that I really brought a light into your life." Dotti did not find my sense of humor even marginally funny.

As suspected, the first date never evolved beyond a very short dinner. And even though I pursued it further, I never heard from Dotti again. I wonder why?

Forty years and six poltergeist agents later, what has been learned? Well, for one thing, poltergeist agents certainly live up to their reputation for quirky personalities.

But are we not missing a vital piece of the equation here? There are easily tens of millions of individuals with similar psychological profiles, even those suffering from seizures, epilepsy or delayed emotional maturation. Yet virtually none of these people display any form of psychokinetic activity. Therefore, there must be another unknown variable that coexists within PGAs to help trigger the onset and continuance of RSPK.

It is theorized that a meta-stable neurophysiological system as related to temporal lobe epilepsy tied to an unstable mentality is at the root of poltergeist activity. But perhaps the answer is more physical than psychological. What if, in reality, certain unique individuals are somehow able to access and modulate an unknown type of energy that "normal" people cannot? Perhaps this extra energy disrupts not only their internal electrochemistry, but also their emotional stability.

What we see as erratic, conflicting behavior may actually be their way of coping with the externalization of surplus energy. The closest analogy in contemporary medicine would be that of psychosomatic individuals who develop numerous physical symptoms for disorders and illnesses they do not have.

This usually occurs when someone internalizes extreme levels of stress and anxiety. If this process continues unabated, it may result in psychogenic disorders, where the mind set of the individual actually brings on a somatic medical condition.

But, what if a poltergeist agent is an example of a psychogenic personality turning the process outward rather than inward? So instead of internal symptoms and physical disorders, we get external symptoms and psychokinetic chaos.

While the field conditions under which I observed RSPK activity cannot be equated to a controlled laboratory environment, they certainly give a more realistic evaluation of the individuals involved. I got to know these people more as friends than as subjects in an experiment.

Little has been resolved in the attempt to discover the science behind poltergeist agents, but I believe that we now have a better understanding and appreciation for what these tortured souls must live with.

END

Chapter 6:
POLTERGEIST AGENTS REVISITED

On most occasions, poltergeist agents are readily identifiable by their highly unique personality profile coupled with a definitive pattern of recurrent spontaneous psychokinetic (RSPK) events throughout their pubescence, adolescence and early adulthood. However, every once and a while, a researcher stumbles across a situation or an individual that does not in any way conform to what we believe we know about poltergeist phenomena. These are the cases where any attempt to resolve the matter in terms of conventional wisdom falls way short of the mark.

In point of fact, there have been several instances where I have met individuals who, for the most part, never recall experiencing any form of poltergeist/RSPK phenomena, nor did they meet any of the criteria already established regarding such generators, yet they suddenly, and for no apparent reason, start manifesting intense psychokinetic storms. The one common element throughout these three particular cases was my presence, which consequently causes one to ponder the possibility of a new, more expanded hypothesis regarding the nature of this complicated phenomena.

Before any apriori judgment or conclusions are reached, it should be made clear from the outset that I have never personally experienced any form of type of psychokinetic activity throughout my fifty plus years of life (apart from that which I investigated in other cases).

Therefore, these effects are not the product of some ignored, deeply buried history of RSPK on my part. However, the question still remains as to why each of the three women discussed herein started experiencing poltergeist outbreaks after they began dating me.

These peculiar series of encounters began when I met a woman named Darlene as she walked into UCLA's Parapsychology Laboratory at the Neuropsychiatric Institute in the late summer of 1974. At first glance, she resembled a very young looking Connie Stevens (maybe some of you readers remember her from 1950-60's television?)

Instead of blonde hair and blue eyes, Darlene had dark brown hair and hazel eyes. Her facial physiognomy was almost identical to that of Connie Stevens. Standing 5'3" tall with a thin buxom figure, Darlene looked very much the part of an actress or model.

Coincidentally, Darlene grew up within the entertainment community and was, in reality, close friends with Connie Stevens to whom she was constantly compared with as a darker colored sister.

Although Darlene looked all of 25, she was, in fact 39, divorced, with one child. This very young physical appearance was later explained as the result of a severe auto accident from which Darlene was brought into the hospital's emergency room almost DOA. After all the reconstructive and plastic surgery, Darlene had skin and muscle tone far superior to that of most college students.

Although Darlene's appearance was striking, she did have several lasting scars from her accident. First, the trauma turned her dark hair grey-white (which of course, she dyed back to its original color). Second, there were substantial scars on her left arm and face, though the prior one was visible compared to the cosmetically reconstructed facial one. Additionally, due to extensive neurological damage at these two sites, all tactile sensitivity in these regions was lost (the areas were numb to the touch).

Shortly after we began dating, Darlene's hair started growing out dark once again and the nerve deadened areas on her arm and face returned to their normal levels of tactile sensitivity, suggesting neural regeneration. Which, as you may know, is not supposed to occur according to contemporary medical science.

These effects caused Darlene to presumptuously conclude that I had something to do with her sudden and dramatic "healing." Being the cautious scientist, I was considerably more skeptical and suggested that perhaps it was simply her own emotional response to being in a new and different relationship that triggered the healing, sort of a psychogenic reaction.

Even though there is a substantial body of medical evidence suggesting that strong positive emotions can result in significant healing and regenerative processes, Darlene did not understand or accept this theory. In all likelihood, this is probably why she did not want the relationship to end though there was absolutely no possibility of our ever getting married, which is what she desired.

My reason for mentioning this particular incident is that as healing is believed to be a product of psychokinesis, perhaps in this case it was a mild precursor to subsequent poltergeist outbreaks. This is to suggest that the same emotional bonding between Darlene and me that resulted in the later RSPK outbreaks was also responsible for the healing. As both events involved unknown types of energy, this line of speculation cannot be ignored or dismissed out-of-hand.

In getting to know Darlene, it immediately became apparent that something peculiar was occurring within her environment. Various small, loose objects like keys, jewelry and sometimes clothes, mysteriously disappeared. Most of the time the objects were found only feet or a room away several hours or days later, like a glass of iced tea or car keys. On other, rare occasions, the missing objects never returned.

As this repeatedly transpired around Darlene, her 18-yr. old daughter, as well as her daughter's boyfriend, while they were at Darlene's Westwood apartment, there was no concern over the possibility that Darlene's teenage daughter might be pulling some kind of practical joke or simply seeking attention.

In fact, the daughter's boyfriend became outraged on several occasions when he lost various possessions while in the apartment. I initially suspected that these RSPK displays were a product of Darlene's interaction with her daughter. However, this theory could never be validated.

Little did anyone suspect that the apports were just the beginning, in a series of paranormal volleys that would result in Darlene repeatedly moving in an attempt to escape the psychokinetic bombardment.

As the phenomena escalated, it evolved, becoming in this author's opinion, more sophisticated in its manifestations. Once the apports began to subside, they were almost immediately replaced by the sounds of disembodied voices, perhaps one of the most unsettling types of phenomena to occur, especially while home alone.

However, the way in which the disembodied voices manifested themselves was, in itself, quite unique. After Darlene and I had left her apartment to see a film or dine out, her daughter would hear our conversations continuing as if we were still there. The disembodied conversations became so pronounced that even friends of Darlene's daughter and neighboring apartments overhead the voices. It was as if our presence and vocal activity were somehow being recorded and played back once we left the premises.

Aliens Above, Ghosts Below by Barry E. Taff

To eliminate the obvious and prosaic possibility that the disembodied voices were simply the result of a hoax, Darlene's apartment, as well as the adjoining ones, were thoroughly examined in search of hidden microphones or speakers. Nothing suspicious was found.

There had been sufficient independent corroboration regarding these voices that the only real problem now remaining was actually recording them. And there was the rub. For although both Darlene and I actually overheard these mimicking voices on more than one occasion, every time we attempted to record them they would abruptly cease. The evasiveness of this phenomenon was truly remarkable.

Unfortunately, in the spring of 1975, circumstances totally unrelated to the poltergeist outbreaks forced Darlene to again move, this time taking her completely out-of-state. Almost immediately after she moved out of Los Angeles and away from your truly, thus ending our relationship, the poltergeist activity totally abated.

Since that time, I have occasionally heard from her and there have been absolutely no further instances of poltergeist activity. The last time Darlene and I actually met was in 1980, and everything around her had long since returned to normal. Our brief meeting was apparently insufficient to initiate another round of phenomena. Assuming, of course, that a casual gathering is all that's required to trigger the onset of this highly atypical form of RSPK, which I seriously doubt.

During the spring of 1975, while teaching a parapsychology course in UCLA's extension, an attractive 25 yr. old blonde named Resa approached me asking if I remembered her. I drew a total blank. She went on to tell me that we attended grammar school together.

Still drawing a blank. Finally, she said that her father was my family's G.P. medical doctor. Still, no bells or whistles, and for the first time in a long time, and I am absolutely positive, to your great relief, that this girl resembled absolutely no other person I have ever known or seen before or since, especially an actress. Well, now that I'm thinking about it.....nah.

Anyway, one thing led to another and we eventually went out on several dates. While I found Resa interesting, and very intelligent, I was not dramatically attracted to her. While sitting in her house talking, her stereo system, turned itself on and one of my favorite record albums (you remember, those pre-CD recording mediums made from black vinyl that always warped?) found its way on to the turntable (interestingly, Strange Days, by the Doors). Strike one, and Resa asked many questions for which there were no definitive or objective answers.

About a week later, while approaching her home (in her car) during a fierce rainstorm after dinner, Resa complained that her automatic garage door opener was broken and that she would have to get out of the car in the downpour to open it. As a gentleman, I volunteered, which may in retrospect, have been an error in judgment.

As we turned into her driveway, Resa inadvertently reached to touch her dysfunctional garage door opener and instead hit my left wrist. The result was a loud and visible electric spark that illuminated the inside of the otherwise darkened car's interior with a purple-blue glow. Suddenly, the garage door opened on its own. Strike two, and now Resa was really being worried about whether we should even remain friends. But why give up on a good thing, especially when the best is yet to come, although she had no way of knowing that.

Several days later Resa invited me over for dinner. Everything seemed very normal and, for once, we both thought that calmness would prevail. Throughout dinner, nothing unusual happened. It was about two hours later while we were on the couch in the living room talking, that the next paranormal event occurred.

An aluminum can of Coke resting on the coffee table next to us suddenly picked itself up and flew across the room right in front of us. Unfortunately, we did not see the can leave its resting place on the coffee table. Our eyes caught up with it in mid-course, before it hit the floor on the other side of the room. Resa's eyes widened in shock as she bolted from the couch and headed for her bedroom. She was not a happy camper.

She ended sprawled across her bed in a state of frenzied shock and fear. As I was attempting to mollify her by getting her to see that she was in no direct danger, a strong electrostatic-like crackling sound was heard in the corner of her room. We both immediately looked up and witnessed the appearance of a humanoid apparition that looked as if it were made of 4th of July sparklers, spitting energy off all its edges.

As the room lights were on when this apparition appeared it was all the more significant in that the image was not a low-contrast, low-light emission in an otherwise darkened room. Unfortunately, we could not distinguish any salient characteristics of the apparition, not even its gender.

Strike three, but the game was not quite over. By this point in our quasi-relationship it appeared that nothing could possibly worsen the situation. Wrong again.

Approximately one week later with only telephonic communication between us, I told Resa about a dream I had about her father. In the dream, her father was floating, face-up, motionless, in a small body of water, seemingly lifeless. Suddenly, Resa appeared and started frantically swimming down towards her father. Upon reaching him she started intense mouth-to-mouth resuscitation, although still under water

Resa's reaction to the dream was cautious and guarded as she was well aware of its symbolic representations, although her father was not ill or particularly old. However, the dream so disturbed her that she abruptly ended the conversation at that point. Given her level of anxiety, what else could she have done in this situation?

About ten days elapsed and Resa called to inform me that her father had suddenly collapsed and died. He suffered a pulmonary embolism while resting next to their backyard pool. Resa rushed to his aid, performing mouth-to-mouth, but to no avail. Resa then remembered my dream and how it accurately predicted these tragic events. Now Resa was angry as well as frightened.

The fact that I dreamt of him underwater is significant for three reasons. One is that he was indeed next to the pool when he collapsed. Two, is the fact that he died of a pulmonary embolism that is, in effect, drowning on your own fluids. Last, but not least, was the mouth-to-mouth resuscitation given to him by Resa.

For obvious reasons this was the straw that finally broke the camel's back in terms of our attempt at a relationship. The poltergeist effects were, in themselves, quite sufficient to scare Resa off.

As if to add some icing to the cake, there had to be a disturbing precognitive dream to wrap things up. Well, another potential relationship bites the dust. Needless to say, that after Resa and I parted company she never again experienced any form of poltergeist activity.

It would be really interesting to talk with Resa today and learn if she had suffered from temporal lobe epilepsy or was seizure prone.

Moving forward to the late summer of 1981 brings us to yet another of these peculiar cases that must remain in sort of a twilight zone in terms of our understanding of this phenomenon at even the most basic level.

Aliens Above, Ghosts Below by Barry E. Taff

I began having dreams about a girl I had never met, which in itself, is not unusual. The dreams were very clear and vivid. The girl was blonde (peculiar, as I am not particularly attracted to blondes) with large blue/green eyes. She had a rather dark complexion (a lot of melanin), a well-structured, faceted face. A very thin nose, and sort of resembled, you guessed it, another actress.

In this case, a very young looking Barbara Eden (from the 1960's I Dream of Genie TV series). In the dream (interesting, given the TV series title I just mentioned), the girl worked at some place where a great deal of money changed hands every day, either a bank or a market I assumed.

Additionally, she wore some kind of uniform, possibly blue or black, although not military or law enforcement. In the dream, she drove a white American compact car with a blue interior and somehow the fact that her mother's name was Mary was evident.

This recurring dream became so pronounced that I had my good friend, who is an illustrator, paint a picture of what this girl looked like. After about three weeks, the dreams finally ceased. At that point, I figured that the matter was over and that the situation would not evolve into anything. Nothing could have been further from the truth.

During the third week in September of 1981 I began teaching my parapsychology class at Beverly Hills High Adult School as I had for several years. As the new students funneled into the classroom I was not really paying attention to any of them as I was busy checking over the class roster making sure that all the necessary paperwork was in order.

Just before the class began I casually looked to my left at the more than thirty students now sitting in their chairs. I was shocked to see the exact image of the girl I had dreamt about for weeks at sitting on the left hand side of the room. She really did look like a young Barbara Eden.

Her appearance was exactly as I had remembered it in my dreams. Trying to be subtle and nonchalant about my studying her features, I noticed that she was looking back at me in a most peculiar and atypical manner. Was I that obvious?

During the break I walked up to the girl and started a conversation with her. To my total surprise, 31 yr. old Linda, said that I looked familiar to her, and asked if we had met before. We had not, except of course in my dreams.

After the third week of my class and following several conversations with her, I suggested that we should get together some time, perhaps for dinner. She readily accepted.

On our first date, I discovered that Linda worked for a local bank that required its employees to wear dark blue uniforms. That she drove a white Ford Pinto with a blue interior and, of course, her mother's name was Mary. One thing led to another and eventually we ended up in a relationship. Isn't it amazing as to how many beautiful women my work has allowed me to meet? Well, at least there is a positive side to being in such a unique line of work.

Everything appeared to be going relatively well except that whenever I discussed my work it made her emotionally uneasy. Odd, as it was because of my work, we met? Additionally, Linda did not share my zeal for movie going or the entertainment industry in general. Well, at least in that respect she was grounded and normal.

Due to occasional work in the entertainment industry, I frequently obtained screening passes, to such films as Poltergeist and E.T., yet she displayed absolutely no interest in attending.

Give me a break. Could anyone really be that dull and boring? I guess so. And as if to make matters worse, like most women, Linda had no interest whatsoever in high performance sports or exotic cars (one of which I owned at the time). In retrospect I really wonder how and why we even continued to maintain a semblance of a relationship for the 8 months we did?

These conflicts of interest started to cause considerable friction in our relationship. Adding further fuel to the fire was the fact that Linda heard her biological clock ticking, very loudly, and I wasn't about to allow her clock's alarm to ring.

She had already been married and divorced once, but without a child. However, at that time in my life I had about as much desire to marry and have children as I did in losing the rest of my hair. Come to think of it, considering most of the women I have met over the years and their reaction to my work, I pretty much feel the same way now as I did twenty-seven years ago.

About mid-summer 1982, Linda's anxiety and frustration over our relationship were reaching a peak. However, she was not verbalizing it with me. As if to silently communicate her anger, resentment and repressed conflicted emotions, poltergeist activity broke out.

It started off somewhat simple as when Linda came home she would find lights on that she had turned off and various doors would be opened that were always kept closed. From there it evolved into dishes jumping out of the sink and landing on the kitchen floor when we were watching TV in the living room. Strangely, they would never break.

As the days passed, Linda came to repeatedly discover in the early morning or late evening, many of her blouses and skirts laid out on the floor and/or her bed as if she were evaluating exactly what to wear for the entire week. To say that Linda was being unnerved and frightened over these psychokinetic incidents would be a gross understatement.

Linda actually thought that I could make these incidents stop, and was agitated when I informed her that I exerted absolutely no influence over these events, nor could I suggest any course of action to terminate their occurrence. At that time it was not clear to me that Linda's unresolved anxiety was at the root of the events.

It is important to re-emphasize here that none of the aforementioned women had ever experienced any type of psychokinetic phenomena before entering into a relationship with yours truly, and this, of course, includes Linda.

Linda was at her wits end, still not verbalizing any of the anxiety and distress arising from the intense desire to terminate our relationship. Something was about to give. The real question was, exactly what.

Several days later, when Linda and I were leaving her apartment early one morning, the large dead bolt lock on her front door threw itself while we were on the other side of the door. This meant that the phenomena had effectively locked us out of her apartment.

In order to get back into her apartment when she returned from work later that day, Linda had to call a locksmith to remove her door. When the locksmith discovered that the dead bolt had been thrown from the inside when no one was there, he did not even want to learn the cause.

This may be overly obvious, but our relationship abruptly ended after the door incident, although I do not think that Linda really understood or fully appreciated the significance of this last psychokinetic event.

Is it coincidence that the "poltergeist" chose to throw the dead bolt and lock Linda out of her apartment when I was leaving with her? I don't think so. It's sort of like her unconscious was saying "I'm going to lock you out of my apartment, hoping that this will get you out of my life!"

Perhaps sublimated anger and frustration were what generated this last psychokinetic event in that it was what Linda needed to do in order to end the relationship within her mind. Perhaps even more telling, is that following this dead bolt situation, after which we never again saw each other, all the RSPK occurrences around Linda ceased, to her great relief.

An interesting sidebar, although not directly related to the poltergeist outbreaks was that on several occasions while washing my hands and face in Linda's bathroom, I saw a very clear image in my mind's eye while looking in the mirror.

The image of a tall, handsome man, dressed in a business-type three-piece suit kept running through my mind. He had medium-brown hair, large blue eyes, with a full beard and mustache. I seemed to know that his name was Michael and that this was the man that Linda was going to marry in the not-to-distant future. There was also the strong impression that their marriage would dissolve shortly after they had a child (but then again, that's a very common problem in today's society).

Foolishly, I told Linda about my impressions, to which she responded that I was simply jealous about the fact that many men were always hitting on her. In that we were not evolving towards either a live-in situation or marriage, Linda's comment was not at all relevant.

To tie down this last case, it should be pointed out that Linda did, in fact, meet the Michael I described and eventually married him. However, what I did not know until about four years ago was that the marriage did indeed end shortly after the birth of their one and only child. How I came upon this knowledge was that one of my friend's wives was shopping at a market in the San Fernando Valley when she accidentally bumped into Linda and remembered her from more than a decade ago when we had double dated.

After they talked about various events in their lives since they had last met, Linda told her of the divorce and her being a single mom. Linda asked how I was doing and my friend's wife filled her in. Then, Linda started recalling my precognitive impressions and, once again, became visibly shaken and disturbed. When asked if she would care to get together with me again, Linda simply shook her head no and quickly walked away. Gee, one would think that I was an attorney or something.

Now that all three cases have been examined in depth, what has been learned regarding these spontaneous outbreaks of poltergeist activity all have this author as the common element.

Could it be that under the proper set of conditions and circumstances some couple's produce what neither of the individuals can accomplish independently? Are some people acting like psychokinetic capacitors and/or batteries in that when a critical breakdown threshold is exceeded the physical environment is then affected? Could one person act as a power supply and the other as a waveguide, focal plane or lens? Until and unless the operant mechanism underlying psychokinesis is identified and scientifically explained, these definitive questions must remain unanswered.

Surely, there have been many other episodes of this type of occurrence between couples that have been either ignored or rationalized away? Others have speculated that this is all the result of some covert psychokinetic gift I possess which only surfaces during very specific romantic scenarios. I do not share that belief.

Either way, we are still left with the uncomfortable notion that poltergeist phenomena and perhaps even psychokinesis in general, may be far more prevalent in the population than once believed, especially when this type of dynamic interpersonal interaction is considered and examined. Only time, careful observation and patience will reveal the answers.

END

Chapter 7:
AN IRREPLACEABLE LOSS
The Life and Death Of A Poltergeist Agent

As Published In:

PSI Journal of Investigative Psychical Research

Vol. 4 (2), 2008, pp. 7-17

True love comes in many forms and occasionally requires us to embark on a very strange, fascinating and unexpected journey through a landscape seldom experienced by others, whose final destination is beyond our comprehension. My friend and colleague, Barry Conrad, took just such an unimaginable trek.

Over the last thirty-seven years as a parapsychologist, having lived through cases like The Entity, Hollymont and San Pedro (An Unknown Encounter) which made up an infinitesimal fraction of my files, I was left with way too many sleepless nights, falsely believing that I'd seen, heard and felt it all. Jaded into complacency, I was sure that nothing could ever really move me again.

To put it simply, I was wrong, dead wrong. There was no inkling that I was on the verge of perhaps the most incredible case of my career, one that would affect virtually every single person I shared my work with.

Early Tuesday morning July 25th 2006, the world lost a very unique and uncommon woman; an articulate woman, possessing incredible intelligence, emotional grounding as well as beauty. However, to film-maker Barry Conrad, the loss of his soul-mate, Lisa McIntosh to cancer, goes well beyond just another human being who has left the land of the living in which the rest of us still reside.

Lisa and Barry met in, what for most, is the least likely to produce a productive and enduring relationship...the Internet. They shared many aspects of life; similar ethnicities, very similar family structures and perhaps what was most important for them, a never-ending interest in the paranormal.

Although the North Carolina native Lisa McIntosh was only forty-two years old when she died, she had dedicated most of her short life to the study of paranormal phenomena. Lisa's interests covered a broad spectrum of phenomena, everything from remote viewing to Ufology.

Interestingly, what allowed her to personally investigate rather than just study many of these aspects even more directly, was her meeting and falling in love with my associate; writer, producer, director, cameraman and paranormal investigator Barry Conrad, a two-time, Emmy award-winning director of photography (DP), best known for his shows; An Unknown Encounter and California's Most Haunted which garnered the highest ratings in the history of the Sci-Fi Channel for a three-hour time block. In fact, Lisa made her producing and acting debut in Conrad's California's Most Haunted and will soon be seen again in "Monsters of the UFO" due out in 2008.

What was not initially known by Barry or myself was that Lisa was far more than just another pretty face whose interests were somewhat askew from the mainstream. In fact, shortly after meeting Lisa in spring of 2001, she spoke of moving from one haunted house to another as she grew up. As the very notion of such is literally an astronomical probability, it strongly suggested that Lisa herself was possibly a poltergeist agent.

A poltergeist agent is defined as an individual, anywhere from pre-pubescence or adolescence into adulthood, who is plagued with varying degrees of psychokinetic [PK] (mind-over-matter) outbreaks. At the dawn of psychical research in the latter part of the 19th century, it was believed that these phenomena were the result of noisy, prank-playing spirits attached or attracted to an individual, which is what the German word "poltergeist" means.

However, evidence collected by parapsychologists over the last 126 years strongly suggests that these incredible displays of psychokinesis have very little to do with discarnate intelligence (dead people's spirits), but everything to do with unusual neuro-chemical brain functions.

In point of fact, since Lisa moved into Barry's house in the summer of 2001, there have been more than 57 separate days of poltergeist events (individual events themselves came to 146, which averages out to 12.5 individual events per day over the course of 5 years) ranging from the sublime to the ridiculous.

So pronounced and dramatic were these incidents that if I myself had not been present to experience many of these extraordinary episodes I would be hard-pressed to believe them. That's how spectacular some of these outbreaks were.

It all began on October 13, 2001 the day after Lisa, Conrad and myself went out to Calabasas to investigate an alleged haunting. However, before we delve into the specific details of the psychokinetic maelstrom that surrounded Lisa McIntosh, several other background essentials must be described so a proper perspective is possible.

Barry Conrad moved into his current home in the Glendale/La Crescenta area during the January of 1997. While Conrad has experienced poltergeist outbreaks in his previous home in Studio City, California back in 1989-90, they only occurred after Jackie Hernandez, the poltergeist agent associated with the San Pedro case An Unknown Encounter, had visited his apartment. Other than these specific incidents related to this particular case, Conrad's life had been totally free of such occurrences. Until Lisa moved in, that is.

Long before the PK volleys began, Conrad shared some fascinating photographs he had taken of Lisa with me. These photos depicted curious luminous anomalies surrounding Lisa, which were bright pink or orange in color. While I thought these images were interesting at the time, I didn't really give the matter any further thought, that is, until other phenomena began displaying themselves around Lisa.

This case is perhaps one of the most perplexing in my files (which now exceed 4,300 cases) in that there were such a high volume of incidents, many of which had multiple witnesses, including myself. Yet, once Lisa became very ill while on location with Barry in Point Pleasant, West Virginia shooting a segment on the "Mothman" for "Monsters of the UFO" and was later diagnosed with Multiple Myeloma in late December of 2004, the frequency and magnitude of these psychokinetic events markedly diminished.

For the purpose of this article, we'll assume that the poltergeist outbreaks around Lisa formally began on October 13, 2001, although according to Lisa's own words, her childhood through early adulthood was littered with classic psychokinetic displays.

Barry Conrad asked Lisa to live with him in the early summer of 2001. During that summer, their existence in Conrad's Glendale home was normal, with not even a glimmer of anything paranormal. Looking back, I believe that this was the calm before the storm.

Aliens Above, Ghosts Below by Barry E. Taff

After Barry and I went out to investigate our first case in which Lisa accompanied us on October 12, 2001, their lives were forever changed as a result. There was nothing particularly noteworthy about this investigation other than marginally higher geomagnetic and low frequency magnetometer readings. The Calabasas, California residents reported the sounds of furniture being moved when it was not. The lid of their washer was torn off by an unseen force and thrown some distance.

Various objects in and around the house had been thrown and broken, doors opened, food moved around, gravel in the backyard thrown into sliding glass windows, toys on the lawn moved, knocking on doors, and file cabinets opened on their own. And let's not forget the old standard of keys appearing and disappearing (apports).

However, most of these events happened long ago, or over the span of many years, and only when the family's younger relatives were present did anything like the aforementioned events occur again.

The very next morning, October 13th 2001, Lisa was upstairs in the bathroom when her hair dryer suddenly turned itself on. Lisa was curious, but not concerned as she assumed that this incident was nothing more than a malfunctioning appliance. Several days later on October 15th while she was working at the computer, it kept shutting itself down for no apparent reason.

Again, Lisa didn't give it a second thought, as PC's (as opposed to Macs) are known to act quirky now and again.

The next event was much more difficult to dismiss as some minor electronic glitch. It was October 17th at around 7:30 p.m. when both Lisa and Barry collectively observed a blinding blue-white flash of light in the foyer of the house from no apparent source. Needless to say, this event caused quite a bit of concern on both Lisa and Barry's part. However, there was still insufficient evidence to suggest that they were possibly dealing with poltergeist activity.

Several days later came the first defining event suggesting that Barry and Lisa were, in fact, dealing with a poltergeist outbreak. Around 1 a.m. both Barry and Lisa are upstairs asleep when they are awakened by the explosive sounds of what comes across as heavy furniture crashing to the floor downstairs in the living room. Barry runs downstairs expecting to find his expensive entertainment center destroyed.

He finds absolutely nothing within the house that could logically explain this classic type of poltergeist chicanery. He goes back upstairs telling Lisa he found nothing. As they are about to fall back into slumber, the extremely loud crashing sounds once again emanate from the first floor.

Barry again runs downstairs, not knowing what to expect. There is nothing to be found Returning to bed he and Lisa spend a very restless night waiting for further activity, which does not occur.

October 26th marked the beginning of a substantial escalation in the frequency, magnitude and nature of events to come. Lisa was upstairs getting ready for bed and Barry is out on a late shoot. Just after Lisa decided to put her book away and hit-the-sack, Barry's dog (Beau, given to him by an ex-girlfriend) decided to jump onto the bed. Beau is very jealous of Lisa's taking her place in bed. Not unexpectedly, Lisa was not too fond of Beau as she was a present from Barry's "ex" as well as being very aggressive and territorial.

As Beau jumps up toward the bed, something interrupted her flight mid-jump. Lisa described it as if an invisible wall or pair of large hands abruptly grabbed the dog in the air. The dog was momentarily suspended in mid-air as if it were defying gravity, then violently thrown or repelled backwards slamming into the wall beneath the window across from the foot of the bed.

Beau is momentarily stunned after which she gets up and shakes as if having a seizure, then lets out a loud moan. The dog then begins to visually "track" something unseen in the bedroom while growling and barking as she hunched down in the corner of the room. The dog quickly runs out of the bedroom. Lisa was almost in shock from the event and immediately calls Barry on his cell who eventually calms her down.

Moving on to November 1st of 2001, it was around 2:30 a.m. as Barry and Lisa were asleep upstairs. There is a sudden loud sound within the bedroom. The high decibel sound of cracking wood or, perhaps that of a high-voltage, electrical discharge.

The event lasted around 3-4 seconds and appeared to come from right next to the bed. Lisa is terrified and starts to shake and cry. Not surprisingly, just prior to the incident, the dog rapidly dives under the bed as if she anticipated the event.

Four days later on November 5th, at around 11:15 a.m. Barry and Lisa are in bed when Lisa repeatedly feels her calf being touched and tapped by icy-cold, invisible fingers. She jumps out of bed terrified. Hours go by before Barry can calm her down.

We now jump to just past Thanksgiving on the 28th of November at 1 a.m. While Barry is downstairs watching TV, he hears very loud pounding coming from the ceiling of the living room (3-4 bangs). He said it sounded like a big sledgehammer being slammed into the bedroom floor. When Barry runs upstairs to investigate, he finds Lisa sound asleep. Nothing in the room is out of place.

The very next day, as if to further inflame Lisa's fears, at around 8 p.m. she observes a can of empty dog food that Beau has dragged into the entrance hall move across the carpet into the living room under its own power. Lisa's alone and freezes in her tracks. As funny as this event is, Lisa's home alone having to cope with all of this without Barry.

It's now December 2nd and everything seems to have tapered off. However, at 5:20 p.m. when Barry and Lisa are lying in bed, they both hear the sounds of someone or something with great weight coming up the stairs and approach the bedroom door. They both freeze. The room's doorknob turns and the door opens. Paralyzed by fear, they both wait for whatever it is to enter the room and reveal itself. Then silence. Summoning all his courage, Barry goes to the door and finds nothing. This incident sounds as if it came right out of a scene of Robert Wise's The Haunting (1963).

Beyond the obvious cliché poltergeist nature of this incident is that fact that just prior to it, both Barry and Lisa felt a strong sense of "overpressure" around their heads giving them both headaches.

The best way to describe this effect is what one feels when diving in a deep pool or scuba diving. This type of physical effect has been the most common physiological reaction to numerous "haunted" environments over the last 37 years, shared by both investigators and residents. However, there does not appear to be a barometric correlation to this sensation.

Jumping forward in time one-half month to December 16th, this author was sitting in one of the comfortable lounge chairs in Barry's living room at approximately 10:45 p.m. with Barry and Lisa watching videos when my chair was violently struck, twice, by an invisible force that felt as if a baseball bat had been used.

My response was simple and direct. I jumped up and out of the chair immediately. Four decades of this work may have somewhat jaded and battle-hardened me, but I am human and do possess a fight or flight reaction, which was certainly forced into action here.

The very next day, the 17th of December also provided a new level of physical intensity related to the PK events. It was 7:30 p.m. as Lisa puts a Pyrex cooking pan into the oven to cook herself some dinner as Barry is out on a shoot. Before the oven even has time to heat up (seconds), the Pyrex pan violently explodes into many shards within the oven shaking the entire kitchen area. Lisa freaks out and immediately calls Barry on his cell to discuss her fragile emotional situation.

Later that same evening Barry arrives home and consoles Lisa. They finally retire for the evening not knowing what is about to occur. At 1 a.m. (which is now the 18th), they both hear the sounds of coins falling and hitting the nightstand next to the bed. A careful search of the bedroom reveals that there are no coins to be found. Lisa's nerves are definitely frazzled at this point.

For the next two months everything seems to have calmed way down as there is not a single event experienced in the house. The world has returned to normal again. At least it would appear so to Lisa and Barry. Comes February 14th of 2002, their peaceful bliss starts to crack apart once again.

It's 7 p.m. and Barry and Beau are at the bottom of the stairwell when both he and the dog look up as they hear what sounds like Lisa walking down the staircase. However, there's no one there. Lisa is in the bathroom upstairs preparing to leave and was nowhere near the stairs. So much for home sweet home.

As the cycle appeared to be starting again, Barry and Lisa were not that surprised when only four days later on February 18th, the next event occurred. While Lisa was in the upstairs bathroom at around 11 p.m. getting ready for bed, she clearly hears disembodied voices "counting down". She quickly comes out of the bathroom to see if the bedroom's TV or radio was on, only to find Barry already in bed. She told him what she had just heard while in the bathroom and he responded that he hadn't heard anything.

The very next morning, the 19th of February at 10:30 a.m. Lisa is again in the upstairs bathroom and something violently pulls on her long blonde hair. She's really starting to panic at this point. Barry left very early that day on a shoot leaving Lisa alone in the house.

Throughout the entire day, the telephone rings incessantly, yet no one is ever on the line. The "Caller ID" reads as if there is no call coming in. Lisa tries the auto-redial function on the phone but it refuses to work.

She then tries another form of auto-redial through the phone company, and it too fails to operate. She eventually calls the phone company in search of an answer. They tell her that they have no indication of any calls whatsoever coming into that phone line during that period of time. Again, classic poltergeist activity. Lisa is at her wit's end.

The next four days were a very short respite where nothing peculiar occurred. But, as all good things come to an end, so did this brief interlude. The next event demonstrated a significant change in the nature of the PK activity as it ventured beyond their home environment for the first time.

On February 23rd while at the Best Buy store in Burbank, California, Lisa is in one of the store's many aisles searching through the vast array of available DVDs when she suddenly feels a hand stroking her hair from behind. She abruptly turns expecting to see Barry behind her pulling a prank. To her dismay, the aisle was empty with the exception of her, and of course whatever touched her hair. Barry was many aisles away at the time. Lisa begins shaking so intensely that Barry had to take her home immediately.

Aliens Above, Ghosts Below by Barry E. Taff

Four days later, Barry and Lisa are in the living room about to watch a DVD when they clearly hear a disembodied female voice moving across the room in front of the entertainment center. The "voice", which was unintelligible, appeared to move from the left wall and exit through the large glass wall where the dog normally sleeps on his pillow.

It is important to note here that the entertainment system was completely off at the time. Another interesting fact to consider is that Barry's home is up on a hill and there are no homes within less than 200 yards. What then was the source of the disembodied voice?

Moving ahead a little more than two weeks, March 16th again showed the intensity of the force behind these psychokinetic events. At 6:30 a.m. the downstairs hallway door leading to the bathroom and bedroom violently slams shut. The force was great enough to shake the entire house and awaken Lisa upstairs; Barry said it was like a cannon shot or loud sonic boom. For obvious reasons, Lisa could not go back to sleep after this event.

The very next morning at 10:30 a.m. Barry and Lisa are in the kitchen when they both feel a strong, cold wind blow through that part of the house. However, all the doors and windows were closed and the heat was on.

Life somewhat calms down for the next three weeks and Lisa is finally able to relax, praying that these events may have finally ended. To her dismay, On April 3rd at 10:30 a.m. Barry walks by one of the dressers in the master bedroom, which still has Christmas lights hanging behind them. Suddenly, the row of multi-colored lights, fly off the wall in front of both Lisa and Barry and hit the floor some distance from the dresser.

Later that same day at 4:15 p.m. I was at Barry's house waiting for them downstairs when I clearly heard what sounds like muffled or garbled female voices in the living room accompanied by an intense feeling of "overpressure". I walked around the bottom floor of the house even going so far as to walk around the outside of the house hoping to find a prosaic explanation for the disembodied voices only to discover nothing.

The next series of events were, in my opinion, the most intriguing for a number of reasons. The least of which is that I spent a good part of the day and evening with Barry and Lisa as we went down to San Diego to investigate another alleged haunted house during which time we were almost continually bombarded by a bizarre array of auditory PK events.

Okay, I know what you're probably thinking here. Why are we going out to distant locations to investigate other people's haunted houses when we have one right under our nose?

As one might expect, I had repeated discussions with Barry about setting up all of our instruments and cameras in his house with the hope of documenting some aspect of the events objectively.

When Barry brought this matter up with Lisa, she was vehemently opposed to such a venture. When I asked her this obvious question, she simply refused to answer and changed the subject. She was very conflicted on this matter. As the old saying goes; "you can lead a horse to water, but you can't make it drink".

Based on what Barry later told me, Lisa was raised in a very religious Presbyterian family that made her believe that these types of events were evil, the result of Satan's own work. If this manner of dogma was drilled into her head as a child that would certainly explain her aversion to my request. Therefore, the notion of poltergeist events being investigated at remote locations posed little, if any, threat to Lisa.

On our way down to San Diego in Barry's van we kept hearing odd ringing sounds. It was not coming from any of our cell phones, Barry's pager or the van itself. While eating dinner at the Hungry Tiger restaurant in Temecula, the same unusual ringing was continuously heard at our booth by us, by other diners and the waitress.

The ringing itself was unusual; always three successive rings appeared to come from around Lisa, then next to me and then in the wall to my right in the booth. These series of rings must have occurred at least a dozen or more times.

It was clearly not Barry or Lisa's cell phone or pager as they all made very distinctive sounds and, were all left in the van and not brought in to the restaurant. After eating we resumed our trip to San Diego and arrived at the woman's house, no further sounds were heard.

We left the San Diego house at 11:40 p.m. and had a two and-a-half hour ride back to Barry's house. Almost immediately, the ringing began again. There was no discernable pattern or interval period to the ringing. Half joking, I began taunting the "source" of the ringing and surprisingly it appeared to respond. We immediately made sure all cell phones, pagers, walkie-talkies, etc. were not responsible for the sets of three rings that appeared to emanate from the front of the van area around Lisa.

When I asked the "source" of the ringing if it was not a random function of nature, it immediately rang in response. I then asked "it" to ring four times for yes and five times for no, giving some indication that whatever we were dealing with was in fact responding to my verbal query.

I asked if the rings were the result of a poltergeist attached to Lisa McIntosh, it immediately rang "four" times in response, which it had not done previously. The next question from me was as to whether "it" was non-corporeal in nature; it instantly fired back a "yes" of four rings.

The "poltergeist" responded in five rings ("no") to many other questions. When I finally asked if the source of the poltergeist was from the distant past, we heard a repeated affirmation of four rings over and over.

By this point in time, Lisa was really freaking out, shaking severely. Lisa's frightful reaction to the escalating events grew so severe that Barry became very upset losing control of the van three separate times, which was more unnerving than the PK events. Fortunately, Barry avoided hitting anything.

The most puzzling aspect of this entire episode was that as the ringing started to taper off, Lisa abruptly falls asleep, which given her heightened state of arousal, anxiety and fear was very unusual, except for the fact that the hour was very late approaching 2 a.m.

As we started approaching Barry's house, the frequency of the ringing dramatically diminished as did it's willingness to respond to any more of my questions.
The last ringing occurred at 1:46 a.m. We pulled up into Barry's driveway at approximately 2:04 a.m. Lisa was sound asleep as it took quite a bit of prodding on Barry's part to wake her.

A peculiar afterthought on this particular PK outbreak is that the next day Lisa remembered that earlier in the day before I arrived "something" kept turning the ringers off on all of the different phones in their house. As Barry has his office in his home, neither of them would ever do such a foolish thing.

The next five weeks were peaceful bliss as everything, once again, returned to normal. But on May 29th while Lisa is upstairs in the bathroom at 11 a.m. she clearly hears Barry calling her. She leaves the bathroom saying that she'll be right down. However, when she comes downstairs she discovers that Barry has been on the phone during the entire time and did not call to her.

Just as summer of 2002 is about to begin so does another surge in the poltergeist activity around Lisa. At 3 p.m. on June 11th, Barry and Lisa are hugging in the garage when the house's back door that opens into the garage violently slams shut without any wind. The force of the door slamming shakes the garage area.

A month and a day later on July 12th at approximately 10 a.m., an autographed photo of Tippie Hedren, with a heavy frame on the display table in the dinning room flies several feet (6-8 ft.) across the room landing near the stone fireplace. Barry and Lisa return the photo to its rightful position and it again finds its way (unseen) to the same area of dining room.

Over the next few weeks Lisa again hears what she believes is Barry calling to her only to run downstairs and discover that he wasn't even home. These events are followed shortly by several incidents where Lisa is looking through their large, walk-in closet off the master bedroom upstairs, when there are loud poundings and knockings right in front of her. She panics and runs downstairs to get away from that part of the house.

Ten days later on August 7th at 5 p.m. the phenomena ascended to a new level in its communicative endeavor. Lisa's upstairs in the office running off copies of California's Most Haunted for Barry when suddenly the computer which was open to MS Word at the time, starts generating its own text in the middle of the screen. The letters "cu" and "et" mysteriously appear on their own without any input from Lisa at the keyboard. Lisa panics and runs downstairs. Unfortunately, Barry wasn't home to console her.

Later that day, after Lisa has stayed out of the house for hours, she returns, emotionally exhausted. Summoning all her courage and bravery she manages to go back upstairs and take a shower. As she was about to learn, this would turn out to be a very bad decision on her part.

While showering, the power in the house suddenly fails, requiring Lisa to find her way downstairs dripping wet and naked to the breakers and reset them. There have been occasional power failures in that region of Glendale, but this event only affected Barry's house. The power came back on several hours later before Barry came home. Lisa was emotionally crumbling at this point.

Four days later on August 11th, it's 3 a.m. and Barry cannot fall asleep so he decides to get some unfinished work done in his office. While at the computer, he clearly hears the sound of heavy footsteps coming up the staircase and approaching the office door. He strongly feels the sensation of being watched and turns, expecting to see Lisa or someone at the room's entrance. There was no one there and Lisa was sound asleep at the time.

Two and-a-half weeks later at 9:15 p.m. and Lisa's upstairs in the bathroom when she hears heavy footsteps coming up the stairs and approaching the bathroom. She panics and starts screaming. Again, Barry was out on a shoot.

It's now September 3rd very late at night. Barry is upstairs working in the office when he hears the sounds of someone or something running around the house and garage making a great deal of noise. His investigation finds nothing to account for the sounds. Earlier that day, Barry recalls an incident when he was positive that he heard Lisa calling to him, only later to realize that she was not even home at the time.

For the next two months the volleys of psychokinetic events seemed to take a vacation as all was quiet in the Conrad home, so much so, that Barry began to worry that something very large was looming just ahead.

The quiet interlude was subtly broken on November 4th when Lisa is in the bathroom upstairs when the shower curtains begin to move as if blown by a strong wind. However, the windows are closed and the heat was not on.

Over the next twenty-five weeks (approx. 6 months) Barry's house is eerily quiet. In fact, this interval is the longest duration when there was a complete cessation of paranormal events. Everything was back to normal and traumatized psyches could mend. Unfortunately, this was a totally false sense of security and serenity, but not for the obvious reasons.

During this half-year period of time, Lisa begins experiencing intense headaches, shooting pains throughout her body, especially in her bones. However, as Lisa had an intense mistrust and hatred of physicians for reasons never discussed, she starts consuming bottles of over-the-counter pain relievers (Tylenol, Aleve, Advil, etc.) per day as opposed to seeing a doctor and getting properly diagnosed. Unfortunately, self-medicating almost always has dire consequences.

It's now late spring of 2003. On the morning of May 13th Barry and Lisa are sound asleep in bed with not a care in the world as they believe the psychokinetic outbreaks are now long gone. At 5:45 a.m. their serenity is abruptly shattered when they are rudely awakened by several loud bangs and knocks coming from the ceiling and walls of the bedroom.

Over an estimated five-minute period, they hear repeated volleys of three intense bangs emanating from various walls around them. Lisa starts screaming and Barry desperately tries to calm her down. Barry then gets up and a knocks back (on the wall), attempting to communicate with whatever is producing the knocks. There is no reply. Lisa is trying very hard to maintain her composure given what's transpiring around her.

There is another break for the next two weeks. On May 26th one of the strangest episodes in this entire case occurs. At around 9:30 p.m., Lisa and Barry are watching TV in the living room when they hear an unusual noise coming from the kitchen. Bracing themselves, they and their new dog Buster, goes to investigate.

CONTINUES AFTER PHOTO SECTION...

PHOTO SECTION

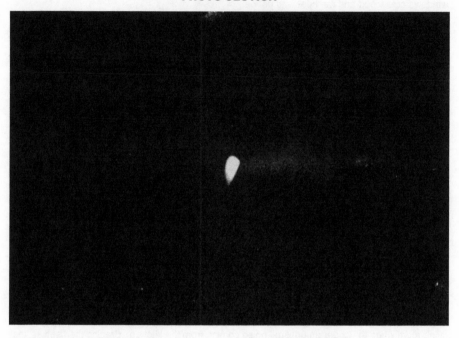

Chap 2- This photograph, of what appears to be an orb of light with a comet-like tail, was the only such example captured during the course of the investigation. It is also the only representation of what was visually observed by the principle investigators and numerous other witnesses during this case. These images were captured with 35mm SLR camera at 1/60 of a second using Kodak Tri-X film, pushed to 6400 ASA in development and employing a deep red filtered flash.

Chap 2- The arc of light displayed in this photograph was not observed by any of the investigators or witnesses. What was seen by all present were large, three dimensional balls of light, (which we refer to as corpuscular masses) traveling at high rates of speed. There is a high probability that these arcs were, in fact, time exposures (due to the cameras low shutter speed) of the fast moving luminous spheres which therefore produced an arc in much the same way stars produce tracks in slow shutter stationary cameras. It is significant to note that the subject of the haunting/poltergeist (Doris Bither) is literally framed by the arc. More importantly is the fact that the arc is not bent in accordance with the walls behind it which meet at a ninety degree angle. A secondary inverted arc can be seen at the left of the frame in front of one of the photographer's heads.These facts lead to the conclusion that these lights are moving in free space and were not projections against the wall. These images were captured using the same camera and film as used in photo 1.

Chap 2- The two arcs shown in this photo appear to be at right angles to each other. Once again, it is very important to note that these free floating spacial images are not bent in conformance to the walls behind them. The same balls of light were observed during this photograph as depicted in photos 1 & 2. Detailed examiniation and analysis of these negatives by the former west coast editor of Popular Photography resulted in his conclusion that these images were not the result of artifacts within the camera or film and that such inverted arcs are a physical impossibility given the optical glass in SLR cameras.

Chap 3- The three balls of light displayed in this photograph demonstrate the high degree of strangeness associated with and documented in this case. Resembling ball lightning or St. Elmo's fire, these glowing corpuscular masses appear to be self luminous (illuminating the carpet beneath them) point sources of light displaying vibrant three dimensional characteristics in their overlapping nature. In fact, one appears to be casting a shadow on the other. Interestingly, their edges or boundaries are sharp, distinct, and well defined rather than defused. These lights are truly enigmatic images that defy explanation. The camera used here was a 35mm SLR with kodak kodchrome film.

Chap 3- This peculiar articulating light formation was dancing on the ceiling when photographed by Jackie Hernandez. Its' texture is very reminiscent of plasma (the fourth state of matter). The eyeball description of this luminous configuration was that of a twisting and contorting miniature sun in the midst of dispersion.

Chap 3- This photograph was taken mere seconds after Jeff Wheatcraft screamed in the attic of Jackie Hernandez's San Pedro home. A twisted plastic clothesline can be seen behind and to the right of Jeff's neck and head. An unseen presence tied a bowline knot in the cord, wrapped it around Jeff's neck and pulled it up over a large nail extending out from one of ceilings rafters. Had it not been for another assistant's presence in the attic at that time, Jeff might have been killed.

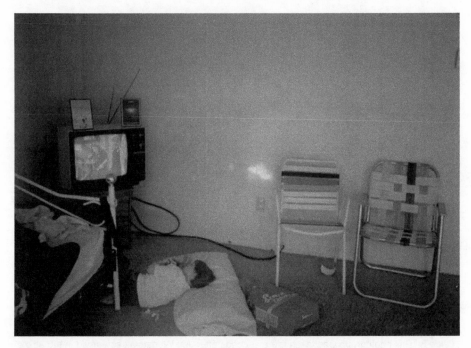

Chap 3- In the middle of the photograph frame, just to the left of the chairs, an anomalous light formation is seen. This image is highly suggestive of an amorphous plasma that is ejecting material or sputtering. This light source appears to be ascending from near the region of the child's head in the lower left section of the frame. There is an unmistakable UFO disc-like resemblance here that is hard to ignore.

Chap 4- These balls of light, similar in appearance to ball lightning were collectively observed by four people when they were photographed. They were electric arc blue in appearance and photographed by a Nikon 35mm camera using Kodak Tri-X film at 1/2000 of a second pushed to 6000 ASA in development. As these anomalous lights were observed by the naked eye and moved as if under intelligent control after being photographed, they could not be reflections.

Chap 4- As in the first picture, these balls of light, now seen several feet closer, were hovering in the front bathroom. Take note of the fact that they now appear in a vertical formation as opposed to the earlier photo where they appeared horizontal. As this positional change was not visually observed, but nevertheless captured on film, it rules out the possibility that the lights were the result of an artifact of the photographic system or a reflection. There was no explanation for such a dramatic change from one photo to the next. Particularly intriguing is the sputtering effect by the right ball of light in the first photo and the upper sphere in the second. The lower left portion of both of these luminous anomalies appear to be ejecting a plasma-like substance, much like high voltage electrical discharge, observed with ball lightning. However, in as much as ball lightning supposedly does not occur in Southern California, there is no explanation readily at hand for these manifestations.

Aliens Above, Ghosts Below by Barry E. Taff

As they enter the dining room, both of them observe a large, dark, amorphous apparitional image, not in the expected shape of a human being, but as a large, distorted letter "M". The image lasts for several seconds as Buster starts to growl and bark at it. Barry and Lisa look at each other trying to understand what they've just seen.

At the time, seeing such an obscure apparitional image had absolutely no meaning to anyone, including this author. In fact, I do not recall any instance similar to this ever being reported in research literature. The significance of seeing a large letter "M" will not become relevant for almost twenty more months.

Later that same evening at 11:30 p.m. Lisa is upstairs getting ready for bed. Barry is still downstairs watching TV when he hears what sounds like shattering glass from the kitchen. Searching the kitchen and dining room reveals nothing. This sound was very similar to what was heard up the bedroom many months earlier and could be the crackling or snapping of high-voltage electrostatic discharge.

The next morning at 9 a.m. Barry was preparing to shave and shower and was unable to find his razor. It never reappears and he must purchase a new one.

On the 31st of May at approximately 9:30 a.m. the downstairs hallway cabinet door violently swings open with enough force to shake the entire house while Lisa and Barry are watching the news on TV. Lisa's terrified and it takes Barry hours to calm her down.

Two blessed months of silence again lull Lisa and Barry into another false sense of security. Their peace of mind is forcefully interrupted on July 28th at around 11 p.m. when they are both up in the office and Lisa feels a "warm hand" touch her right ribcage area which causes her to jump and start screaming.

There is another six-month interval when there is very little, if any, activity to report, most of it being sparse reoccurrences of banging and knockings or Lisa and Barry thinking they've heard each other calling.

Not until January 24th of 2004 does anything dramatic happen again. At 5:40 p.m. Barry, as usual, is on his way home from a shoot. At home, Lisa puts a chicken into the oven within a Pyrex pan. After less than five minutes there is loud explosion in the oven. The oven's door blows open and shards of the Pyrex glass pan are propelled out of the oven barely missing Lisa.

Fortunately, she was on the other side of the kitchen nowhere near the front of the oven. Oddly, given the fierce nature of the explosion, the chicken itself, was untouched. It's as if the glass was blown out laterally away from the chicken. However, there was no way Lisa was going to attempt to once again roast that chicken after witnessing this event. This was now the second incident of this specific type, as the first one occurred on December 17, 2001.

Maybe the poltergeist "chickened out" if you'll excuse the pun, but things dramatically "simmered" down for the next three months until the 24th of April. At 7:55 p.m. Buster (the new dog) awakens from his slumber in the downstairs bedroom, walks out and intensely stares and then begins barking at the steps leading upstairs.

Barry comes over to see what's going on, as Buster is normally a very calm dog. He looks up and sees nothing unusual. Cautiously going upstairs, Barry sees a bright blue flash of light without any apparent source.

As he turns around he notices that a framed photo from the bookshelf is lying on the floor. He places it back onto the shelf and walks away. Only moments later he again finds it on the floor, several feet away from the shelf. Fearing for Lisa's sanity, Barry doesn't tell her about this event.

Another thirty-eight days pass and everything has once again turned calm. But on June 2nd the calm is broken at 11:50 p.m. while Lisa and Barry are up in the bedroom watching TV. Something unseen slams into the door of the cabinet holding the TV producing a loud crack, startling them. Once again, Lisa's is in a state of heightened anxiety.

Three weeks later, there is another event strongly indicating that these phenomena are associated with Lisa and travel with her away from her residence. Lisa accompanies Barry who went to the mid-west for work, after which he decided to visit his father in Ohio. It was a very pleasant trip and Lisa really enjoyed meeting many of Barry's family members.

However, on June 24th at approximately 6 a.m., while Barry and Lisa are sleeping at Barry's father's house, their bedroom door begins to intensely shake and then repeatedly slam itself shut over the course of 10-15 seconds. Later that morning, when Barry goes to take a shower, the power in the house repeatedly quits only to abruptly turn itself on again.

What makes this event all the more compelling is that these events have never occurred prior to or since Lisa visited Barry's father's house. Over the last several decades since Barry moved to California, he has frequently gone back to visit his father in Ohio. There has never been an incident such as the aforementioned one in his father's house.

Since Barry has moved into his Glendale home, he has had numerous 4th of July barbecues with his friends. As usual, the food as well as the company was great and some guests stayed well beyond midnight into early the next morning talking out on the patio by the pool.

At around 1 a.m. on the 5th of July, several guests are still talking when Barry walks back into the house and discovers a large, heavy, lobby card (poster) that was leaning against the wall is now several feet away lying on the floor. A little later, after Lisa extinguished the Tiki torches around the edges of the pool in the back yard, she sees several of them reignite on their own. This had never happened before.

It takes ninety days for the phenomena to reassert itself. On October 4th at 3 a.m. and again at 9 a.m., Barry and Lisa clearly hear a disembodied woman's voice seemingly coming from the downstairs area. When Barry goes down to investigate, there is no one present. There are several more incidents of this type during that same day.

Two more months pass until December 4th at 10 p.m. when Barry is walking upstairs he hears something hit the wall right below the staircase. He goes to check and finds that his manual toothbrush is now lying beneath the stairwell next to the wall.

Over the following days to weeks, Lisa becomes very ill with a high fever and severe muscle and bone pains. Barry finally convinces her to go see a doctor, which she hesitantly does.

The news is very bad. Lisa is diagnosed with Multiple Myeloma, a very tenacious and debilitating form of bone cancer. The lethality rate of this cancer is close to 100% as there is no known medical cure, although there have been some indicators that a particular form of magnetic polarization therapy significantly destroys the cancer without killing the patient.

However, under current FDA guidelines, only pharmaceutical intervention can be labeled as a cure. Lisa is given intense chemotherapy, which appears to be working. However, she must consume powerful prescription pain meds, which make her very sleepy.

Aliens Above, Ghosts Below by Barry E. Taff

The diagnosis of Multiple Myeloma is most startling given what was seen by Lisa and Barry on May 26, 2003. The observed apparition of a large, dark letter "M" now has a very disturbing and foreboding significance. Was Lisa's unconscious mind trying to communicate with her conscious mind what was really going on within her body the only way it could long before she was diagnosed? This possibility, in and of itself is absolutely incredible and connotes high-strangeness beyond anything this author has ever heard of.

As Lisa fights her way back to health it appears that the chemo is doing its job. Lisa's blood work shows her to be in remission. However, in order for the remission to be considered complete, she must stay that way at least five years. As is quite common with this type of virulent cancer, Lisa bounces between remission and relapse.

On January 1, 2005, at 5:45 a.m. Barry and Lisa hear a loud explosion as if something crashed onto the floor. Buster refuses to go downstairs, but Barry does and finds nothing to account for the noise.

Over the next several months Lisa's health vacillates from good to bad. She begins losing great amounts of weight, as she cannot eat. The pain and incredible fatigue associated with her cancer comes and goes. By early summer of 2005, she appeared, once again, to be in remission and starts going out of the house with Barry.

On July 17th of 2005 Barry and Lisa accompanied me out to a new haunting case on Cielo Drive within Benedict Canyon of Beverly Hills. If Cielo Drive rings a bell, it should. More than thirty-nine years ago on August 8, 1969, the followers of Charles Manson viciously murdered Sharon Tate and four of her friends.

A stone's throw away, maybe less that one hundred feet down the block, a new house was built in 2002 and was occupied by the son of the builder. Not surprisingly, the construction crew, the resident and many of his friends, have experienced a wide range of paranormal phenomena including apparitions, psychokinetic displays as well as disembodied voices.

However, we had absolutely no way of knowing upon our arrival just how utterly unique this specific property would turn out to be. Our instruments indicated bizarre and totally unprecedented magnetic field amplitudes and polarities throughout the entire house combined with an ambient electromagnetic background anywhere from 20-100 times normal. This house was a compass needle's worst nightmare.

After this first visit, Barry, Lisa and I came away from this house feeling physically ill. In fact, after turning beet red, I had passed out at the bottom of the stairwell where the highly localized geomagnetic field (GMF) measured out at 1,700 milligauss [mG], when 300-500 mG is normal. While both Barry and I had relatively strong adverse reactions to the high amplitude geomagnetic fields, as have about 67% of those visiting, Lisa's response was far more severe.

In fact, there's a distinct possibility that her spending some 6-8 hours in the Cielo house pushed her back into a series of intense relapses from which she never recovered. However, I am not saying that the energy in the house was responsible for her untimely demise, but it possibly hastened its arrival. It then was not surprising to later learn that this specific location is listed by the U.S. Geological Survey as a geomagnetic anomaly site.

Had we known that this property had such strong, positively polarized magnetic fields associated with it, we never would have allowed Lisa to even step foot on the property, let alone within it.

Over the course of almost four decades, nothing even close to these levels of energy has been experienced around here during such investigations. As mentioned earlier, there is substantial body of clinical evidence indicating that exposure to negatively polarized magnetic fields substantially inhibit the growth of many types of cancers, while positively polarized magnetic fields appear to rapidly accelerate their growth and proliferation.

It goes without saying that neither Barry nor Lisa ever returned to the Cielo house. I, on the other hand have visited that location more than twenty (20) times over the course of a year and have gotten sick on virtually every occasion.

Before you assume that I am a masochist with a death wish, let me assure you that it is simply a matter of my intense scientific curiosity overwhelming my logic on occasion. In my opinion, the Cielo case offers more potentially rewarding information towards unraveling this aspect of the paranormal than any other location I've visited during the course of my career. I may return to this location if I am paid to do so on a shoot or able to bring more sophisticated instrumentation into that environment to better study it.

However, there is one specific requirement that must be met before I ever return to this location again. It is that I fashion a head-to-foot suit out of Giron or Mu-metal to shield my body from the high intensity magnetic fields. I may look like a chunky alien, but at least I will no longer get physically ill from being in this house.

As the summer of 2005 ends, so does the phenomena's dry spell at Barry's house. At midnight on September 26th, Lisa and Barry are about to go to sleep. Suddenly, there are extremely loud banging noises heard throughout the house preventing their rest. Buster goes nuts believing someone is at the door.

These poundings last for several minutes and then cease. At 3 a.m. there is another volley of loud pounds accompanied by footsteps coming up the stairs. Buster again goes wild. During this time Lisa has been very ill from the ever-growing cancer.

For the next eight months Lisa's physical condition rapidly deteriorates and the PK outbreaks stop. Lisa has started radiation therapy in hope of turning her condition around. She has lost much weight, has numerous tumors throughout her body and is very fatigued.

Lisa knows that she's dying and tells Barry that she just wants to be free of the constant physical pain she's had for almost two years. Lisa promises Barry that if there is a way, she will attempt to contact and communicate with him from "the other side."

At 11 p.m. on July 16th 2006 there is a very loud explosion heard at the front of the house. No source is found.

Over the next nine days Lisa physically degenerates and lapses into a coma from which she never emerges. As she requested to be brought home from the hospital to spend her final days in a familiar environment there is round-the-clock nursing/medical care.

Approaching two in the morning on July 25th, Buster runs to the stairwell and begins intensely barking as he looks up to the top of the stairs, as if he could sense something Barry could not. Half and hour later, the nurse tells Barry that she believes Lisa is about to pass. Barry rushes to her side and holds her hand.

Though she's in a coma, Lisa seems to be aware of Barry's touch and responds ever so slightly by very gently squeezing back. Lisa takes one last, painful breath of air and stops breathing at 1:50 a.m. Lisa no longer feels the incredible pain from the consuming cancer within her body. She is, at last, forever free of it.

Barry's eyes along with many of his friends and Lisa's twenty-three year old daughter well up with tears. There is silence in the large room as everyone gently lowers their head.

Aliens Above, Ghosts Below by Barry E. Taff

This brief moment of silent prayer is sharply broken by the sound of numerous doors within Barry's large house opening and closing on their own accord. This is shortly followed by lights in the patio and throughout the house flickering on and off. Was this Lisa's attempt at communication, or simply another one of the many PK incidents occurring in and around the house?

Four days later on July 29th at approximately 12:45 a.m. Barry is in the kitchen talking with Lisa's daughter's boyfriend while she is in the bathroom. An ice cube materializes (apports) into the space directly between them, hangs motionless in the air and then falls to the ground. Barry just takes it all in thinking that perhaps this is "contact" from a discarnate Lisa. The boyfriend doesn't believe in the paranormal. His eyes widen in horror as he immediately bolts out of the house.

After a sleepless night, Barry awakens late the next morning and goes to his office. For some unknown reason the front office door will not open. Something's preventing it from moving. Barry goes around through the bathroom and enters the office through the other door. He is astonished to discover many tapes he had recently shot for his current project are wedged up against the front door preventing it from opening. No explanation. Does this represent "contact'?

Several extremely anguish filled days later, Barry and a friend are reviewing footage they are editing when they suddenly both hear and feel the whistling of cold wind moving through the house.

It's now early 2007 and Barry's house has returned to its normal ambiance that does not include poltergeist activity. This case presents a unique and fascinating opportunity to evaluate one of the major theories within parapsychology related to poltergeists.

As discussed earlier, modern academic paranormal researchers believe that "living, breathing" people, are the physical generators of recurrent spontaneous psychokinetic activity, better known as RSPK. Moreover, there is a truly enigmatic psychodynamic relationship between these unique individuals and the electromagnetic environment in which they live.

As research has indicated, a high percentage of these "poltergeist agents" or PGAs, are either seizure prone or epileptic. When these physically unique individuals take their prescribed meds to quell their seizures, the psychokinetic outbreaks cease as well. This more than suggests that the same region of the brain responsible for mediating seizures and epilepsy may also mitigate psychokinetic phenomena as well.

Strangely, most people suffering from seizures and/or epilepsy do not manifest poltergeist phenomena, while the majority of PGAs seem to be either seizure prone or epileptic. This observed mind-body nexus suggests that this might be a unilateral effect and that there is a missing or unknown variable here, which has yet to be discovered. My own case files clearly demonstrate this unexpected relationship. If we had only known what questions to ask many decades ago, the database on this matter would be absolutely enormous.

This case is unique and stands on its own for many reasons. Examining this case strictly from a medical perspective is perhaps the best starting point. According to the oncologists who dealt with Lisa and Barry, she is, perhaps, the youngest person on record to contract and so rapidly die from Multiple Myeloma as this form of cancer is normally associated with elderly patients, although its etiology is totally unknown.

As was keeping and building the database on this case, entering data usually within hours after it occurred, we have the unique opportunity to retrospectively observe the longitudinal patterns that developed over the course of five years. The collected data strongly suggests that, in this particular case, the waxing and waning of the psychokinetic outbreaks were directly correlated with Lisa's physical health.

When Lisa first started feeling sick enough to consume vast amounts of over-the-counter painkillers starting in late 2002 until May of 2003, we see the first major drop off in activity. It was as if her body was marshalling all of its energy to fight off the initial onslaught from the pathogens.

After Lisa became very ill around Christmas of 2004, necessitating her reluctant visit to a physician resulting in her being diagnosed with Multiple Myeloma, we again see a significant attenuation of phenomena. When she began to physically degenerate and required radiation therapy as a last resort, the RSPK activity around her almost completely abated.

Since Lisa's passing in late July of 2006 and the minute flurry of events that followed, it feels more like the last capacitive discharges from her physically depleted system.

Although one cannot draw any conclusions from any single case, the accumulated database, which is far more comprehensive than discussed herein, and its biomedical correlations, may finally point us in the right direction in terms of understanding this type of phenomenon.

Generally speaking, in the majority of poltergeist agents I've personally investigated or read about, the phenomena dramatically tapers off or completely ends well before ones 30's or 40's. To the best of my knowledge, there has not been a single case where a documented and continuously active poltergeist agent dies and the phenomena abruptly stop.

The normal course of events is one where the poltergeist agent simply ages and matures, "growing out of" their paranormal "condition". I would think that the probability of a relatively young individual dying during the course of a poltergeist outbreak is extremely low. Therefore, such data would very likely not exist. If, in fact, it does, no one within the paranormal research community is aware of such at this time.

This case is more than simply amazing; it's incredible, for it finally provides a physical, perhaps even causal link between the material world and the seemingly non-material, paranormal one.

I've had the privilege and pleasure of knowing and working with Barry Conrad as a research associate for eighteen years. In that time I've learned what a kind, gentle, intelligent and giving person he is. His dedication to parapsychology is rivaled perhaps only by my own. I've met every woman he's dated since meeting him in 1988.

Lisa was, in every respect, a breath of fresh air in Barry's life of failed relationships with emotionally damaged women who frequently took advantage of his magnanimous nature while sharing absolutely nothing in common with him. Moreover, Lisa was a breath of fresh air in everyone's life that came to know her.

I had such admiration and respect for her, having talked with her extensively since meeting her in 2001, that I would have chosen her as a mate over every woman I've known in my five decades on earth.

Both Barry and I keep asking ourselves why did Lisa have to die at the tender young age of 42? In a world of over 6 billion souls residing on this small rock in the heavens, why was Lisa forced to give up her existence and the love she shared with all her friends, family and especially Barry? Why here, why now? What's the point and meaning of it all?

In a strange twist of fate, the loss of Lisa to my colleague and best friend Barry Conrad may have inadvertently provided us with a vital key to unlocking the very domain she dedicated her all-too-short life to.

Let the loss of Lisa's physical life be seen as a new beginning in unraveling at least one small fraction of the paranormal. Barry's loss may have given the rest of us incalculable knowledge that we might never have otherwise acquired.

Lisa…. if there is any portion of you still residing within the physical world we call life, please hear the call from Barry and the rest of us. Your untimely death was not totally in vain. You will never be forgotten. As long as we remember you, keeping you alive in our hearts, minds and dreams, you are still with us. Thank you for being you. The world desperately needs many more enlightened beings just like you. You are truly one of kind.

Let this not be your final goodbye.

END

Chapter 8:
ANATOMY OF AN EBE

In the May, 1982 issue of OMNI Magazine, there appeared an article entitled "Smart Dinosaurs," which included a photographic model of a dinosauroid----what many researchers believe dinosaurs might have evolved into had they not been rendered extinct some 65 million years ago, by way of what many believe to have been a cataclysmic meteoric bombardment.

The dinosauroid man is constructed very much like a human being. He is a bi-pedal, humanoid creature, and bears more than a striking resemblance to collective descriptions given by hundreds, if not thousands, of people who have claimed UFO abductions over the last 40 years. Is it mere coincidence that this dinosauroid image dramatically matches the reported form of what many UFO researchers refer to as an Extraterrestrial Biological Entity or EBE?

Adding fuel to this speculation is evidence collected by the late UFO researcher Leonard Stringfield and published in his monograph, The UFO Crash/Retrieval Syndrome, Status Report II   (MUFON, 1980).

In this status report, Stringfield offers a collective summary of comments by various anonymous medical examiners, who supposedly examined deceased alien bodies retrieved from crashes between 1947 and 1980. The following tentative morphology refers to an alleged alien humanoid measuring 3 1/2 - 4 1/2 feet tall and weighing 40 pounds. Forget Fox-TV's Alien Autopsy, this is the real thing.

- Two round eyes without pupils. Under heavy brow ridge, eyes described variously as large, almond shaped, elongated, sunken or deep set, far apart, slightly slanted, appearing "Oriental" or "Mongoloid."
- By human standards, the head is large in relation to the limbs and torso. It has been compared with a 5-month old human fetus.
- No ear lobes or protrusive flesh extending beyond apertures on each side of the head.
- Nose is vague. Two snares are indicated with only slight protuberance.
- Mouth indicated as a small "slit" without lips opening into a small cavity, and appears not   to function as a means of communication or as an orifice for food ingestion.
- Neck is described as being thin and in some instances not visible because of the garment on that section of the body.
- Most observers describe the head of the humanoid alien as hairless. One source said the pate showed a slight fuzz. Bodies are described as hairless.
- The torso is generally described as small and thin. In most instances, the body was observed wearing a flexible, metallic garment.
- Arms are described as long, thin and reaching down to the knee section.
- One type of hand consists of four fingers and no thumb; two of the fingers appear longer than the others. Some observers have seen fingernails; others none. A slight webbing effect between fingers was noted by three authoritative observers. Other reports indicate types of hands with both less and more than four fingers.
- Legs are reported as short and thin. Feet of one type are described as toeless. Most observers describe feet as covered. One said alien foot looked like an orangutan's.
- Skin is not described as green. Some claim beige, tan, brown or gray with a tannish or pinkish cast. One said it looked "almost bluish-gray under the deep freeze light," in two instances, the bodies were charred a dark brown in the wake of an alleged crash.
- Skin texture is described as scaly or reptilian, and as stretchable, elastic or mobile

over smooth muscle or skeletal tissue. No striated muscle, no perspiration, no body odor.
- No teeth
- No apparent reproductive organs. No genitalia. An absence of sexual organs suggests that they were perhaps atrophied by evolutionary degeneration, or the possibilities that some aliens, and perhaps all, do not reproduce like human beings, or that cadavers studied may have originated through cloning or other artificial means.
- To most observers, the humanoids appear to be "formed out of a mold," sharing identical facial characteristics rather than individuality displayed by humans.
- Brain and its capacity unknown.
- Colorless liquid present in body, without red cells; alien circulation not oxygen carrying. No lymphocytes. No food or water intake known; in one known retrieval, witness noted that no food was aboard. Absence of digestive system, gastrointestinal tract, alimentary canal and rectal area.
- More than one humanoid type. Life span unknown. Descriptive types of alien anatomy may be nor more diverse than those known among Earth's Homo-sapiens. Other recovered alien types or other grotesque configurations, or human, are unknown at this time. Origins also unknown.

Stringfield also came in contact with a physician who in the early 1950's allegedly performed an autopsy on an EBE. The witness described the body as follows:

SIZE: "The specimen observed was 4 feet, three and three-eighths inches tall. I cannot remember the weight. It has been so long, and my files do not indicate the weight. I recall the length well, because we had a disagreement and everyone took their turn measuring."

HEAD: "The head was pear-shaped in appearance and oversized by human standards for the body. The eyes were Mongoloid in appearance. The ends of the eyes furthest from the nasal cavity slated upwards at about a ten-degree angle. There seemed to be no visible eyelids, only what seemed like a fold. The nose consisted of a small, fold-like protrusion above the nasal orifices. The mouth seemed to be a wrinkle-like fold. There were no human lips as such----just a slit that opened into an oral cavity about two inches deep. A membrane along the rear of the cavity separated it from what would be the digestive tract.

"The tongue seemed to be atrophied into almost a membrane. No teeth were observed. X-rays revealed a maxilla and mandible as well as a cranial bone structure. The outer 'ear lobes' didn't exist. The auditory orifices present were similar to our middle ear and inner ear canals. The head contained no hair follicles. The skin seemed grayish in color and seemed mobile when stretched,"

In November 1979, additional word was received from the medical authority concerning the nature of alien skin. Under magnification, the tissue structure appears mesh-like, or like a grid network of horizontal and perpendicular lines. Clarifying an earlier reference that describes the skin of the entity as "reptilian," this new information suggests that the texture of the granular-skinned lizards, such as the iguana and the chameleon, may be similar to at least one type of alien humanoid.

I do not believe it is a coincidence that the bulk of reported encounters with EBEs or alien humanoids, such as the ones allegedly ejected from the 1947 Roswell, New Mexico crash and as described in Budd Hopkins' Intruders, Witnessed and David Jacobs' Secret Life, share many features in common with the aforementioned anatomical/physiological descriptions.

An interesting hypothesis is the possibility of another star system where the predominant life-form was reptilian, as was our own planet many millions of years ago. In this hypothesized star system, however, dinosaurs evolved into erect, bi-pedal beings that resemble humans only in the vaguest of terms. Therefore, instead of hominids and eventual homo sapiens, dinosauroid men/women evolved. This hypothesis offers several intriguing perspectives regarding the appearance, behavior and possible motives of EBEs.

For one, if EBE evolution is indeed reptilian, they certainly would look considerably different than we do, although not totally dissimilar, in that they would share common bi-pedal characteristics. The objective differences might well include scaly skin, webbed hands and/or feet and a totally different brain structure incorporating elaborately divergent functions, especially as their mid-brain, [specifically lacking an amygdala (pleasure center)], and stem would have its origin from reptilian as opposed to hominid roots. It's important to remember here, that the limbic system of homo sapiens is believed to be a reptilian vestigial.

These physical differences might result in a species inability to sense color as we do, to feel or express emotions as we do, to eat the same foods as humans and, most important, the tendency not to exhibit a strong sense of territoriality and possessiveness, which in human history, invariably leads to war.

However, they might still harbor the fundamental underlying trait of higher lifeforms---- the need to know and understand the universe in which they live. But the lack of an adrenal and/or endocrine system and sexual organs, as we understand them, might result in a radically different biological entity, with perceptual processes that disallow or prevent the organism from perceiving reality and its many complex social elements as we do, and as we so often take for granted.

Try to imagine what life would be like without emotions such as love, hate, fear, excitation, etc., and without consumption of the foodstuffs we so enjoy and yet require for survival.

If EBEs do not procreate and biologically age as we do, they would have very little if anything in common with us----with the exception, of the "need to know." At the most basic of levels, the decision-making, reasoning and judgment of such entities would not be governed by passion or sentiment, but by cold, hard, rational, pragmatic logic. Their orientation and agenda, whatever it may be, would certainly be self-centered, not human centered, as altruism would very likely not be a word contained in their lexicon.

Such a dramatically different species of life would certainly look at human beings as quite peculiar indeed. We would appear as large, hairy creatures with rather primitive technology (compared to theirs, which may employ paranormal forces the way we commonly use electromagnetism) whose primary occupation is tribal warfare and entering strange metal boxes that spew toxic gases into the atmosphere and emit bright lights after dark (automobiles).

Though a dinosauroid-evolved EBE would probably not experience the same emotions and thought patterns as do homo sapiens, due to the major anatomical and physiological differences, certainly they would exhibit curiosity in our behavior, which is no doubt enigmatic by their standards. Much reported alien behavior evidences that sort of curiosity. However, is this the curiosity of a neutral observer or an intervening experimenter?

It's a sociological truism that when the spiritual or cultural ethics of a civilization fail to keep pace with its technology, that civilization is doomed, leading to the kind of inexplicable behavior that only humans display. We are the only Earth species that prey upon themselves---- and not for food or other survival needs. As the theorized EBE's forebrain, mid-brain and stem would have evolved from reptilian roots, perhaps they might lack one of the primal ingredients inherent in this twist of human nature: violence.

It might explain how a technologically advanced civilization survived its "catastrophe" era, in that ethnocentrism with its territorial fears and paranoia never existed to begin with, eliminating national boundaries as we currently know them on Earth. How much greater progress in all endeavors could a civilization make that was not hampered by these self-destructive tendencies?

During the course of numerous abductions, the abductees report a form of telepathic contact with their abductors. But even with this advanced form of communication, the aliens appear extremely naive concerning very common aspects of life on Earth. Such things as fruit, vegetables and colors seem as alien to them as eating a shoe would be to us.

The reason for this paradox might be quite simple. The EBEs evolved from reptilian ancestors, which would have given them a 65 million year jump on Homo Sapiens just in biological terms. Their survival requirements would in no way resemble anything we are even vaguely familiar with. This would be comparable to humans trying to understand insect life's needs, attitudes and motivations based on its own social structure.

An intriguing incident was reported in John Fuller's The Interrupted Journey, in which abductee Betty Hill is communicating telepathically with the alien captain of the vehicle in which her and her husband Barney were abducted. At one point, the EBE captain told Betty that they frequently re-visit Earth and would like to see her again. There was some indication during this exchange that such a return visit would require an exceedingly long time span, at least in terms of a human life.

Betty informed the alien captain that when they returned, she would not be able to see them again, for in all likelihood she would be dead due to age. Strangely, the alien humanoid could not comprehend the concept of biological aging and death. Betty tried her best to explain what death was and how the passing of time caused us to age, but the EBE still remained puzzled.

However, is it not odd that the EBE captain could comprehend the passage of time relative to his interstellar voyage, but not to biological atrophy or aging? Wouldn't it seem that these temporal facts would be inherently linked? If this aforementioned exchange did, in fact, occur as described, it strongly suggests that human beings have absolutely nothing in common with their EBE abductors and therefore may not have any basis for cultural contact at this time.

The most fascinating scenario is one theorizing that EBEs are entities genetically engineered for the expressed purpose of traveling across the vast, interstellar void. Their unique physiological and anatomical makeup, lacking the necessity for the assimilation of food and excretion of waste matter, apparent agelessness in real time and absence of oxygen carrying blood, makes these creatures perfect candidates for a truly advanced civilization to develop or breed specifically for extended duration space travel, especially if long-term environmental controls and/or superluminal speeds are unobtainable.

As recent news has taught us, the task of genetically engineering a life form for highly specific applications is no longer confined to the realm of science fiction. In the laboratories of some of the most advanced genetic engineering facilities, recombinant DNA techniques are being used right now to mate biological elements that under normal conditions would never intermix without eons of random mutation.

Many of these labs are now creating recombinant strains of bacteria and viruses that might prevent damage to crops all the way to altering damaged DNA material within a mature human body.

Given this acknowledged potential of genetic engineering, it is well within reason to presume that a more technically advanced species may have mastered their own genomes, their full set of chromosomes with all inheritable traits, and can manipulate life forms at their whim and discretion.

This speculation dovetails with Budd Hopkins' and Dr. David Jacobs' hypothesis regarding EBEs conducting massive, possibly even longitudinal genetic hybridization experiments during abductions for reasons we can only guess at.

There is, however, one vital piece of information that must be considered at this point. There is good reason to believe that we cannot totally trust our perception in and around this phenomenon (UFO's, EBE's, etc.).

A substantial body of evidence exists suggesting that whatever we are dealing with here has the ability to alter our perception to induce both auditory and visual hallucinations. Moreover, to make us remember "events" that were never experienced at a conventional sensory level.

Such "scanned memories" are perhaps implanted within our brain through some unknown method of induction, to make us see, feel, hear, taste and smell virtually anything "they" desire. If this is true, then we cannot rely upon any of our perceptual processes when dealing with such a truly advanced and manipulative abductor.

While it's intriguing to speculate as to the method of such incredible technology, its purpose is certainly understandable. Just look at the way we modify and manipulate the environment of lower life forms to study their behavioral responses.

As we humans attempt to better understand and comprehend the intelligence, reasoning and emotional qualities of other species on earth, we stage elaborate experiments in order to determine how these animals respond to different stimuli.

While our feeble efforts at communicating and experimenting with other intelligent life forms cannot be directly compared to purported alien methods, they are essentially similar in nature. That is, to produce a specific response to given stimuli. A stimulus tailored to the subconscious needs, wants and fears of the subject. In this case though, we are the subjects!

What is particularly fascinating about the purpose of scanned memories is that we again see suggestive evidence that whatever these "things" are as related to UFOs and abductions, they are not that much unlike us. Their behavior and methodology are not totally dissimilar from our own.

Maybe the reason we see such commonality here is that we are in some strange way related to these beings. That our thoughts and behavior are modeled, in part, on those who may have created us! Or is it simply the way in which any advanced life form uses its technology to achieve its goals? Something to think about, huh?

One thing we can assume with some confidence is that if we are being visited by a races of extraterrestrial beings, it does not appear to be the same race described in ancient Biblical texts (unless the transmission of information from that era was incomplete or inaccurate, what is not unlikely). On the basis of their behavior, these beings are not totally benevolent, in that we may find ourselves looking out from within their test tubes.

In conclusion, for all their differences, there are remarkably striking similarities between these EBEs and human beings. They do to us what we do to lower life forms on our own planet, and most certainly would do to any less advanced life forms we might discover on other worlds. The fundamental difference is that they are far more knowledgeable and advanced than us at studying numerous biological specimens. And all indications strongly suggest that we are the ones now being studied----and under someone else's looking glass! How does it feel being on the other end of a microscope? - END

Aliens Above, Ghosts Below by Barry E. Taff

Chapter 9:
YOU CAN'T GET HERE FROM THERE, OR HOW TO PROPEL A UFO

It's been frequently repeated by skeptics and debunkers the likes of the late Phillip Klass and Dr. Carl Sagan that not only do UFOs not exist, but even if there were such devices as extraterrestrial "starships," they could not traverse the enormous interstellar distances between Earth and say Zeta Reticuli...a mere 37 light years, due to the time factor.

Based upon conventional theories of propulsion and the fact that the fastest man-made object to leave the solar system, Pioneer, was traveling at a mere 86,000 miles per hour----the speed of light is 186,000 miles per second----that's a mind-stretching 670 million miles per hour----we're nowhere near attaining light speed, let alone superluminal velocities (faster-than-light), a la "warp drive."

At our current stage of technology, the underlying reason why we cannot achieve even a substantial fraction of light speed, let alone faster-than-light travel is based on some very fundamental principles put forth by Einstein that have yet to be violated, except perhaps in speculative theory.

However, Einstein himself stated that even though he determined it was physically impossible for any object with rest mass to achieve or surpass the speed of light, we would eventually succeed at accomplishing such a feat.

It is extremely unlikely that such a monumental technological leap will be achieved through the use of symmetrical, chemical propulsion, as in contemporary rocket engines. Since the dawn of heavier-than-air flight, we have essentially relied on the same fundamental aerodynamic mechanisms to propel ourselves; pushing air over winged surfaces to obtain lift, and shoving air back or out the rear of a vehicle (propeller, jet or rocket) for thrust.

We have changed little from the Wright Brothers' first flight at Kitty Hawk to the SR-71 Blackbird's Mach 3+ at 85,000 feet (although the "official" top speed of the SR-71 is claimed to be 2,193 mph, strong evidence from reliable sources suggests that it was more like Mach 6+ or, approximately 4,400 mph with an operational ceiling of greater than 112,000 feet), the Space Shuttle (Mach 25+), or even the canceled National Aerospace Plane (NASP).

Before the program was cancelled, the NASP was envisioned as a single-stage-to-orbit trans-atmospheric vehicle that would take off much as a conventional airliner, climb into the ionosphere and above using slush hydrogen-fueled scramjets (supersonic combustion ramjets) and rockets, attain low Earth orbit (LEO) and return under powered flight like an ordinary jet. Allegedly, the NASP program was terminated in the late 1990's due to insurmountable technical hurdles.

One of the many "deep black" projects covertly deployed by the U.S. Air Force is the Aurora, perhaps better known today as "Senior Citizen", "Sentinel" or more simply the F-100 (an interesting numerical designation, as the original F-100 was the U.S. Air Force's first supersonic fighter in the 1950's).

Designed and developed by Lockheed Martin's Skunk Works, this newly designated F-100 hypersonic aircraft is a Mach 15 (roughly 11,000 mph) strategic reconnaissance follow-on replacement to their SR-71 that was retired in the early 1990's, claiming budgetary restraints and superior methods (satellites) for collecting remote sensing data.

Aliens Above, Ghosts Below by Barry E. Taff

The F-100's are supposedly based at Nellis Air Force Base's (AFB) Area 51, Beale AFB in northern California and Mildenhall (United Kingdom) RAFB and manned by a crew of three.

When their powerful, pulse detonation wave, liquid methane-fueled, combined-cycle scramjets kick in, they create a sound like the air itself is being torn apart accompanied by a high-pitched screeching noise. Supposedly, the F-100's engines can be heard more than 30 miles distant, hardly anyone's definition of acoustic stealth.

The F-100's titanium, Inconel and metal matrix composite fuselage are that of a tapered black delta configuration with blended engine nacelles and twin, inward canted vertical stabilizers with 75° swept-wing configuration. In many ways, the F-100 bears a striking resemblance to one of the proposed designs for the NASP. The F-100 may indeed be America's first trans-atmospheric spaceplane, capable of wave-riding voyages at altitudes exceeding 200,000 feet.

Considering the relatively unorthodox design of the F-100 (generically similar in some ways to the Navy's canceled A-12) and its Mach 15 cruising speed, it could easily be mistaken for an unearthly craft, except of course, that it cannot silently hover. But the problem is that we are still flying with wings and a tail (vertical stabilizer). Albeit faster and with greater maneuvering ability, but our basic method of flight has remained essentially the same for more than a century.

Until we radically alter the way in which we propel aerospace vehicles of all types, we will be limited to the mundane, yet seemingly complex, flight we are used to, and similarly be forever tied to near-Earth voyages. Given that, we certainly cannot achieve instantaneous acceleration/deceleration, extremely high-g turns and endoatmospheric speeds in excess of 20,000 mph, which UFOs appear to do quite readily.

There is, however, an alternate means of flight that theoretically will allow us to do within our atmosphere almost everything a UFO does and at the same time provide us with quantum leaps in aviation technology, such as traveling to any spot on Earth within less than one hour! The method of which I speak is generically known as "field propulsion."

Perhaps the best way of describing field propulsion and how it differs from conventional forms of aerospace propulsion systems is to imagine a vehicle, say a 35-foot diameter disc that is surrounded by an artificially generated electromagnetic field (EMF). This teravolt (trillion volt) electromagnetic or electrostatic field incorporating a rectified radio-frequency, waveguide antenna.

If generated at the proper frequency, pulse envelope and power utilizing convoluted, rotating mercury plasma within a superconducting torus, it should produce a polarized "electro-gravitic," quasi-gravitational inertia field, roughly equivalent to repulsive gravitation, or more simply, anti-gravity, which can induce lift, thrust and maneuvering forces by acting against the ambient gases in the Earth's atmosphere as well as the Earth's electromagnetic/gravitational fields.

For those of you who are up on the concepts of torsion field manipulation as related to Zero Point technology, the aforementioned technology might appear familiar. An interesting potential side effect of this form of torsion field manipulation is that of temporal dilation and displacement, a.k.a, time travel!

Moreover, the vehicle's EMF decouples it from Earth's gravitation, therein allowing it to sort of "float" on gravity much the same way a boat does on water. As this field is uniformly generated around the craft, it is defined as asymmetrical in nature, for it does not originate from a single point on the vehicle such as exhaust from a jet or rocket that is symmetrical in nature.

Aliens Above, Ghosts Below by Barry E. Taff

To achieve lift, all one must do is create a varying polarity structure surrounding the vehicle, where the polarity on the bottom of the craft is the same as the Earth below, causing repulsion in the same manner as two magnets of the same polarity. To descend, the polarity is simply reversed. For horizontal thrust, or vector thrusting to maneuver, different polarity configurations are created around the vehicle to react accordingly with the electromagnetic/gravitational environment.

Such discrete field polarity control can only be achieved if the outer hull of the vehicle was composed of a high-temperature superconductive composite material. This type of flying would not be considered "aerodynamic" in any sense of the term, as there is no re-direction of airflow over dynamic control surfaces. For a more in depth discussion of the nature of field propulsion as related to UFOs, read Unconventional Flying Objects: A Scientific Analysis by Paul R. Hill from Hampton Road Publishing Company, 1995.

There are numerous advantages to this method of flying. To begin with, it's somewhere between 15 to 45 times more efficient than jets or rockets, and does not combust and exhaust its fuel into the atmosphere, thereby polluting it. Although the primary reason for its efficiency is that most of the specific impulse energy is not lost in the form of heat, there would be an artificial field of high-power microwave radiation which could pose a biological hazard, that is, if one were foolish enough to stand near such a vehicle during take off or landing.

Field propulsion also offers the advantage of engendering little if any G-loading as the entire vehicle and everything within it are being uniformly motivated by a field as opposed to being pushed by a symmetrical force such as jet or rocket. The field-induced impetus of the craft causes it to become its own center of gravity.

Even in hypersonic acceleration/deceleration and/or sudden high-g turns, the passengers and cargo would move as one with the vehicle, rather than continuing in their original direction of motion. What is being described here essentially is a functional reduction of mass and inertia relative to the Earth, which have always been daunting problems regarding advanced aircraft performance especially as related to pilot's gravity induced loss-of-consciousness.

The physics behind this are extremely complex and are, as yet, not fully understood. What is posited here is that there exists a definitive relationship between electromagnetic field forces and gravity that can be exploited for use in both endo-atmospheric as well as exo-atmospheric propulsion. The best premise is that of the Grand Unified Theory (GUT) of modern theoretical physics, or what Einstein referred to as his Unified Field Theory, which links electromagnetism to the strong and weak nuclear forces and finally to gravity.

In essence, what field propulsion offers is the ability to neutralize the inertia and/or mass of the vehicle relative to the Earth. The side effects of that "gravitational de-coupling" include reduction of dynamic loading of the airframe to almost zero, reduction of atmospheric drag coefficient and frictional heating to a negligible point, and virtually eliminating the sensation of acceleration and deceleration on passengers.

Thus, a VTOL (vertical take off and landing) field propulsion vehicle would ascend at perhaps Mach 12-15 to around 200,000 feet or more, then horizontally traverse the intended distance at say, Mach 30+, and when finally arriving at its destination, vertically descend at Mach 12-15 again. All this would be accomplished in less than one hour, or before you could finish reading an issue of Time Magazine, and with absolutely no sensation of movement.

To many, all of the above may sound like something out of a grade "B" science fiction film. But if one examines the work and research of T. Brown, John Searl, James Cox and Alan Holt, all the aforementioned potentials become far more than simple speculative theory; they are potential reality.

Aliens Above, Ghosts Below by Barry E. Taff

Then why has no one yet developed, built and deployed such an obviously superior and efficient vehicle? There are numerous reasons, chief among these being one of pure power. Power in terms of that utilized to motivate the vehicle and that of many companies that has a vested interest continuing to sell large quantities of chemical fossil fuel for jets and rockets to government and private sources. The power of this chemical lobby is quite formidable and it's unlikely that they would tolerate any "rocking of the boat" regarding their dominance and control.

Those who wonder about the notion of the U.S. government and/or military or a covert faction of it, having secretly developed UFO technology, with or without the assistance of extraterrestrials, only have to look at what we are still flying, building and developing to get some degree of clarification.

For those who harbor paranoid beliefs regarding such joint ventures between us and alien technology, let them cast their memories back to January of 1986, when the shuttle Challenger exploded, taking seven astronauts with it.

If we really had the super-advanced technology demonstrated by UFOs, why would we still be playing around with F15E's, F16's, F117's, the F-22 Raptor, the F-35 Joint Strike Fighter (JSF) and the B-2, as well as the obsolescent Space Shuttle? If this is nothing more than a cover ploy of disinformation, it's the most expensive one in history----hundreds of billions if not trillions of dollars spent just to misdirect public attention. I don't think so.

However, on the other side of the coin we must at least consider the claims of individuals like Bob Lazar, an alleged physicist who claims that he worked for EG&G at Dreamland's (Groom Lake) Area 51-S4, where he conducted back engineering on recovered extraterrestrial discs....UFOs.

His story has its merits and unfortunately, its drawbacks. Lazar's description of the alien antimatter reactor sounds like little more than a highly efficient thermo-electric generator. He never quite explains precisely how using "element 115" produces anti-gravity. Let us not forget the fact that element 115 has been created (and surpassed). To no one's surprise, it did not stabilize as Lazar predicted.

Additionally, his description of the so-called gravity generators depicts crudely designed, mechanically articulated, armatures, rather than an electronically scanned, active arrayed system. However, the most disturbing aspect of Lazar's incredible story is that he was given access to sensitive, highly classified information and material, such as alleged alien time travel exploits and how they subsequently influenced and manipulated human history, that he did not have the "need to know" given his alleged position at S-4.

This conduct on the part of whatever government agency he worked for flies in the face of virtually every informational compartmentalization protocol of "eyes only" data used within the military/intelligence community. Unless, of course, some or all of Lazar's story is disinformation, wherein the folks he worked for intentionally provided misleading and fabricated data to him knowing he would violate his national security oath and divulge it to the public. The other possibility is that Lazar and his "story" was nothing more than fabricated disinformation, as I suspect the Alien Autopsy show from Fox-TV was in the 1990's.

In other words, they fully intended for Lazar to do what he did! The question is, if this theory is accurate, did Lazar know he was disseminating disinformation? Remember, the best disinformation is truth hidden between lies, or vice versa.

The overall result being that when the lies are uncovered and the entire story and those associated with it are discredited, any truth contained therein is equally discarded. Moreover, the best place to hide the truth is between lies! This is the best way to have the baby thrown out with the bath water. A classic disinformation ploy used by the military and intelligence community.

Even if we totally disregard Lazar's claims, what about the late Lt. Col. Philip J. Corso and the information contained in his book The Day After Roswell? Corso is not as easy to dismiss as Lazar given his verifiably impeccable military and intelligence background. Although, in some ways, his story is even more problematic than Lazars' as he asks us to believe that much of our modern technology was directly derived from the recovered extraterrestrial craft that crashed at Roswell in 1947.

If indeed lasers, fiber-optics, integrated circuits (computer chips) and super-strong composite materials were all the result of alien technology transfer, is it not then conceivable that we also were able to successfully unlock the secrets of the crashed UFO itself? Not necessarily.

Perhaps we could get the thing to hover and fly at some rudimentary level, but understanding its complex construction and propulsion might be beyond current human understanding. By comparison, imagine taking a modern automobile back in time about five thousand years.

Our ancestors, who once over their fear of the thundering machine itself, could very likely get the car to start and possibly even drive it. But on what roads? However, once it ran out of gas, do you think they would understand that you have to fill its tank with petrochemical fuel (gasoline)?

How about a spark plug for igniting the gasoline to drive pistons, connecting rods and a crankshaft? Do you think they would grasp how its engine/transmission and differential worked if any piece of the powertrain failed? What if a tire blew out on a rock? Would they know what it was and how to patch and re-inflate it with compressed air?

Sure, our ancestors were very bright and industrious given their early positioning in the homo- sapien family tree, but I don't believe for one second that such innate wisdom would have enabled them to repair a modern automobile, especially considering its sophisticated electronics.

I think you get the picture here. We might be in a similar situation with recovered or back engineered UFOs? If we truly understood how such technology functioned and could easily replicate it with existing materials, would it not behoove us to do so?

But then, of course, there are always those individuals who say that the U.S. military has indeed built and possibly even deployed such devices, but are keeping the technology under wraps due to its world-changing and possibly even world conquering potential. In other words, we do not want to share the ultimate weapon system with any of our neighbors, fearing that they might use such technology against us.

There is ample evidence that UFOs utilize some form of electromagnetic force field propulsion to neutralize and decouple from gravity. A noteworthy side effect of a vehicle propelled through an EM force field would be invisibility to all forms of radar (Doppler, Phased Arrayed, Ultra-Wide Band, Over-the-Horizon Backscatter and Millimeter-Wave, etc.) as the microwave field generated by its propulsion system would absorb, diffuse and scatter the incoming radar wave and prevent significant return for it to be "painted" on a radar screen.

Similarly, an EM field propelled vehicle would not be detectable through infrared tracking, for it does not expel hot gases in an exhaust plume behind it to generate thrust. Therefore, a field propulsion vehicle would be the ultimate stealth aircraft, something already acknowledged in UFO research, as such aeroforms frequently fail to appear on radar tracking and acquisition systems.

At the same time it neutralizes gravity, EM field propulsion emits a powerful field of microwave radiation. There have been frequent close encounters wherein observers have been burned and even radiation poisoned by what appears to be a combination of microwaves, ultraviolet and perhaps even gamma rays, such as in the Cash-Landrum Case.

The actual power supply/source aboard a UFO is certainly beyond speculation at this point, with the exception however of some type of Zero Point engine. However, in a human engineered vehicle, the power plant could be either superconducting magnetohydrodynamic (MHD) or a compact, rotating bed nuclear reactor about the size of two large beach balls, whose power output can reach or exceed several gigawatts (billions of watts) per pulse.

Either of these powerplants would be more than suitable for the needs of an endo-atmospheric field propulsion vehicle with sustained cruising speeds exceeding Mach 35.

When it comes to interplanetary or interstellar travel, we must take a giant leap into speculative propulsion systems in order to conquer the inconceivable distances involved. Even with the most advanced nuclear or thermonuclear propulsion systems currently on the drawing boards, starships would still take very long periods of time to achieve only a small fraction of light speed and would require a virtually inexhaustible quantity of fuel to do so.

There is, however, an alternative to attempting to reach light speed through linear acceleration methods. The technique would be to "jump" to light speed or even superluminal (faster-than-light) velocity without having to deal with the problems of increased mass/energy normally encountered. In simpler terms, time is space and space is time.

If you take away or shorten the space between where you presently are and where you want to go, you automatically shorten the amount of time it takes you to get to your destination.

For example, if you are asked how far you live from where you work, you might say "half and hour." In point of fact, you do not live half an hour from work; that's simply how long it takes you in your car to travel the distance between the two locations. If you lived further away, you answer might be 45 minutes or one hour, while if you lived several blocks away, you might say "ten minutes."

How does one go about changing space so that distant interstellar journeys do not take hundreds, if not thousands of years?

Look at a standard 8 1/2 x 11-inch piece of paper, and place a dot in the lower left hand corner, then another dot in the upper right hand corner. It is automatically assumed that the shortest distance between the two points is a straight line, such as drawing a diagonal line from the dot at the lower left to the one at the upper right.

But what happens if you take the sheet of paper and fold it so that the two dots are now touching each other, creating a sort of warped or convoluted section? By bending the paper, you have effectively removed the distance between the two dots, thereby reducing the time required to get from one to the other, or more precisely, zero. In reality, space-time may function in much the same way.

If one could generate sufficient quantities of power----perhaps, let's say, through the use of regenerative antimatter and induce a quantum singularity resulting in a gravitational collapse (bending or warping) of space, this would create what is known as a white or worm hole.

By rapidly repeating this process in succession, one might be able to travel thousands of light years in clock time, especially when taking into account time dilation; the closer one approaches the speed of light, the slower time moves for the traveler relative to the observer.

Visualized in its most simplistic form, you'd have something akin to a "warp bubble" wherein the space in front of your starship is compressed, while the space behind it is expanded. The resulting "wave" would propel you through what is no longer linear space faster than that of light.

And believe it or not, NASA/JPL's own Breakthrough Physics, Faster-Than-Light (FTL) Group has theoretically proposed such a superluminal warp drive mechanism, even though they have not the foggiest idea of how to build, let alone fund, such an extremely costly venture given the world's current economy, its weaponization potential and lack of interest.

Moreover, even if we had the starship Enterprise in orbit right now, we don't have anyone else's interstellar address, so to speak. So what do you do? Just casually travel around the universe at superluminal speed looking for sentient neighbors who might want to sit down and break bread with a war-obsessed race of beings such as us?

So what we have now is reminiscent of Star Trek's warp drive, and if this theory is fully extrapolated, a fuel supply is NOT required. Think for one moment. What is the most abundant element found aboard a starship such as the Enterprise, apart from the materials from which it is built? Well? Have you figured it out yet? And no, it's not oxygen, but you're getting very close.

It's carbon dioxide, what we all exhale as long as we live and breathe.

Whether there are 5 or 5,000 crewmembers aboard a starship, their exhaled carbon dioxide could be converted back into breathable oxygen by separating and revitalizing it through a nuclear reactor (as in nuclear submarines). The remaining carbon could also be revitalized and turned into carbon and anti-carbon for power, when it is brought back together and annihilated. Thus, an inexhaustible supply of power would be available with even a small crew, considering the cubic volume of carbon dioxide a person exhales daily.

There is an even more intriguing element that seems to be potentially pliable enough if properly utilized to generate a warp field, a.k.a. bubble or wave. In Chapter 13 (It's About Time) you will discover what said, extremely toxic (as lethal as plutonium without being radioactive) element is, and why it appears to be so critical for creating your highly localized, artificial wormhole to drive a starship.

In fact, this particular element was so critical to the efforts of the Axis powers in World War II that the very last and the largest U-Boat to leave Nazi Germany carried many tons of this substance for delivery to Japan in the closing months of the conflict. I've always wondered why there was such a sudden and seemingly desperate, covert shipment of this specific element between these countries?

The "official" military explanation never made much sense or ever held much water, which is exactly what this submarine's shipment ended up doing at the bottom of the Pacific Ocean, forever contaminating its waters. Again, Chapter 13 will fill in all the blanks and connect the dots here, as strange as those might be.

If you can guess the answer, that's really saying something about your critical and analytical thinking process. Congratulate yourself for a job well done and thinking outside the box.

Back on Warp Drive (and no, that's not my address), if you'll excuse the pun, intergalactic trips should pose no real problems, except perhaps for the navigation and the paradox effects created by traveling at superluminal speed. Even though little if any time would pass for those aboard a warp-driven starship, those left behind on Earth would experience a great passage of time during the flight; you in a superluminal vessel might age days to weeks while your friends back on Earth would have turned to dust, for many thousands of years would have passed for them.

Remember, even Einstein stated that at light speed one could circumnavigate the entire universe in only forty years. But that forty years must be lived at light speed! In reality, most distant interstellar voyages would require speeds well in excess of warp 9.5. It would probably require close to warp 150+ at least. Even then, it leaves those "suspended" in warp-driven superluminal trips somewhat lonely, as time on Earth would still pass at an incredibly accelerated rate.

Alan Holt, a NASA physicist, has theorized and proposed a manner by which to circumvent this temporal problem called "Field Resonance Propulsion." This system would allow one and his or her ship to literally "apport" or leap anywhere in spacetime, once the resonance of the intended destination was plugged into the vehicle's navigational/guidance systems.

In theory, Holt's Field Resonance Propulsion would even surpass warp drive, in that it would get you where you wanted to go instantaneously, while warp drive, even at factors exceeding 1,000+, would still consume time in a dilated manner, even though attaining extremely high superluminal velocities.

To a stationary, neutral observer, both propulsion systems would cause the ship to appear to literally vanish in the blink of an eye, while warp drive might consume time to accomplish its travel, while field resonance might not. In either case, the very thought of a large ship disappearing before one's eyes brings to mind many reported sightings of UFOs as witnessed by Earthly observers. Is it possible that a similar method of propulsion is employed by UFO occupants?

In a way, superluminal propulsion brings forth the notion of time travel being directly associated with interstellar travel. In reality, such may indeed be the case. For in order to travel amongst the stars at speeds in excess of light without the necessity or carrying infinite quantities of fuel, and without having multi-generational ships (which is highly impractical), traveling through time or at least a far greater understanding of it might well be a prerequisite for manning the helm of the starship Enterprise at warp 200. Perhaps future, superluminal, interstellar spaceships might be more time machines than space-traveling machines.

So as we have seen, the technology utilized in what might be UFO propulsion is not that far fetched or beyond our ken, even at this stage of the game. However, before we can start planning our interstellar voyages, we must develop a practical field propulsion vehicle strictly for Earth-bound travel that will fly circles around F-16's and F-22's and allow us to conserve our precious fuels for more important needs.

Until a commercially based field propulsion transport is built and deployed, thus replacing jet airliners (it would have few in any moving parts, no explosive on-board fuel or pollution----including noise) and expendable launch vehicles, including the highly inefficient space shuttle, even considering a vehicle with interstellar capability possessing faster-than-light potential is beyond our conceptual reach. As it is, the age of our jet airliner fleet is such that it poses a serious safety threat to all who fly, evidenced by ever increasing numbers of crashes.

If we can currently build and fly a field-propelled superluminal vehicle, just imagine what future technology will provide----but that's if those technicians who design and develop future aerospace vehicles are willing to look beyond conventional propulsion modes.

Aliens Above, Ghosts Below by Barry E. Taff

Now that we potentially can get THERE from HERE, it's a lot easier to gain a glint of understanding on just how "they" (the alleged ETs) might get here from "there." Especially given what may well be several thousand years more advanced technology.

Isn't it intriguing the way the science fiction and fantasy of the past has a way of turning into the science and technology of the future. When I first watched the tour of space dock in Star Trek: The Motion Picture (1979) it brought tears to my eyes. I was truly overwhelmed by the magnificence and majesty of seeing the starship Enterprise in its full glory on the huge screen before me.

Deep within my heart and mind I knew, and still know today, that humankind will eventually build the equivalent of the Enterprise. If we survive as a species without destroying ourselves with the power such technology brings us, we will indeed develop and deploy superluminal "starships" capable of traveling vast interstellar distances.

It is no wonder then that during a presentation made before UCLA's School of Engineering Alumni by Ben Rich, former head of Lockheed's Advanced Development Company (Skunk Works) shortly before his death, he casually discussed the fact that the supposed inherent difficulties regarding interstellar travel have been more or less resolved and that a great deal of our former understanding of such technical barriers were incorrect.

One specific quote from Ben Rich at this alumni meeting went something like this. "We have things flying at Groom Lake that would make George Lucas drool." Yeah, but, how would have Gene Roddenberry have reacted to such knowledge? Unfortunately, we'll never know.

He went on to say, that we currently possess the technical skills for interstellar travel in real time, like in Star Trek, but it very likely will not be commercially developed or utilized in the near future. Could it be that along with learning how to control space and time comes the lack of need for chemical propulsion and the use of fossil fuels?

Do you think that such an evolutionary step forward in human motility, a.k.a. propulsion, would finally shake us loose from our petrochemcial addiction? The problem is that by the time we reach the stage of field propulsion and warp drive, we will have long exhausted our finite supply to fossil fuels and probably our existence as well.

After Rich's address I casually strolled up to him and asked if what we was referring to in terms of interstellar propulsion and travel in real time was developed by Lockheed or acquired.

Rich's response was to look at me as though I were an alien as he was perplexed by my question and its cryptic nature. He finally replied: "What do you think?" Immediately, I said, the latter (acquired as opposed to developed). Rich smiled and responded; "You know, you might be right." The really sad part is that I was the only one in attendance who asked a question like this after Rich's presentation.

Isn't it odd the way the U.S.'s space program simply fell apart after the Apollo missions? The Space Shuttle was outdated and obsolete long before the lowest bidder built it, of course. You probably already know that the original design concept for the Space Shuttle was far more sophisticated and was envisioned as a true space plane with a powered return from space as opposed to being a low-tech glider. This design was never adopted due to its cost. Gee, what else is new?

Given that any manned return to the Moon and potential Mars missions are still designed around crude chemical propellant vehicles (rockets) that are nothing more than a rebuild of what we used close to a half century ago, it's unlikely than manned spaceflights will continue beyond the near future due to its costs and lack of any major technological advances in propulsion technology.

Personally, this author believes that there are indeed brilliant and visionary propulsion engineers out there that have figured out how to effectively and efficiently conduct manned planetary exploration now, as we've just discussed. However, the real problem has more to do with the potential socio-economic and political infrastructure fallout from harnessing and commercializing field propulsion powered by Zero Point Energy (ZPE).

So much for seeing a Star Trek future any time soon. I guess many of us Trekkers will have to sit tight, age as slowly as possible while remaining in space dock awaiting our departure orders. Praying might not hurt either. END

Chapter 10:
ABDUCTION CENTRAL?

You can hardly turn around anymore without running into some information regarding alleged UFO abductions. From the tabloids in the checkout line at the supermarket to books such as Dr. John E. Mack's Abduction: Human Encounters with Aliens or Bud Hopkins' Witnessed.

If recent Gallup and Roper polls are statistically accurate, as many as 5 million American citizens believe that they have been abducted over the last thirty years, most of which began in childhood and evolved generationally into adulthood. Considering what these numbers might be like on a global scale is staggering and very disturbing in terms of their epidemic proportions. In essence, it appears that the earth's population is part of an immense longitudinal study, the purpose of which is unknown as are the perpetrators.

Or, a unique form of psychopathology has reached epidemic proportions. Even more disturbing are those who contend that these perpetrators are indeed known. That virtually all abductions are part of an elaborate, covert conspiracy conducted by radical factions of our own intelligence/military/government for the purpose of influencing and eventually controlling social consciousness.

That these all-too-human abductors are in possession of some of the most advanced technology on Earth (or anywhere else, for that matter). Technology which supposedly (I refuse to use the word "allegedly" here) is capable of altering consciousness to induce controlled hallucinations or delusions that conform to abduction scenarios.

In point of fact, what little mind-altering technology does exist, is nowhere near the level of sophistication required for such precise mental manipulation. But that does not stop certain individuals from piecing together unrelated and isolated tidbits of information to draw irrational and insupportable conclusions.

If this hypothesis were true, what would be the purpose of such an extended pretense? If you intend on altering and controlling social consciousness, to what end? To make us think we are being abducted by extraterrestrials? Why? Do you think that Orson Wells' 1938 radio broadcast of War of the Worlds had more of an effect on some people than others?

Or maybe it set some very sick minds to wondering precisely how much panic and social chaos would actually result from contact with extraterrestrials? What do think would be the likelihood of these human perpetrators being caught in the act of their staged abductions over the course of four decades? By chance alone, I would say pretty high.

In the same vein, there are others who theorize that abductions are little more than electromagnetically induced hallucinations caused by anomalous plasmas or transient magnetic fields. And while vaguely generic sensations commonly associated with abductions have been stimulated within the brain by magnetic fields, this does not   automatically mean that abduction experiences are all generated by this method.

That is equivalent to saying that because we can make a true-to-life motion picture about going to the moon, NASA's Apollo lunar program was a hoax and we never landed at Tranquility Base in July of 1969.   Just because we can realistically simulate or recreate something does not mean the actual event upon which it was based never occurred.   That is very faulty logic.   Remember the earlier discussion of Ockham's Razor?   Well, if it was ever applicable, this is the place.

Now that we have wasted enough time and space recounting the least probable explanations regarding abductions, let's move on to what the evidence tends to suggest and support.

From analyzing data from more than three decades, it appears that no geographic region of the planet is immune to the abduction phenomenon nor is there any perceived demographic pattern discernible at this time. In this respect, Southern California has been no exception. It's been a literal hotbed of activity since at least the early 1970's, although no data exists to determine precisely when such heightened activity began.

In the years of 1974 through 1977, few if any ufologists believed that extraterrestrials were virtually waltzing into people's homes within densely populated cities and abducting them for examination and experimentation.

Even after books like The Interrupted Journey by John G. Fuller and its 1975 NBC-TV movie The UFO Incident, starring James Earl Jones and Estelle Parsons, and Bud Hopkin's book Missing Time (1981), most UFO researchers found it difficult to accept or even believe that E.T.'s were so bold and brazen as to come directly into one's home and kidnap them right out from under their family's noses.

It was extremely hard for investigators to even come to grips with the notion that large numbers of people are being abducted to begin with, never mind why it always seemed to occur in remote, desolate locations, far from major population centers.

However, by 1999 things have dramatically changed regarding UFO abductions and our perception of the potential magnitude of their occurrence. For one, most ufologists now generally agree that abductions do, in fact, occur. That they appear to be transpiring at an ever increasing rate and that such events may have been occurring for many decades. In fact, of the various types of Close Encounters (CE), I-V, IV being an abduction, it now appears that CE-IV's may be the most common variety.

With the publication of Budd Hopkin's second book, Intruders, and its subsequent CBS-TV mini-series (1992), Whitley Streiber's best-seller Communion, its resulting low-budget motion picture and the following books of Transformation and Majestic, not to mention David M. Jacob's Secret Life: Firsthand Accounts of UFO Abductions and Tracy Torme's intriguing film Fire in the Sky (Paramount, 1993), Showtime's Roswell (1994) and a seeming wave of abduction reports from around the world, the entire UFO research community is well aware of the fact that these forces, or beings may, in fact, frequently violate our most sacred privacy to serve their own selfish needs.

Unfortunately, the closed-minded attitude existing more than two decades ago also pervaded my own mentality that caused me to overlook what might have otherwise have been two very significant abduction cases; one in 1974 and another in 1977 where I was actually present during the abduction!

In the summer of 1974, while working out of UCLA's Parapsychology Laboratory in the Neuropsychiatric Institute (since disbanded), I was referred by Dr. Annis, a psychiatrist at the NPI, to one of his patients, Ann, who complained of strange, diminutive night visitors who did horrible things to her.

Under normal circumstances Dr. Annis would have assumed (with good reason) that Ann's fears were the result of paranoid delusions of supernatural persecutors, however, her stories had a strange ring of reality and truth about them that is why I was consulted. Dr. Annis felt that as he could be of no assistance to her, perhaps I and our lab could be. Was he wrong on that account!

Needless to say, when I first met with Ann [not her real name] (who lived in the Mid-Wilshire district of Los Angeles) and heard her stories, I was very skeptical of her claims regarding nocturnal presence's. I spent several hours talking with her about her experiences, her personal background and any and all associated matters.

My conclusion was that Ann was unquestionably suffering from acute trauma and anxiety brought on by some unknown stimuli. Her background revealed no evidence of any childhood abuse or neglect that might lead to nightmares or fantasies of being manipulated and sexually violated. Similarly, there were no other relationships in her past or present that would even suggest that her "visitors" were the product of a stigmatized imagination.

When Ann finally felt more comfortable talking with me, she confided more details than she had to Dr. Annis, perhaps because I was about the same age she was at the time, twenty-six. Her story, now quite common by abduction accounts, was that several small humanoids (my word usage) appeared from out of nowhere within her bedroom, and before she could put up a struggle, rendered her semi-conscious through some form of paralysis.

The next thing Ann recalled was lying on her back on some type of metallic table in a roundish room, also metal-looking, that was emitting brilliant light from the walls and ceiling. Around her were three or four humanoids.

Her description of the "funny-looking men" is again very reminiscent of what we are now very used to hearing: 3-4 feet tall, hairless, slim with very large, inverted pear-shaped heads with no outer ears, no apparent nose except for two vertical slits and no lips except for another horizontal slit where the mouth should be. Ann's most disturbing memory of their physical appearance was their eyes. Large, dark, reflective and almond-shaped, angling up away from the horizontal at about 15 degrees. Sound familiar?

While these humanoids were examining her she never heard them audibly speak, but seemed to sense their words in her mind, as if telepathic in nature. Though she said it was as clear as if they verbally spoke, their slit-for-a-mouth never once moved. Their skin, according to Ann's recall, was greyish-brown and leathery in texture. They did not have five fingers. The shape of their hands, which included webs between their three fingers and an opposing thumb-like digit, looked reptilian to Ann, who still found herself in a state of total muscular paralysis, except for her autonomic nervous system.

As the humanoids began a more detailed examination of Ann, her memory began to cloud over as the beings kept repeating to her that she had nothing to fear, she would feel no pain and would not remember these events. Ann's memory concluded at this point with the apparent insertion of some type of probes into various bodily orifices: nasal, mouth, ear-canal, rectal and vaginal.

Despite the suggestion of no pain, these probes were very physically irritating and caused her to scream and cry. At the point, just before Ann lost consciousness, she remembered one of the humanoids placing its hand over her head, telling her not to feel any more pain and to simply relax. Ann then blacked out.

While conveying these details to me, her emotional state became more intense, eventually ending in a crying binge that lasted for quite some time. Her distress required immediate attention to calm her down as she was on the verge of hysteria.

After hearing the above story, I was startled and really did not know what to believe. Ann was a well-educated, intelligent, emotionally balanced woman who, other than her supposed dreams, demonstrated absolutely no overt or covert signs of emotional disorders. In fact, everything in her life until that point was as normal as apple pie.

However, her level of fear and anxiety was so acute that I reluctantly agreed to spend several nights on the couch just in case the humanoids returned. After several nights on a very uncomfortable sofa with no visitations, I convinced Ann that everything would be fine and to call me if anything unusual occurred.

About two months or so later she called back, saying that the humanoids had reappeared in her bedroom and basically replicated the same procedures they had performed originally. However, this time Ann said that she was pregnant but could not account for it as she was using birth control that until then proved very reliable. The last thing Ann wanted was an unplanned pregnancy, especially when she had not been sleeping with anyone in many months!

Upon hearing this update, I was very reserved in my opinion regarding this entire affair as it was extremely "strange" and felt more than likely could be explained very prosaically. The real shocker came several weeks later when in literal hysteria, Ann called late one evening to inform me that her fetus had disappeared from her womb, and that the little humanoids were the ones who removed it!

After visiting with her again and calming her down, I tried to convince Ann that perhaps she had nothing more than a hysterical or false pregnancy, which is not that uncommon. However, Ann was not dissuaded by my attempt at logic, especially as she swore that she did not have an abortion, that she really was pregnant, with tests to clinically confirm it, and could not explain who fathered her child or what caused it to disappear.

During another lengthy discussion Ann told me of her encounter in which the little humanoids took her unborn fetus away. It again had all the earmarks and keynotes of what is now reported quite frequently by Hopkins, Jacobs, Mack and others. There was little I or anyone else could do to bring peace to Ann's mind. Eventually I was able to convince her that none of these events were in fact real, but simply the products of night terrors and that she would eventually overcome her anxieties and fears regarding them. Well, she never really recovered in full.

Her present life, what little is left of it after two failed marriages and numerous jobs she was unable to keep, is primarily due to a dramatic change in her personality. Ann was not the recipient of any form of therapy regarding her alleged encounter with whatever phenomena she experienced.

Remember, back in 1974, there were no support groups for such individuals or psychologists lending any credence to such events. Had the proper therapy been received, there is a good chance that her life today would be far more stable and rewarding. I have not heard from or of he since late 1986 and have been unable to locate her. I cannot help but wonder what might have been learned and how her life and emotional makeup might have evolved had I been less myopic in my apriori judgment of her experiences?

The second case occurred in July of 1977 and was far more personal as it involved a young woman named Judy (not her real name). I originally met Judy during the investigation of poltergeist activity within the apartment she shared with her ex-boyfriend. The thirty-year-old woman was a model and an aspiring actress (surprise?) who bore a striking resemblance to a cross between a young Elizabeth Taylor and Joan Collins, or more precisely, a large-breasted clone of Stepfanie Kramer from the 1980's Hunter TV series.

After my investigation of her case in the Mid-Wilshire Los Angeles area during which time we recorded some audible phenomena, Judy and I grew to become quite close friends. During this time I discovered that she was extremely "gifted" in the sense of being overtly telepathic, clairvoyant and precognitive, which allowed her to work with us in our UCLA psi development group. Over time, our relationship blossomed into a romantic affair and everything was going along quite smoothly. So smoothly, in fact, that we were about to become engaged.

About the only oddities in the relationship were Judy's occasional intrusions into my own inner thoughts when she would literally tell me what I was thinking about, though she had no knowledge of such information through our relationship or our current conversation. This happened with such regularity that I began accepting it as normal. Her psychic talents were multi-faceted in the respect that she was very helpful in looking for missing persons and/or property, cases that we investigated many times each year.

Another interesting phenomenon occurred once while I was massaging Judy's lumbar region that always gave her pain. In the midst of attempting to rub out the pain, a ball of brilliant light, similar to ball lightning and about the size of two large male fists, literally emerged from her lower back and ascended straight toward the ceiling.

The ball of light was self-illuminating and lit up the otherwise dimly lit room. Both Judy and I bolted at the appearance of the glowing sphere that disappeared into the ceiling without so much as a sound.

As time moved on, various types of paranormal phenomena continued to occur while I was around Judy. Several times, while visiting her new house in the Hollywood Hills, all the clocks, which normally kept perfect time, suddenly and for no apparent reason, began desynchronizing. Each clock was keeping its own special time, none of which were accurate. In fact, one of the clocks in the den actually jumped off the wall, landing several feet from the location where it hanged.

As I first met Judy under conditions and circumstances strongly suggestive of recurrent episodes of spontaneous psychokinesis, or what is more commonly referred to as poltergeist phenomena, I felt that this might just simply be another outbreak of the activity. However, nothing could have been further from the truth as I was about to discover.

Having first met Judy in February of 1977, we had now known each other for approximately five months, as it was July. She had a personal background of enduring emotional hardship and stress related to the untimely death of her older beloved sister from lung cancer and the very early death of her biological father from alcoholism.

These are obviously very heavy burdens for anyone to bear, but even more so as Judy's newly acquired stepfather was a deputy station chief in the CIA and was never really around. Meanwhile, her mother did not really raise her either, but hired a governess, as she was busy hobnobbing around the world with other diplomat's wives. Therefore, Judy grew up essentially without any real parental guidance. No abuse to speak of. But certainly neglect through absence.

Given all this, Judy displayed exceptionally normal patterns of behavior and appeared very well adjusted and balanced in terms of her interaction with others. Whatever emotional scars remained from her youth, they seemed well healed. Admittedly, her generic psychological profile was very consistent with that of most poltergeist agents. However, in mid-July of 1977 all of Judy's sense of reality, well-being and peace of mind was forever shattered.

She woke up one morning and was very disturbed by a dream she had the previous evening. At least she first thought it was a dream. While still under the covers, Judy turned toward me in bed and began telling me of her nightmare. She remembered being paralyzed and bathed in an intensely bright blue light, during which she was levitated out of bed, through the walls of the bedroom, ending up in a strange round metal room bathed in blinding white light.

Suddenly, she found herself lying on some sort of pedestal-like metal table in the middle of a room, surrounded by small bi-pedal creatures with big heads and large dark eyes, without pupils, or lids. The beings were very strange looking according to Judy, as they did not have any ears, nose, lips or hair.

Judy became very frightened and attempted to get off the table, only to discover herself restrained at her neck, waist, wrists and ankles by some sort of invisible mechanism. The next thing she recalled was a sense of paralysis followed by one of the little creatures bringing a large, round eye-like device down over her body and running it from her head down to her toes.

During this strange "scanning" procedure, Judy could see different colored lights going on and off on a wall near her. Then another one of the diminutive entities brought out a small, strange-looking tubular device and began inserting it into her nasal orifice, her ear, mouth, rectum and finally her vagina. The insertion of this "probe" or whatever it was, was extremely painful and Judy began crying, even while relating the dream to me. After the pain subsided she lost consciousness and finally woke up back in bed.

My first question to Judy was whether she was at all familiar with any UFO stories or literature or had ever seen The UFO Incident on TV or read The Interrupted Journey. Her reply was "no" and that she never really had any interest whatsoever in UFOs or even believed in them (this was before Close Encounter of the Third Kind). Judy asked me why I asked her about UFOs after having such a weird dream or nightmare. I answered that I was just curious, that's all.

When Judy got out of bed my curiosity turned into shock and hers into horror. For around Judy's wrists, ankles, waist and neck were black and blue bands of discoloration as if she had been held in tight restraints for some time. Equally disturbing was that Judy was bleeding from her nose, left ear and her uterus, although she was not menstruating at the time.

Were these the remnants or scars of a physical examination performed by extraterrestrials who abducted her while she slept and her interpretation of the event was a nightmare? Or was it a form of stigmata? More puzzling is that we were sleeping right next to each other in the same bed and I slept the entire night through undisturbed. How could any agency have removed her from the space directly adjacent to me without waking me?

To say that these wounds and scars strongly suggest mishandling by someone unfamiliar with the frailty of human anatomy and physiology, and that the experience was traumatizing, would be the greatest understatement of the century.

Even for someone who had been studying ufology for more than 16 years, I couldn't bring myself to accept the possibility than an alien entity, or entities, may have entered her house in the middle of the night within the densely populated Hollywood Hills and abducted her right out from under my arms.

Twenty-two years ago, no serious ufologist believed that such events occurred, especially right in front of them. Of course, we now know differently as it's been frequently reported that abductors can collectively turn off an entire group of people while they remove just one individual. When the others are turned back on or "unfrozen," they are startled to discover that one of them is strangely missing as was the case with Betty Luca in Raymond Fowler's The Andreasson Affair: Phase I & II.

In that I did not take Judy's "dream" or encounter seriously and felt that it might be form of psychogenic reaction formation, Judy did not seek or receive any form of therapy for her experience (not that such was even available then).

Since 1977, Judy's personality has almost completely disintegrated into a vegetative state in that she has become a religious zealot who literally lives and breathes to worship Sai

Baba, a supposed East Indian avatar. In her deluded thought process, she now believes that it was Sai Baba who actually visited her on the night of her encounter.

Supposedly, Judy has allegedly had repeated nocturnal visitations by this being/entity/avatar when it has performed somewhat similar procedures on her. Her emotional state is so fragmented and disassociated from reality that she has been unable to hold down any form of employment, keep any close friends or relationships (except of course for those others who are also Sai Baba devotees) and has gone through numerous interpersonal relationships and several failed marriages. Judy was obsessed with the notion that she must exist only to serve Sai Baba.

Following her first abduction in 1977, her psychic abilities became so tainted, distorted and contaminated by her deluded sense of spirituality that they were virtually useless for all practical purposes of research and/or law enforcement.

Interestingly, following Judy's abduction and persisting for some time, she experienced repeated outbreaks of poltergeist activity and apport phenomena, which she naturally attributed to Sai Baba.

The most intriguing event to follow Judy's initial abduction, was when one of her close friends, a Sai Baba devotee herself, also claimed to have had an abduction-like experience totally independent of Judy's, in fact, without her ever knowing about it. This also launched her into spiritual zealotry.

Later, she desired to have a child with her husband. She went to visit Baba in India thinking she had to ask his permission in order to have a child, (Judy and her friend(s) went to India at least once a year "to be one with Baba") Nevertheless, Baba gave Judy's friend his blessing and of course told her to have a child if that what she desired.

Several months after Judy's friend conceived, she went to have a routine examination during which a sonogram was performed. The ultrasonic image revealed that there was no fetus in her womb, although she manifested every clinical symptom of pregnancy!

What's particularly interesting about this missing fetus is that it followed closely on the heels of what appeared to be another alleged abduction as described by Judy's friend, who of course, believed it was all the work of Baba, who took away her child due to some sin or infraction on her part.

It is incredibly coincidental that another incident of an abduction-like scenario wherein a woman's fetus may have been removed from her by what might have been extraterrestrials is related to a woman who very likely was abducted in 1977 while sleeping inches away from me in the same bed. Or are all of these coincidences simply because this is the field of research I am in, therefore I have a greater probability of running into this sort of experience?

There may or may not be any direct proof or hard evidence that alien entities were in any way involved in the aforementioned experiences, but the circumstantial evidence in terms of vestigial scars certainly speak for themselves and there isn't the slightest indication that either of these women discussed here inflicted their bodily wounds on scars upon themselves, nor would they have desired to.

I lost contact with Judy in 1984 and did not hear from here again until late in 1992 when we accidentally connected. She was again married, a fourth time, now to a Baba devotee. According to her and her husband's testimony they have both been repeatedly abducted.

Although, in all fairness I must say that Judy's state of mind has devolved considerably, even from its fragmented 1977 condition, which places her evaluation and judgment on such matters in serious doubt. When last we spoke she was confusing dates and events more than four years apart and insisted that they occurred the same year.

Digressing to 1976, the lab received a call from Allen (not his real name), a high-paid executive at a local TV station who lived in Canoga Park within the San Fernando Valley. Allen phoned the lab due to numerous occurrences of poltergeist phenomena such as exploding and levitating crystal dishes; flying bookends; large flying balls of light; three-dimensional humanoid black shadows; loud banging noises, disembodied voices in the bedroom and glowing vaporous clouds moving throughout the house. This appeared to be another classic poltergeist case. Time however, would prove otherwise.

Several months later Allen and his wife took a car trip to Northern California during which time they observed an unusual aerial anomaly. While driving in a remote area one night they witnessed a bright light descending from the sky, which they assumed to be either a plane or a meteorite.

As it got closer they became more intrigued and decided to follow it to the best of their ability. When they came around a bend in the road they saw an object hovering some 200 feet in the air.

At this point, about several hundred yards distance, their engine, lights and radio failed. The object began a final descent in a falling-leaf motion. During this time, Allen and his wife noticed a bright reddish-orange glow emanating from all around the seventy foot diameter, low-domed disc. The glow extinguished itself when the vehicle landed.

Shortly thereafter, several small humanoids disembarked the craft and began, what appeared to be taking environmental samples. Allen and his wife were petrified with fear. Suddenly, one of the beings spotted them in their disabled car. The creature raised his arm, pointing a tubular rod with a glowing tip in their direction. There was a pulse of brilliant white light and then everything went dark. That was the last thing Allen and his wife remembered.

When they awoke, the UFO was gone and their car worked perfectly. It was not until some time later that Allen discovered that they had lost more than two hours of time. They both attempted to forget what they had seen but that did not help much.

During their trip, and for several months to come, they found themselves becoming very irritable, anxious and disturbed by terrifying nightmares. Additionally, both developed very confrontational, argumentative and irascible attitudes on virtually everything, which was highly atypical given their easy-going personalities.

Eventually, both were put through independent regressive hypnosis and recalled a rather classic abduction scenario involving a standard examination and numerous invasive procedures. The end result was their divorce and Allen's inability to calmly interact virtually anyone. After leaving his job at the first TV station he moved on to another local station from which he also was fired and then another and so on. Allen has since moved out the Los Angeles area and has not been heard from since 1989.

Moving to 1979, one of our most disturbing cases appeared in a small, remote suburb of the San Fernando Valley known as Sunland, which in those days was very sparsely populated. The call came from a Mrs. Valdez (not her real name), a divorced, forty-something woman with a daughter of 18 and a son of 22, who claimed that she was seeing apparitions.

During the initial interview, Mrs.Valdez spoke of soft-glowing greyish humanoid apparitions that would peer in through the windows, move about the house during frequent accompaniment of poltergeist activity.

In fact, Valdez informed us that the small gray apparitions seemed strangely interested in her car and its headlights. On other occasions she observed large fireballs rolling down the hillside next to her home, occasionally colliding with it, causing it to shudder intensely. While we never witnessed anything, Mrs. Valdez's children frequently did, which caused them to eventually move out of the house.

At one point during the interview, I asked Mrs. Valdez approximately when all this phenomenon began. She thought for a moment, with her eyes shifting back and forth in her head while in recall, and told me of one evening about one year earlier when she was taking a stroll in the canyon behind the house.

While walking during the early evening, she first heard a peculiar buzzing in her ears accompanied by a high pitched whine. She looked over to her left and saw what she described as two gigantic pie plates stuck together, about the size of her house, surrounded by a blue corona, hovering low in the canyon; more simply, a flying saucer. She was absolutely terrified and immediately turned and ran back to her home. It was after that encounter that all the paranormal phenomena began. This case immediately took on an entirely different flavor.

Although we have had numerous other cases that began as paranormal experiences that evolved into a UFO encounter, this was the first in our file that began as a UFO and then manifested paranormal phenomena. However, it is quite common for individuals having CE-III's & IV's to experience significant paranormal fallout following their UFO encounter.

After frequent contact over a short period we were suddenly unable to reach Mrs. Valdez. Eventually, her children contacted me in an effort to determine her whereabouts and it was at that point that we all became very concerned. When returning to Valdez's house, it was in perfect condition. Everything was where it should be, except for Mrs. Valdez.

Her clothes were all present, her money, car and virtually everything was as it should be, except for her. There was absolutely no indication of any foul play even when the police were called in. It was as though she vanished right off the face of the earth. Which is perhaps exactly what occurred?

In ufology, there is a category known as CE-V (Close Encounter of the Fifth Kind), which theoretically is an abduction experience from which the abductee never returns. Now admittedly, this is one of those untestable hypotheses in which it cannot be proved or disproved.

However, given the high strangeness that preceded her disappearance, one cannot totally dismiss the possibility that she was abducted by someone other than a criminal of earthly origin. To this day, no trace of Mrs. Valdez has ever been found.

In late November of 1986, before I learned to turn my telephone's ringers off and my answering machine on with its volume control turned all the way down when I went to sleep every night, I was blown out of a deep sleep when the phone rang at 2:30 a.m. On the other end of the line, I heard two women, apparently hysterical, screaming something about a direct confrontation with what sounds like extraterrestrial humanoids. After they calmed down we agreed to meet that afternoon.

Teri (not her real name), a 20-year old UCLA student, lived at home with her parents in the elegant Bel-Air sector of West Los Angeles. The story they told to me began when Teri awoke from what she assumed was a dream, where she had been within a metallic-walled room with small, humanoid creatures that were examining her with various instruments, including intravenous needles placed in both of her arms. As she reached full waking consciousness and opened her eyes, she saw small, humanoid creatures standing on either side of her, withdrawing needles from her arms.

Aliens Above, Ghosts Below by Barry E. Taff

The young woman began screaming at the top of her lungs, which caused her dog to run into the room where it encountered the two humanoids. The dog growled as it started to approach one of the creatures, who, suddenly thrust his four-fingered hand out toward him. The dog whimpered back in fear and ran from the room howling. Every time Teri screamed, the other humanoid would place its hand over her forehead, attempting to tranquilizing her. By this time, Teri's mother overheard the commotion.

Upon entering her daughter's bedroom, the mother also witnessed the creatures. Both Teri and her mother described the two humanoids as approximately 4 feet tall, with reptilian textured greyish skin and heads massively disproportional to their bodies. Deeply set within their hairless heads were large, almond-shaped black eyes, angled upwards.

The mother immediately began screaming in fear, which caused the two humanoids to jump back as if startled and touch a circulating hemisphere of light attached to what appeared to be belts on some kind of uniform they were wearing. They then allegedly lit up in a flash of bright light and literally "blinked out."

Trying to recover from what they had just experienced, Teri's mother tried turning the bedroom lights on. They then noticed that the power in the house was out. Simultaneously, they noticed what appeared to be a large, reddish-orange ovoid object through the picture window in the bedroom. It was silently hovering up above the edge of the house, causing it to vibrate in resonance. They watched the strange craft as it slowly departed.

Needless to say, the mother and daughter were terrified and confused by the whole experience. Once calmed, however, the mother attempted to rationalize the event as a possible practical joke played on her daughter by one of her many friends. I casually asked the mother if any of her daughter's friends resembled the entities she observed or knew how to vanish in a flash of light.

After careful thought she answered, "no," but that did not rule out the possibility in her mind! Whatever the origin of the event, both women were prescribed mild tranquilizers by their physician to overcome their anxiety.

During the next ten days, other strange events transpired. Furniture began moving around the house by itself, the front doorbell would ring incessantly at 3 a.m., even after it was electrically disconnected. After more than a week of this poltergeist-type activity, Teri awoke early in the morning to see the humanoids back in her bedroom.

However, on this occasion they had no apparent interest in her, but instead were carefully examining her books, furnishings and the pet snake she kept in a large glass cage in her bedroom. The creatures displayed particular fascination with the reptile. Perhaps they thought it was a distant relative?

Finally gaining her senses, Teri began screaming. Her mother and father--he had been out of town at the time of the first encounter—came running into the bedroom. Both terrified parents observed the two diminutive humanoids. The father yelled out while the mother began screaming, and the entities responded as they had before--by touching the center of their belts and disappearing in a flash of light.

The parents thought that this "joke" had gone far enough. Neither would accept the possibility that what they saw and experienced really was what it appeared to be. They took their badly traumatized daughter to a psychiatrist, who automatically assumed that the whole affair was nothing more than a shared hallucination that time and therapy (with the proper compensation, of course) would easily resolve.

This abrupt, but all too predictable psychiatric evaluation did not resolve the fact that

Teri did, in fact, have bruises and wounds indicative of a crude physical examination by someone not totally familiar with human anatomy and physiology, or else just plain crude.

With no evidence of drug usage, Teri was scarred with inexplicable puncture marks. After the first encounter, she had bled from her uterus, and yet was not menstruating at the time. Since these events, which took place in late 1986 and early 1987, Teri has packed all her belongings, closed her bank accounts, shut off her phone and left, leaving no notice of her destination. Although there is no evidence of foul play, she has not been heard from since. As her parents did not in any way cooperate in any follow-up with this author, her condition or location remains unknown.

Late one evening in January of 1988, I received a phone call from a young woman named Laurie, an attorney who lived in the fashionable Brentwood district of Los Angeles. Sounding as though she was in shock, the woman attempted to convey a story to me as her boyfriend listened in on the extension.

Several nights earlier she was about to go to sleep after reading in bed. Her boyfriend was already asleep. As she turned off the lights and started to pull the covers over her body, she noticed the presence of a small "man" on the right side of her bed, where her boyfriend was sleeping.

Laurie said that it was a very peculiar looking man, who was about 3 1/2 - 4 feet in height, with greyish-tan skin that looked like leather or the skin of a snake. His head was very large with a pointed chin, there was the absence of a protruding nose or outer ears, and the large dark eyes Laurie described as Oriental in appearance but not completely horizontal.

Laurie tried to scream, but found herself almost totally paralyzed. Except for her breathing, heart and eye movement, no voluntary functions within her body seemed to work. A tingling-like static electricity coursed through her body, she said, and apparently caused the paralysis.

Suddenly the little being reached across the bed, passed her boyfriend who was still sound asleep. As it attempted to touch her she saw its hand, which had four fingers with webs between the digits and talons, or claws at the terminus. The hand drew closer and Laurie heard the words "do not worry, I am not going to hurt you, I just want to examine you" clearly in her head.

More frightened than ever, Laurie again attempted to scream, but in vain. However, just before the creature touched her, Laurie's boyfriend jostled and tossed in bed. The little "man" was apparently startled and jumped back, lighting up in a blinding white flash of light and vanishing. After several seconds, Laurie's paralysis waned, and she emitted a piercing scream, waking her boyfriend.

Also an attorney, her boyfriend was quite skeptical when she told him about her experience, although he knew Laurie to be logical, grounded and pragmatic, and not prone to fantasy or hysteria. Knowing that, he was convinced that perhaps something did occur. Was she spared being abducted due to her boyfriend's restless sleep?

We may never know--but since the event, Laurie's personality has dramatically degenerated, so much so that she continuously moves from one residence to another in fear of being found again and she has great difficulty in maintaining day-to-day functioning on her job. Normal sleeping is all but history for her at this point.

The above stories represent only a small fraction of the cases I, and numerous associates have investigated over the last three decades. Other cases from the Los Angeles neighborhoods of Palms, Beverly Hills, Manhattan Beach, Venice, Marina Del Rey, North

Aliens Above, Ghosts Below by Barry E. Taff

Hollywood, Burbank and Long Beach have accumulated faster than we are able to process them. However, at this time (2009), there seems to be a substantial lull in activity.

What is particularly disturbing about this entire matter is the way some segments of the public as well as the research community is evaluating and interpreting these abductions. There are those who perceive such abductions as a form human spiritual evolution and look upon the abductors as being totally benign, despite their direct invasion of our privacy, kidnapping against our will and grossly invasive medical procedures.

It appears that some of these individuals are identifying with their abductors such as the victims of terrorist kidnappings often do, as in the case of Patty Hearst and the SLA from the 1970's.

Such a perspective is not only naïve, it is downright dangerous given the scope and implications of the abductions. There is strong suggestive evidence (Intruders, Hopkins, Secret Life, Jacobs, Abduction, Mack) that the earth's population is being used for some type of genetic hybridization experiments in which human eggs and sperm are being employed to produce a crossbreed between extraterrestrial life and homo sapiens.

In essence, this reduces us to little more than laboratory guinea pigs living out their lives in a controlled environment or test tube in which the experimenter can, at their discretion, intervene and manipulate our reality. Stop for a moment and consider the way in which the modus operandi of these covert abductors parallels human behavior.

Initially, they locate their prey, victim or intended target in the field. They then tranquilize or immobilize them, after which they transport them into their laboratory environment within which they perform numerous invasive procedures and experiments.

Once they are completed their work, the specimens are possibly tagged with some type of transponder and returned to the original environment from which they were taken. Sound vaguely familiar? It should. Except for the sophistication of the technology and methodology, this is precisely the same way we human's capture and experiment with animals in the field.

To those individuals holding on to the naive notion that these alien entities are possibly our benefactors, think for one moment as to the way animal laboratory researchers treat their caged, experimental specimens! Not a pretty thought, is it? And there is every reason to believe that that's exactly how they view us; like hairy, primitive earthno-biologic lifeforms, to be used as they desire.

But let's go beyond this one aspect and question why these abductors are allegedly using our DNA building blocks to create a hybridized lifeform. Do they intend to re-populate the earth after we have destroyed it through an ecological or nuclear holocaust?

Do they know something about our future we do not? Are we heading towards the same fate as the dinosaurs after an asteroid or comet impact? Or are they going to use our genetic material to populate a planet orbiting a star in some distant solar system, possibly replicating what they did here on earth several million years ago with some minor variations?

At the same time, I do not in any way subscribe to the insupportable, untestable and paranoid conclusions put forth by Dr. David M. Jacobs in his latest book, The Threat, The Secret Agenda: What The Aliens Really Want and How The Plan to Get It. Perhaps Dr. Jacobs has spent a little too much free time watching bad sci-fi movies wherein the extraterrestrial entities are here to take over and control the Earth by slowly replacing us humans with hybrids. Has he seen Invasion of the Body Snatchers and its awful remakes one too many times, or what? Get Real!

154

This may be a great idea for a big-budget Hollywood blockbuster (I hope he has a good agent for selling the motion picture rights) but I believe that this absurd hypothesis will gain little, if any support in ufology other than some intense collective laughter. It will be fascinating to watch the media feeding frenzy regarding this particular book. Talk about ammunition to once again trounce and discredit ufology. Jacobs has supplied not an M1 Abrams battle tank, but a multi-megaton, thermonuclear bomb.

Are what looks like a massive, ongoing "experiment" by extraterrestrial visitors accelerating or is it simply a case of people bored with their mundane existence who are fabricating stories to make otherwise dull lives more exciting? In a strange, twisted form of logic, it might be said that if these abductions are not the product of alien intervention, then the human race might be experiencing a form of mass psychosis far more threatening than any potential extraterrestrial biological entities.

Short of that, all we can do is speculate----unless, of course, the phenomenon operating here comes forward to display itself more openly before humankind. Only time and incredible patience will tell.

END

Chapter 11:
UFOS: THE BOTTOM LINE

If Ufology as a whole was forced into a court of law in an effort to prove that the Earth is indeed being visited by highly advanced, technically superior extraterrestrial beings possessed of seemingly metaphysical instrumentality, what would serve as evidence to convince a jury, beyond reasonable doubt, of this premise or theory?

A review of the more substantial pieces of documentation published over the last 50 years shows numerous instances of what, on the surface, appears to be very compelling evidence regarding extraterrestrial UFOs. Such books as Above Top Secret by Good, Clear Intent by Fawcett and Greenwood, Sky Crash by Randles, Butler and Street, Witnessed by Hopkins, The Day After Roswell by Corso, and of course UFO Crash at Roswell by Schmidt and Randle, and most significantly, UFOs and The National Security State by Richard M. Dolans, Majic Eyes Only: Earth's Encounters With Extraterrestrial Technology by Ryan S. Wood as well as many of the Freedom of Information Act (FOIA) documents released by the FBI and CIA, are highly suggestive that something of an extraordinarily strange and unknown origin is, and has been, regularly violating our airspace with impunity.

However, as impressive as much of the aforementioned material may appear, it lacks even one essential piece of hard data; something physical or tangible to show a judge and jury. In this respect, all the superb research efforts on the part of hundreds of dedicated ufologists has yet failed to produce a single piece of physical evidence that would stand as irrefutable or incontrovertible proof of extraterrestrial production.

This is not to imply that there has not been a diligent effort on the part of most researchers to uncover such a smoking gun. But given what might be the most elaborately orchestrated conspiracy in the history of any government to obfuscate, deceive, misdirect and manipulate its public in terms of the real truth underlying UFOs, it's highly improbable that there would be any loose pieces of hard evidence simply lying around somewhere waiting for the likes of Stanton Friedman to pick up and bring to the world's attention.

About the only kind of hard evidence capable of persuading a trial jury would be either an actual UFO vehicle itself or an alien being, dead or alive, in the flesh. Admittedly, this is a very tall order, and may not be possible in the near future given the incredibly tight security around such potentially earth-shaking evidence.

In this regard, perhaps more emphasis should be placed on the work of the late Leonard Stringfield, whose research and publications into Crash/Retrievals may eventually provide that piece of "hard" evidence to convince a disbelieving world that the nightmare has already begun. With the exception of the Roswell case, which can stand on its own merits, Crash/Retrieval investigations, once cleaned of all disinformation possibilities, promises the most rewards in terms of objective data.

Since 1978, Stringfield has published nine pieces of literature specifically dealing with Crash/Retrievals. At the time this article was originally published in 1992, the most recent document from Stringfield was UFO Crash Retrievals: The Inner Sanctum, Status Report VI.

This particular report opens with a most intriguing piece developed from a statement provided Stringfield by Sgt. Maj. Robert Dean (ret.) as concerns an alleged previously classified study entitled "Assessment: An Evaluation of a Possible Military Threat to Allied Forced in Europe," that was established in early 1961 at the Supreme Headquarters Allied Powers,

Europe (SHAPE), which was, and is, the military arm of NATO.

Although dated in terms of the cold war situation, this assessment, in and of itself, appears to be far more than a simple acknowledgment of UFOs, for reference is made to "several" extraterrestrial civilizations and a "process" or "plan," suggesting that far more elaborate information was collected that we never made available for publication, or even review.

Additionally, there is a direct mention of crash/retrievals supported by photographs, bodies and exotic "plasti-metals" that were beyond our understanding at the time. With today's technology base, these so-called plasti-metals sound suspiciously like matrix composites being used in aerospace, or at least a highly evolved generation of such.

Given the early dates on the study's initiation and publication, one can only wonder what follow-on data has been collected since the mid-1960's. While not providing hard, objective evidence we can yet examine, this study certainly establishes a fascinating paper trail...one that can definitely be followed.

Moving forwards in time brings us to page 50 of Status Report VI and the early 1970's where a high ranking U.S. Army officer, a source of great integrity, conveys to Stringfield what is perhaps one of the most terrifying events in ufology. This report contains information, which, if verified, may generate more questions that it answers; in it are the purported claims of Special Forces soldiers in the Vietnam (actually Cambodia) who came upon a landed UFO and aliens collecting and sorting human body parts!

The result of this gruesome discovery was an intense firefight between G.I.'s and the aliens, where the entities were using some type of hand-held, directed energy weapon and we were, of course, left with good old M-16's. According to testimony, heavy losses were taken on both sides, although it required a direct head-shot to kill the alien beings as their apparent metallic-like garment was bullet-proof. After the protracted firefight, the aliens withdrew, loading their bin full of human body parts into their vehicle and abruptly departing the area.

Following this incident, all surviving soldiers were rounded up and intensely de-briefed, interrogated and sternly warned never to divulge what they had experienced in the jungles of Cambodia. Can you imagine the public's response if this information was formally acknowledged to the world? Can you spell the word panic. ?

The very idea of alien beings landing for this grotesque purpose smacks of the kind of frightening stories coming out of John Lear and others. Although sounding much like a scene out of the motion picture Predator, is this the only incident of its kind that transpired during the Vietnam war? Why, one may ask, were the aliens so frantic to collect body parts to begin with?

Another startling story regarding what may be yet another, New Mexico crash/retrieval is revealed by Stringfield on page 41 of Status Report VI from a source, Chuck Oldham, of Landsdowne, Pennsylvania. The alleged witness was a former military officer with a high security clearance. While serving in the military, he had a special clearance that enabled him to access a restricted library (prior to 1970) that held data on nothing other than the government's investigation and study of UFOs.

If true, it is astonishing that there would an entire library dedicated to UFOs within the military industrial complex. Due to the highly sensitive nature of the information, no data is provided which could be used to identify him or the location of the base.

Although provocative in content, the most tantalizing portion of the interview is the tail-end where the U.S. military/government's withholding of their knowledge is discussed. Admittedly, we have all heard, and by now are quite familiar with, our government's supposed reasons for debunking UFOs. However, particularly interesting about one aspect is that from the very beginning of our military's investigation and study of UFOs they have always emphatically stated two constants.

One piece of propaganda has been the ardent denial of the existence of UFOs, period. Secondly, the official line was that these phenomena, whatever they are, do not represent a threat to our national security. These two statements are incompatible and contradictory. For if there are no UFOs to begin with, why be concerned with a possible threat to national security? Is this yet another example of a not-so-brilliant oxymoron, like "military intelligence?"

Something beyond strange is going on here. It strongly smells like our government may be concealing something about UFOs and their occupants that far outweighs the simple concept or understanding that our planet is being, and has been for quite some time, visited by intelligently controlled extraterrestrial vehicles.

Based on the amassed evidence, there is good reason to suspect that even if an ultra-black faction of the U.S. government has indeed developed a formal relationship with one or more extraterrestrial races, this in and of itself would not constitute sufficiently damaging information to withhold from the public.

What if that which has been learned during the course of dealing with alien entities is so potentially devastating, though perhaps not in terms of a possible invader or conqueror, that it could literally rip apart the very fabric of our planet's social structure?

Another portion of Stringfield's Status Report VI describes the testimony of a purported Major General in the Air Force, who reveals his knowledge of UFO crashes and aliens dead and alive. He also told Stringfield's source, on Cheri Manet, of a "very high level cover-up" extending to "the highest office in the land."

Exactly what would shake our belief systems? We are already pretty much aware that UFOs exist and represent technology far superior to our own, and that they have been flying around our skies for at least fifty years. So what's so damned shocking? Certainly not what we already assume or suspect.

Given the media exposure to the entire concept of alien life and UFOs in general, from Unsolved Mysteries, The UFO Report,, Sightings, to Close Encounters of the Third Kind, E.T., Communion, Aliens, Predator, Fire in the Sky, Roswell,, Contact and Intruders, what could possibly be left to our imaginations that hasn't already become part of our cultural mindscape?

As a modern telecommunicating civilization, we have been slowly acclimated, conditioned and even begun accepting the notion of alien life visiting Earth and directly interacting with its population. How would our government's release of currently classified UFO data result in the breakdown of society's socio-economic infrastructure as well as that of the military industrial complex?

Certainly, not losing faith in our government's ability to protect us against supposedly hostile aliens! No contemporary western nation particularly enjoys knowing that a technologically superior presence can willfully violate its airspace leaving them virtually incapable or responding.

There is absolutely no evidence or reason to suspect that the U.S. population would suddenly lose trust in its government if such were acknowledged for there has never been a direct or implied threat from hostile extraterrestrials. Unless of course, one is to believe the paranoid mentality allegedly demonstrated by our military in the late Lt. Col. Phillip Corso's book The Day After Roswell.

158

Aliens Above, Ghosts Below by Barry E. Taff

We as a nation became painfully aware not too long ago of just of how underhanded, deceitful, corrupt and unscrupulous our government officials, whether elected or not, really are. Let me count the ways; The Warren Commission Report, Vietnam, Watergate, Iran-Contra, Whitewater, Travelgate, Monica Lewinsky, George W. Bush's administration disinforming congress on weapons of mass destruction the Iraq supposedly had. Should I continue? All one must do to understand our governments continuing covert nature is simply keep up with the news.

Judging by the popular response to the more than thirty year informational blitz on UFOs/ETs, most people find the subject amusing, curious and interesting, but their concern about such matters is relegated to occasional lectures, movies, reality-based TV shows and after-hour cocktail party discussions.

Unless UFOs affected individual lives to the point of influencing decision-making processes on such issues of family, job, income, health and religious convictions, such information would not have any significant impact on society in general.

What facet of UFOs could possibly affect people's lives at these dramatic levels? Certainly not concern over national security matters, nor the worry that every time an inferior culture meets or confronts a superior one, the prior is either assimilated or destroyed by the latter, at least in human history. Well then, what's left?

Again, reference must be made to Stringfield, but this time a passage from page 44 of his Status Report III, which tells of a pathologist who allegedly performed an autopsy of an alien body, and who was ultimately silenced. Stringfield writes, "His last message reiterated through his colleague, concerned a hypothesis which postulated that early man, possibly Cro-Magnon or before, had been genetically altered, or hybridized, with an alien of superior intelligence to form homo-sapiens. According to his rationale, atrophied human-like organs such as evidenced in the alien's genitals, suggest Earth-related evolutionary ties that are beyond coincidence.

In essence, according to the pathologist, primeval Earth had become an experimental test tube for a new race whose development required periodic watching. Provocatively, the hypothesis, which was presented at a secret high-level medical conference (with Russian attendance), does answer a lot of basic questions about the UFO, i.e., their cyclic visitation, some biblical events, the lack of open communication, the lack of overt hostility, and a plausible explanation for abductions of random subjects for what seems to be physical examinations.

Also, it would explain the prolonged high-level international secrecy. If world governments have medical and other back-up evidence to support the hypothesis, then the posture of silence takes on a new meaning. Perhaps they (world governments) assume that Man's concept of himself in his world would be shattered".

Bullseye! In all probability, this information is the missing link as to why the world's governments, or the U.S. more specifically, will not divulge virtually any UFO data to the public, that is, total denial. Stringfield's evidence, if existing in physical form, could unquestionably be the most devastating blow to the human psyche since the beginning of recorded time on this planet.

Think for one moment how an area like the Middle East might react if the U.S. government officially announced the aforementioned data, which in essence says that human beings are not necessarily made in the image of God, but perhaps in that of a hybridized reptilian humanoid!

As many zealots in this world are always more than happy to run into a suicidal jihad, or holy war, screaming the name of their God, might not such a declaration trigger severe hostilities toward those who released such blasphemous or sacrilegious information? Tempers might flare and a world war of the nuclear kind might result for offending and insulting their long-standing Moslem beliefs.

How about all the people in the Western world who attend church or temple on a regular basis? Would such a proclamation affect their attitudes about the God-head and themselves? To say the least, it would spiritually knock the whole human race down a few notches and on its collective behind! Humbling as that may be, could we live with such a systemic shock?

Most of the ethnic and religious attitudes within various cultures on Earth are deeply ingrained within the unconscious, and while not looked at as hardened facts, have become part of what makes humans so proud of their unique individual heritage's. In one fell stroke, all of that history might be forever dispelled and destroyed, replaced by a far greater truth and reality.

The question of who we are and from whereas a race of beings we stem is perhaps one of the most profound questions facing us. It is at the very root and core of our being. Human being, that is.

How degrading would it be to have our biological and theological history re-written into little more than a cosmic experiment? Just think of the difficulties we are currently experiencing regarding interrelationships between different ethnic races on Earth; black, white, brown, red and yellow. What would happen if "grey" was suddenly added to that list?

If indeed the circumstantial evidence presented here is valid, whose best interests are served by maintaining a tight lid of secrecy on government UFO knowledge? Surely our negligent and relatively inept government knows full well the irrevocable ramifications of declassifying such potentially destabilizing information; planetary chaos followed by socio-economic infrastructure collapse.

Other than those few individuals, proportionately speaking, who really want to know the truth regarding UFOs----some scientists, researchers, UFO journalists, scholars, etc.----most people would not benefit in any way whatsoever by the release of such information. Is it possible that the world's governments might actually be doing the right thing for one of the few times in their existence?

Or is it simply the knowledge that a government cannot rule or govern a body of people rendered apathetic, hysterical, self-negated and panic-stricken by having their reality turned upside-down and inside-out----a race with an inconceivable and unimaginable past as well as a very problematic and uncertain future?

Perhaps the answer is so obvious that we normally would not even think about? Perhaps the U.S. government is just a little concerned over whether a disenfranchised population would still pay homage to their not-so-powerful government and write that check to the IRS every April 15th? It might be just that simple.

Although in actuality, it might be even simpler than that. If Philip Corso was correct, from the beginning, the UFO cover-up may have been about money and little else. If the technology recovered in the Roswell crash included a powerplant/propulsion system that draws its energy from space-time itself, that would indeed be cause for concern to governments whose economy and existence is based on non-renewable sources of energy.

If such seemingly "perpetual" technology (which by the way is disallowed by the U.S. Patent Office) was ever made public it would forever end the oil companies monopoly currently running and ruining our planet. What would it be like if there were no more gas stations, no electrical/gas companies?

If our planes, trucks and trains were motivated by, lets say, self-contained zero point energy systems? If all our energy concerns were suddenly derived from a ubiquitous, unlimited source, freely available to all, trillions of dollars would be lost in such a devastated economy.

By comparison, the recent Enron and WorldCom bankruptcies would seem like a bad hair day. Do think that the powers that be would allow such a dramatic transition of "power" to occur? I think not. But what if our supplies of fossil fuels were exhausted and we had no alternative? Would oil company executives rather die with their money or save a planet and improve its living conditions? Difficult decision, huh?

The most disturbing and credible possibility is that both of the aforementioned theories are valid with regard to why the United States and many other world governments will not acknowledge the existence of UFOs. Just think of the implications of such revelations.

First, our cultural, ethnic, and religious heritage(s) are rendered moot and secondly, as if that weren't enough, the world's economy is shattered. Well, at least there's one positive thing that would come out this massive socio-economic chaos; the nations of the Middle East would no longer have us by the short hairs, as our dependence (along with the rest of the planets') on their oil would forever be eliminated.

Maybe if people were slowly conditioned to this new reality----or new world order---- their response might not be so self-destructive; just maybe, we are being protected from our greatest enemy; ourselves. If given the power of rendering this monumental decision, what would you do?

END

Chapter 12:
BRAIN HOLOGRAMS: THE LIGHT WITHIN

We all know what an apparition or ghost is, don't we? Or should I say that we all know what an apparition is not?

It is not a solid, liquid, gas or plasma, at least not as we understand them. It is not a tangible item the essence of can be distilled into a test tube and analyzed. Nor can it, on most occasions be photographed, although there exist some supposedly authentic pictures of such phenomena. In fact, on most occasions, this phantasmal image is not even seen by everyone within the room in which it appears. In other words, the ghostly image can be highly selective in the materializations.

Perhaps the most intriguing aspect regarding the apparition is that it has absolutely no trouble whatsoever in appearing within a completely sealed room, or in leaving the same. Physical obstructions apparently pose no problems for it either, giving this manifestation a quality greatly desired by mortal beings; that is, the ability to be gone in an instant without leaving behind any remnants or tangible proof of presence.

Another striking feature of the ghostly form is that it frequently possesses normal optical qualities of matter, such as three dimensions with full parallax (the apparent displacement of an object when seen from different directions). However, on occasions, apparitions have appeared as translucent and even slightly glowing at their edges, if one can refer to an apparition as having edges.

Now that we have attempted to define what the apparition is not, the question still remains as to what it is. Throughout our currently understood universe, there supposedly is no comparable physical manifestation resembling or possessing similar attributes to that of the spectral apparition. With modern comprehension of matter, energy and mind, the historical appearance of the apparition constitutes a major contradiction to many of our physical laws. Or does it?

What if, within our present technology, there existed a physical process that produced a photographic image almost identical to that of the apparition? Well, strangely enough, such a process does indeed exist, a process that displays its image or picture in a non-material three-dimensional form, including parallax; holography.

Almost anyone alive today in the Western world has seen numerous examples and types of holograms. From glittery magazine covers, to print advertising campaigns, to security logos on credit cards to advanced medical imaging systems and entertainment, holography is in wide commercial use. If you do not remember ever seeing such images, you are certainly in the minority.

Shortly after the invention of the laser in 1964, Dennis Gabor was studying various ways to improve the resolution of the electron microscope when he accidentally discovered holography. The invention or creation of holography was deemed so significant that Gabor was awarded a Nobel prize for it.

Unlike conventional photography, a monochromatic light source such as a laser must be employed in order to create a hologram. It is primarily through the use of the laser that the complex essence of the hologram is produced, an effect which incoherent light cannot produce.

Aliens Above, Ghosts Below by Barry E. Taff

A hologram is created by splitting a laser beam so that half of it reflects directly off the object being photographed (subject beam) onto the photo-sensitive medium (film), while the other half of the beam is reflected off a mirror (reference beam) onto the same medium. The result is a convergence and interference pattern of wavefronts or fields.

Both of these wavefronts are present at the same time and, as a result, become permanently associated with each other in the film's emulsion. The information carried in both the subject and reference beams are spread over the entire hologram, so that any part of the hologram can reproduce the entire image. Moreover, it can be said that the information is equally distributed throughout the entire photographic medium.

Each holographed object has different spatial frequencies associated with its feature spacing (the distance between physical objects in the image), making the hologram a Fourier series of periodic feature correlated fringes. More simply, there is a direct ratio between all the information from the subject contained within both light beams striking the film.

The hologram as viewed by the unaided eye is quite unintelligible, and gives no hint of the image embodied within it. A cursory examination of it tempts one to identify the visible structures (concentric rings, specks and the like) with portions of the subject or object holographed. Such an identification would be quite incorrect. The visible structure is purely extraneous and arises from dust particles and other scatterers on the mirror that supplies the reference beam.

The pertinent information recorded on the hologram film can be seen only under magnification and consists of highly irregular fringes that bear no apparent relation to the object. It is quite unlikely that one could learn to interpret a hologram visually without actually reconstructing the image.

When the hologram is placed in a beam of coherent light, however, the images embodied in it are suddenly revealed (although there are white light holograms that can be seen in normal, incoherent, ambient light). The identity between the reconstructed waves and the original waves that impinged on the plate when the hologram was made implies that the image produced by the hologram should be indistinguishable in appearance from the original object. The identity is in fact realized.

There are different types of holograms that, depending on how they are produced, display uniquely diverse types of images. The "virtual image," for instance, which is seen by looking through the hologram as if it were a window, appears in complete, three-dimensional form, and its three-dimensional effect is achieved entirely without the use of stereo pairs of photographs and without the need for such devices as stereo viewers. Basically, the image floats in space between the holographic film and the light source illuminating and reconstructing it.

Holographic images have additional features of realism that do not, and cannot occur in conventional stereo-photographic imaging. For example, as the observer changes his viewing position, the perspective of the picture changes, just as it would if the observer were viewing the original three-dimensional scene or object.

Parallax effects are evident between near and far objects in the scene; if any object in the foreground lies in front of something else, the observer can move his head and look around the obstructing object, thereby seeing the previously hidden object. Moreover, one must refocus one's eyes when the observation is changed from a near to a more distant object in the scene.

In short, the reconstruction has all the visual properties of reality, and there is no visual test known that can distinguish the two.

Even more astounding is what is known as the "real image," which when viewed by an observer finds the hologram suspended in space between himself and the photographic film. This image has all the aforementioned properties but is somewhat more difficult to view.

It should be understood that the hologram is the most complex form of artificial information storage mechanism known. So complex, in fact, that many optical physicists and computer scientists have been attempting to develop a viable holographic computer storage mechanism for more than twenty-five years.

However, the technical hurdles are such that it may be a considerable time before we are word processing on optical computers with a holographic storage mechanism. There were rumors back in the early to mid-1970's that a group had developed holographic television and VCRs. However, it never appeared either at the scientific or commercial level.

Holography is unique unto itself, possessing qualities totally unknown in any other man-made artifact. However, from all indications, the image created by holographic techniques appears to possess many if not all of the primary factors observed in apparitional sightings, including full three-dimensional form with parallax, but without substance or mass (remember, photons have no rest mass).

Although present holographic methods are essentially restricted to photographic film, it is possible that in the relatively near future holograms may be projected into the empty space where apparitions are generally seen. The aforementioned real image might well be the dawn of an advanced stage in holography, one that could possibly totally mimic the apparition.

There is another form of hologram known as a multiplexed image, which is where numerous successive images are placed within a single frame or frames of film. This technique can store vast amounts of data and even produce a moving or motion hologram. Thus, multiplexing brings us even closer to commonality with real-time apparitions.

The properties demonstrated within holography are so uncommon and extraordinary that they inspired Dennis Gabor and others, not long after the birth of holography, to hypothesize on the possibility that the human brain has multi-variant processes akin to holography.

In fact, it is the one cogent theory of memory and brain function that seemingly encompasses much of our thought processes. In this regard, a respected neuropsychologist from Stanford University, Dr. Karl H. Pribram, published the first and what is considered by many to be the penultimate book on this theory; Languages of the Brain: Experimental Paradoxes and Principles in Neuropsychology .

From the work of Pribram, Gabor, Westlake, Swigert and others it appears that many neurophysiological functions such as our brain's neural network, spatial filtering, pattern identification, and even recall itself has distinct holographic qualities. There is even circumstantial evidence that the firing of many our brain's neurons may be synchronous or quasi-coherent in nature, properties similar to that of a laser.

One particularly fascinating property of the hologram is that each part or any portion of it, no matter how small or the fact that it has been multiply fractured, can reproduce the entire initial image. Thus, the hologram can be broken into many small fragments, each of which can be used to reconstruct a complete image.

As the pieces become smaller though, the resolution (the distinct quality of the image) and information is lost, since resolution is a function of the aperture of the imaging system. This curious property is explained on the basis of an observation made earlier: each point on the hologram receives light from all parts of the subject and therefore contains, in an encoded form, the entire image. Again, put more simply, the information in holograms is equally distributed.

This amazing reproductive property of the hologram is especially significant when related to the brain, in that when large portions of the human brain or cortex are damaged or removed, memory and functional integrity are not lost.

Even attempts at short-circuiting various areas of the brain have failed in reducing memory functions. It is also interesting to note that in memory tracing, there does not appear to be any one portion of the brain specifically reserved for any one particular type of memory.

Consequently, certain information cannot be traced to a localized site (although current neurophysiological research may dispel this belief). Could the hologram then be a simple, small-scale replication of cerebral functions?

Another interesting similarity between the brain and the hologram is that in both cases massive amounts of information can be impressed or stored onto a relatively small space. With a hologram, many images can be superimposed on a single piece of film on successive exposures. Each or several images can then be recovered without being affected by the other images or affecting them.

This overlaying of images, or multiplexing, is done by using a different spatial or temporal frequency carrier for each picture, just as many radio messages can be transmitted between two sites simultaneously by the use of different carrier frequencies. The grating carriers (property of depth) can be of different frequencies, as in radio communication. Moreover, since the film is three-dimensional there is still another degree of freedom, that of angle.

In the brain, there is also a limited or finite amount of space, yet we continue to assimilate, process and integrate new information and knowledge throughout our lifetime.

Since the brain itself does not physically grow beyond adult maturity, we must then assume that all acquired information is somehow impressed or encoded on or over the same cerebral or cortical space.

The encoding of information might well be accomplished through neuronal activity and could be referred to as a "neural hologram." The brain would then serve here as an immense, convoluted, multiplexed hologram, per se.

Perhaps during the process of remembering, we are re-creating the initial spatio-temporal frequency carriers on which the event was fixated, consolidated and stored, which would allow the image and accompanying information to be recovered and recognized.

The limits of such a neuro-holographic storage capacity would certainly be viewed as astronomical in view of the over 10 billion interconnected nerve cells in the brain, each with over a hundred synaptic connections. The combinations of spatio-temporal frequency carriers available in this network of nerve fibers would literally be infinite in number.

Lending even further support to a comprehensive holographic brain model is the previously discussed factor of the hologram's decreasing resolution with corresponding decrease in size. It is a well-established fact that when the human brain atrophies and shrinks with age, recall and recognition capability diminishes as does intellectual and cognitive capacity, a state that is generally manifested as senility.

Thus, with a smaller cerebral medium available, information and image resolution would decrease, paralleling that of the hologram. This effect might not apply to surgical removal of diseased or damaged brain tissue, but only to natural degeneration of nerve cells with age.

There still, however, remains the delicate question as to how much atrophy can occur and still leave a large enough cortical medium for distinct and clear resolution and recognition of information. For some individuals, although massive cellular degeneration occurs from aging, acute senility is not seen. Such individual differences along with the fact that men's brains appear to experience greater shrinkage at an earlier age, are far from being understood. Nevertheless, this particular aspect lends itself nicely to a holographic theory of brain function,

Another particularly fascinating parallel between the brain and holography is that there does not appear to be any loss of information or energy in either system regarding work functions. In standard photography, a great deal of information is forsaken due to the restrictions of only two dimensions, while in holography, all the information relating to the subject is retained.

Perhaps the most direct connection between neuro-biological systems and holographic processes is evident within virtually every one of our cells. From molecular biology and genetic engineering it is well known that the DNA comprising our genome is equally distributed within every cell of our body. What this means is that the DNA from almost any cell within us can be used to replicate us genetically. The equally distributed nature of our DNA could certainly be looked at as holonomic in nature.

Experiments in hypnosis have revealed that the subconscious mind essentially remembers virtually everything an individual experiences and is capable of recalling the entirety of its past through proper induction and conditioning. It has long been speculated that those individuals who are "in touch" with their subconscious mind have near photographic memories and exhibit some degree of voluntary control over their autonomic nervous system.

Perhaps it is this type of person who can easily re-create a previously employed spatio-temporal carrier frequency on which memory information might be contained. Could it be that what we are describing here is a "coherency of thought or mind," similar to that of coherent light?

Excluding computers with RAM, ROM, etc., it was long believed that only living organisms with some form of consciousness possessed actively, associative memory, that is, the ability to recall and interrelate experiences and events from an earlier time. However, the hologram also appears to possess this quality in a form appropriately known as a "ghost image," which is vaguely similar to a real image in that it appears suspended in space before the plate.

In "ghost imaging," the object being holographed is removed from the system, but the information contained within the converging wavefronts of light from splitting two laser beams actually retains an associative memory of the object and reconstructs its exact three-dimensional image, even though the object is no longer physically present. The light is "remembering" what was at a specific point in space in an earlier time.

This particular type of imaging or perception is sometime referred to as internal duplicates and could possibly serve to explain hallucinations----a situation where intense internal imagery is projected externally (to that particular individual) and appears to be real due to its three-dimensional characteristics.

In this respect, holographic ghost images occurring within the human brain might account for such phenomenal experiences of mind as deja vu, dreams, eidetic imagery, illusions, out-of-body experiences and even phantom limb pain, all of which could be defined as the reconstruction of a displaced or removed informational source.

Could this holographic ghost image truly be the essence behind apparitions? Is what we observe in such cases an "optical memory" of the past that is mediated and oriented by living or discarnate consciousness?

In an attempt to reinforce this theory of paranormal ghostly images, we turn towards thermography. Researchers have taken thermal images of an empty parking lots at 7 p.m., and were able to observe the outline of cars that stood in that same lot at 4 p.m. that same afternoon. Could this be considered a ghost image or a reconstructed interference pattern? Or are we simply seeing the residual infrared image? Or is there really any difference?

Proceeding on this assumption, it is quite probable that some type of reconstructed holographic image could be responsible for a large percentage of hauntings and ghostly materializations, especially those where the apparition concerned simply continues to replicate previous behavior patterns of individuals who once lived or traumatically died in that environment.

Could it be that a particular, and as yet unknown, set of environmental conditions can actually reconstruct the optical and perhaps even acoustic interference patterns from the past on which the initial information and image of an event were stored and now contained?

Perhaps even this reconstruction is mediated at some level by the presence of consciousness? This effect, however, would not totally account for acts of discrete intelligence or communicative attempts by apparitions. Or would it?

Even the fact that many instances of ghosts and apparitions are not collectively observed might be explained by extending the analogy between the holographic brain and the paranormal. Perhaps in the instance of an independently observed apparition, the image (supposing it is holographic in nature) would possess a spatio-temporal carrier frequency that does not fall within the perception bandwidth of everyone attempting to observe it.

This theory would be similar to the way a radio can only receive stations that are within its frequency bandwidths, such as AM or FM, or the way cameras require special film or filters in order to register infrared or ultraviolet radiation.

However, it is possible that these highly subjective experiences can be more rationally and logically explained in terms of phase angles or the relationships between the phenomenon and the observer. That is, the spatial relationship between the two. For example, when viewing a conventional hologram, say a 90-degree multiplexed image, if your observational perspective is not within the 90-degrees of required viewing angle, within which the reconstructed light is displayed, you will not see the image.

Moreover, the proper spatial relationship must exist between the illumination source, the hologram itself, and the observer, in order for the image to be seen. In physics terminology, this spatial relationship is known as the phase angles and may help in explaining this most perplexing problem regarding apparitional images.

It could be that the viewing angle of a particular apparitional image may at times be extremely narrow, whether by design or volition, thereby allowing only the individuals within the small degree of arc to witness it, while others outside of it, see nothing.

Then of course, we must concern ourselves with whether or not the apparitional image is truly an objectively real image as opposed to an internally generated, subjective hallucination. However, if this is the case, what is the source of the subjective image?

Whether or not interference pattern reconstruction or ghost images do indeed relate to apparitions remains to be seen. However, such an intriguing analogy should not be ignored and laid to rest simply because it deals with the paranormal. For it is quite obvious that the parallels between these two disciplines are substantial and far more than simple coincidence.

Aliens Above, Ghosts Below by Barry E. Taff

If within the super-intricate neural network of the human brain and the central nervous system there exists functional processes analogous to holography, then perhaps this form of imagery can be externalized under the proper conditions and made visible to an observing eye or camera. Considering this holographic model of consciousness as plausible, then perhaps the overall action of the brain or mind in this respect might be termed a bio-laser effect.

What if, for example, one could project a "mental hologram" of their body into the next room, it conceivably could perform feats totally impossible for their physical body to even consider; de-materializing, walking through furniture and walls, and even becoming translucent.

Interesting, how this type of projection is beginning to sound more and more like a ghost or apparition, is not it? Except of course that it's being generated by a living person, as opposed to a deceased one. Although, I wonder if there really is a fundamental difference between the two?

In a study conducted at the turn of the 19th century entitled The Census of Hallucinations, a detailed analysis of anecdotal apparition cases was correlated. From the results of this census, it was somewhat established that certain gifted individuals did, in fact, possess the ability to project an apparitional image of themselves, or some image firmly implanted in their subconscious minds to another person, even to the point of excluding any form of suggestion.

In brief, the outcome of this particular study was quite dramatic, although its significance has yet to be fully understood due to the lack of existing technology regarding the paranormal.

With all the analogies between the hologram and the brain firmly "in mind," (excuse the pun) what are the possibilities of employing laser holography in a sophisticated investigation of ghosts, hauntings and apparitions?

Could the parallels between brain functioning and holography provide us with a new tool for direct informational induction into the brain for use in education----a means to effectively increase the rate and magnitude of learning a million fold, possibly even to the degree of rendering books as obsolete as steam locomotives? That is not even considering the advances possible in areas of psychiatry, psychotherapy and analysis.

Would the similarities existing between the apparition and the hologram produce a greater probability of photographing with a laser beam what may not even be there physically there to begin with? For with holography, as in conventional photography, one can supposedly only photograph what can be seen.

Although, as we have seen, there have been those occasions where cameras have recorded or captured "things" that were not visible to the naked eye, and conversely, there have been those instances where a camera would not photograph something clearly observed by the unaided eye. Within both holography and thermography, effects of this nature have been frequently seen, a fact that tends to disprove standard photographic principles.

Hypothesized neuro-holographic models do not in any way upset classical neurophysiological concepts, but rather enrich, clarify and consolidate detailed research findings. This theory reinforces many areas of psychology by providing a plausible mechanism for understanding phenomenal experiences of mind, especially those that science has for so long refused to deal with on an empirical basis.

I wonder if it's merely coincidence that each and every cell within our body contains all the genetic information required to reconstruct or replicate the entire body? Perhaps whoever or whatever designed and created us was following a grand scheme regarding a holographically

168

ordered and linked universe?

Exactly what these analogies will bear over time is anyone's guess. However, judging by the disdain modern medicine has for parapsychology, it's unlikely that any substantial progress will be made in the near future.

The laser and holographic techniques may not become a new tool in the arsenal of paranormal investigators, especially when considering its cost and complexity, but it might shed some new "light" on a very old subject; laser light that is.

BIBLIOGRAPHY

Collier, R.J., Burkhardt, C.B. & Lin, L.H., Optical Holography, Academic Press, N.Y., 1971

Gabor, D., Kock, E. & Stroke, G.W., Holography, Science, Vol. 173, 1971, pp. 11-23

Gabor, D., "Nobel Prize Lecture, December 13, 1971," Science, Vol. 177, 1972, pp. 299-313

Gabor, D., Improved Holographic Model of Temporal Recall, Nature, Vol. 217, 1968, pp. 1288-189

Gabor, D., Associative Holographic Memories, IBM Journal of Research & Development, Vol. 1, 3, No. 2, 1969, pp. 156-159

Pribram, K.H., Languages of the Brain: Experimental Paradoxes and Principles in Neuropsychology, Prentice-Hall, New Jersey, 1971

Swigert, C.J., Pattern Identification and Spatial Filtering in a Neuron Network Model, International Journal of Neuroscience, Vol. 2, 1971, pp. 249-264

Westlake, P.R., The Possibilities of Neural Holographic Processes Within the Brain, Kybernetik, Vol. 7, 1970, pp. 129-153

END

Chapter 13:
IT'S ABOUT TIME

The technically correct answer to the question of "how tall are you?" is when?" The reason being that when you walk during your daily activity, it mildly compresses your spine and causes you to lose height, leaving you marginally shorter in the evening than in the morning. This shrinkage in height can be as much as one whole inch in some individuals. Certainly not a welcome thought for short people.

Similarly, on the next occasion you are asked what time it is, the appropriate reply should be "where?" Although this response may appear to be somewhat more abstract than the one regarding height measurements, it is still the most precise answer possible. For as we currently understand time, it is fundamentally based on spatial concepts and theories.

The space existing in one exact location today is not the same space that occupied that region a million years ago, nor is it the same space that will be there in an eon from today. From relativistic theories, it appears as if all energy and matter are in constant motion; moving through the universe by some unknown flow process (Kozyrev, 1968). It may well be this flow process that we perceive as time.

More simply, time could be change of space, or the movement of it to be more exact. In other words, time changes space, and as we will see, space changes time as well.

Time might also be referred to as the distance in space between two events relative to a perspective observer, which mechanically speaking might be expressed as cause and effect. But in physical reality, time is quite different at different spatial locations, both here on Earth and throughout the universe as well (Kozyrev, 1968; Terletskii, 1973).

To illustrate this time differential more clearly, all we must do is to take notice of the time zones that we have created on Earth to compensate for changes in the environment. Due to the Earth's axial rotation, it was necessary to create various zones of time in order to conveniently organize society due to the varying progression of the sun across our skies.

For example, if you are in California watching a live television broadcast of a football game originating from the east coast, you are actually watching an event occurring three hours in the future. That is, three hours forward in time relative to your present time zone reference.

If the sports event, let's say a Formula One road race happened to be coming from Silverstone in England, you would be witnessing an event approximately eight hours ahead in time as we interpret it. While if we could carry this sporting event to the moon, it would appear to be even further displaced in time according to our present comprehension of time and space. This is, of course, disregarding the fact that light requires only 1.23 seconds to reach the moon. The point being made here is that time essentially is space, or the distance it imposes between events.

To gain a greater understanding of this premise, let us look at some basic concepts of relativity and cosmology.

When viewing stars in the night sky, the light we see emanating from those heavenly bodies left many of them long before humans evolved as life forms on Earth. If we could amplify, collimate and resolve that starlight intensely enough, we would observe all the events that transpired in that star system relative to its past, which happens to be our present. If the star system in question happens to be three million light years away, we would then observe events occurring in that space approximately three million years ago. We are in essence seeing through time, into the distant past to be exact.

If we begin to travel towards this particular star system in a ship of sorts, we would view more and more current light, in other words, we would observe an entire panorama of that star system's past and eventual present, while at the same time traveling further and further into our Earth's future.

Similarly, if there were intelligent beings existing in this distant star system, and if they possessed similar astronomical viewing instruments, they too could observe light emanating and reflecting from other celestial bodies; including light from our Earth.

However, if these stellar inhabitants did observe Earth light from that great distance with optical imaging systems identical to ours, they would surely witness the earliest beginnings of our ancestral fore-bearers. For the light they would be capturing, would be that of Earth three million years ago, not Earth as it is today.

Unless some unique superluminal viewer was employed, the extraterrestrial's observations might lead them to conclude that Earth was still in its infantile stages of homo sapien development, and barely beyond that of its Jurassic age.

Perhaps at some future date we may invent and employ superluminal-viewing devices that somehow captures or catches up with the light that has left the Earth ages ago.

If this feat is accomplished, we could for the first time in our brief existence in the firmament truly "see" how the Earth, the solar system, and the universe with all its life, evolved. For carried on that light, for out in space, may lie all the information of past eons. In the depths of interstellar space, eternally recorded on light in a manner we have yet to fully fathom, might be all the knowledge of the ages; immortality preserved and equally available to all who possess the intelligence and tools to retrieve and decode it. It is there for the taking, it is now our task to discover how to access it.

But surely such an optical recording process is still occurring this very moment, and perhaps by understanding and learning to work with it here, the obstacle of treking deep into space after it may seem less difficult.

One method might involve the use of infrared holography, a special photographic process that captures images and information of what was in a space prior to the camera being present and after the event has occurred. This wavefront reconstruction and resulting interference pattern, known as ghost imaging (Collier, 1971), may be the primitive beginnings of a superluminal viewing system.

Realizing that it is possible to perceive certain elements of the past, is such then true of the future? Is there such a thing as future light? Presuming that all past events are somehow recorded or encoded on light and broadcast throughout the universe, is a similar process then occurring regarding the future as well?

One theory (Tiller, 1972) suggests the possibility that all information within our universe is being simultaneously propagated both backwards and forwards in time. The mechanics underlying such a system is at present beyond our comprehension, so therefore, we deem it as no more than theory.

But due to the fact that a positron appears as an electron wandering backwards in time (Gardner, 1967), the notion of omni-directional informational propagation through time cannot be totally dismissed. Moreover, the possibility then exists that information is continually flowing forward from the past and backwards from the future, therein forming a continuum in which the past, present and future simultaneously co-exist, separated by spatial-temporal properties.

The greatest barrier in attempting to understand time is our current belief in the finality of the velocity of light. This supposedly absolute factor is one that in theory cannot be exceeded in a physical realm due to properties of inertial mass. This steadfast theory regarding the invariance of light has only recently been dented by astrophysics and elementary particle physics.

However, with the postulation of negative and imaginary masses and negative spacetime, the probability for the existence of superluminal velocities becomes somewhat greater. Phenomenon has already been observed that more than marginally exceeds the speed of light (Taylor, 1969; Terletskii, 1968).

For example, there is the Russian discovery of Cerenkov Radiation of elementary particles. This radiation, first fully analyzed by P.A. Cerenkov in 1934, is the shock wave of radiation emitted by a particle traveling faster than light in a crystal dielectric medium; it is the radiation equivalent of the sonic boom or the bow wave from a ship traveling faster than the surface water waves. The speed of Cerenkov Radiation has been charted at velocities greater than three times the speed of light (Terletskii, 1968),

Another interesting phenomenon in elementary particle physics is a recently postulated particle named tachyon; from the Greek term "tachys," meaning swift. This theoretical enigma supposedly exists only in a superluminal state and can possess a velocity close to a billion fold of light (Taylor, 1969; Kreisler, 1973).

Tachyons appear to be intimately associated with Cerenkov Radiation in that they supposedly are the superluminal particle that emits this radiation. Although tachyons have been mathematically postulated, and the foundation upon which their theoretical existence is based in sound, they have not as yet been detected (Kreisler, 1973).

The problem here, and the intriguing property of the tachyon is that, in theory, this particle loses energy as it speeds up (from light velocity), until it is traveling infinitely fast, when it has absolutely no energy at all. Attempting to detect an infinitely fast particle that possesses no energy poses rather perplexing problems, some of which will be discussed further on in this chapter.

Within contemporary physics, both energy and momentum, in the special theory of relativity, increase indefinitely as the velocity of a particle approaches the speed of light. Therefore, it would take an infinite amount of energy, in theory, even to get a particle speeded up to the velocity of light.

What this essentially means is that we cannot take a particle traveling slower than light and speed it up until it is going faster than light because this would require an infinite amount of energy. That the energy does increase in the way expected from the special theory of relativity has been found in high-energy particle accelerators; within four thousands of one percent of the velocity of light in the electron accelerator at MIT (as of 1975), and their energy increase exactly agrees with that postulated in special relativity.

There appears, however, to be no reason why a particle cannot exist which is already traveling faster than light. Such a particle may well be the tachyon. Its energy and momentum would be imaginary if it had real rest mass; but because this latter quantity is not directly observable while energy and momentum are (and are real), then it is necessary to choose the rest mass of the tachyon to be imaginary.

Aliens Above, Ghosts Below by Barry E. Taff

Due to these factors of energy and momentum, a tachyon is, in principle, not capable of carrying information, as we currently understand it. Nor does it ever decrease to a sub-light velocity. Only if a tachyon interacts with a luxon or bradyon particle would information be transferred (Terletskii, 1968). Such an event has not yet been observed.

Another superluminal phenomenon occurs when converging microwaves meet in a feed tube and produce a radiation or compression wave traveling at approximately 1.5 times light speed. While in the depths of space, astronomers have recently observed quasars that appear to be separating or traveling away from each other at velocities greater than five times that of light.

The theoretical cause for such supposedly unnatural phenomenon might possibly be linked to gravitational lensing effects generated by curved or warped space-time caused by the presence of enormously massive object (possibly composed of dark matter) between Earth and the image source.

When discussing gravitation, however, we must temporarily shelve current notions regarding luxon propagations, for gravity, due to its enigmatic properties, has been referred to on occasion as instantaneous causality (Misner, 1973), or that dreaded phrase "action-at--distance," which physics doesn't deal with very well. Although no speed of propagation has yet been determined concerning gravity, some physicists speculate that it may, in fact surpass that of light, if indeed gravity is propagated at all.

There is still a heated controversy regarding the form in which gravity itself might propagate; by particle (gravitons), wave or field? This is not even considering how gravity is propagated, and as to whether or not it attenuates identically to electromagnetic energy on a macro-scale, or whether it is a function of space-time itself. Currently, there is talk of a sort of anti-gravity, a repulsive force that may be what allows the universe to infinitely expand and prevent it from collapsing back into a primordial fireball from which it allegedly arose.

Regardless of the modality by which energy achieves superluminal velocities, one major problem looms ever present in relation to time; that is the principle of causality.

A principle that requires that the cause of any event, precedes effect. A superluminal particle such as the tachyon would violate this principle by seemingly being absorbed prior to its emission. Time would then appear to flow in reverse; an obvious paradox.

For example, if there was a rifle that shot forth tachyon "bullets," the target would appear to be impacted before the tachyon bullet was propelled from the rifle's barrel. This phenomenon in itself may indicate the possibility that a tachyon possesses negative energies.

We may consider an observer watching a tachyon move from one point A to another point B. Another observer moving fast enough with respect to the first observer (though no faster than light) will see the tachyon apparently moving with negative energy; and also being emitted after it has been absorbed.

However, the second observer can reinterpret what he sees by saying the emission of a negative energy particle is equivalent to the absorption of a positive energy particle. In other words, the second observer can interpret what he saw as the emission of a negative energy particle from point B and afterwards its absorption at point A.

Such a reinterpretation kills two paradoxes with one stone, since it avoids both the resulting violation of causality as observed by the second observer and the negative energy tachyon seen by him. Traveling into the past has been avoided by reinterpreting the order of emission and absorption of tachyons of negative energy; this reinterpretation has not led to any other reason why tachyons cannot be detected. Because of this, experiments have been and are currently being performed to find tachyons (Kreisler, 1973). But one can easily imagine the difficulty regarding such work, wherein time appears suspended and even to flow backwards.

Inasmuch as tachyons would essentially move backwards in time due to their superluminal velocity, their eventual detection poses some very disturbing situations. For example, at time index T+1 you activate your tachyon detector and lo and behold, its registering voluminous amounts of the superluminal buggers.

Then, at time index T+2 you arbitrarily decide not to generate the temporally retrograde particles. Hmm. This creates somewhat of a dilemma in that you have detected something that was never created or generated to begin with! See the massive temporal, if not paradoxical conundrum here? In essence, you have changed the future, or is it the past?

Believe it or not, there have been serious experimental efforts in the attempt to demonstrate what is called "retroactive psychokinesis," which in layman's terms is the ability to alter or affect the past with your mind. Although this runs contrary to everything we take for granted about our forward ordered temporal universe, the researchers involved with retroactive psychokinesis actually claims success in their efforts.

At time T1, they digitally record and verify random number generation in a solid-state memory. Then at time T2, a gifted psychokinetic agent attempts to alter what was recorded earlier in time. At time T3, they check the memory and discover to their amazement that the sequencing of numbers is no longer random.

Rather than assuming that the psychic altered the electronic memory in real time regardless of the physical distance between the agent and the memory, they jump to the outlandish conclusion that the psychokinetic effect went backwards in time to T1. To avoid the anticipated skepticism from even their own ranks, the researchers say that the past was not changed, it was just "altered." I do not think that semantics will save them from their own ignorance and arrogance, do you?

Just for laughs let's devise our own little retroactive psychokinetic thought experiment and see what happens. At time T1 we all sit down and concentrate on the fact that President John F. Kennedy was never assassinated. At time T2 we go to check our convenient encyclopedia to see if we have changed the past and are shocked to discover that JFK is still alive and well, having served two terms in office.

Then suddenly at T3, we cannot remember why we are even looking up JFK's life to begin with. It seems that in changing or altering the past, our (as well as everyone else's) memories of the original event, as well as all written records of such, are now consistent with the new present or future. Our previous memories of JFK's death no longer exist, because that event never occurred to begin with.

Back in physical reality, another prime example of enigmatic spatio-temporal events involves antimatter with its negatively charged proton (anti-proton), positive electron (positron) reversed positron spins in their orbits and magnetic moments. One current notion in physics suggests that time in relation to antimatter would flow in reverse due to its theoretical properties of negative energy and mass.

If an antimatter world or universe existed, its sequential time flow might then be the reverse of ours if viewed from our positive space-time frame.

However, if we could somehow exist within such an anti-environment, time might appear to flow quite normally. The point being made here is that all these perceptions of temporal ordering and flow are relative to the perspective observer and their subjective reality. But considering the bi-temporal meanderings of the positron, the possibility of time reversal effects cannot be completely dismissed. In fact, there is absolutely nothing forbidding such reversed time effects (Alfven, 1967; Gardner, 1967; Sachs, 1972).

Perhaps if we stretch our imaginations even a bit further we can envision antimatter with its negative or anti-mass manifesting negative or anti-gravity (Burbridge, 1968; Gardner, 1967).

The not-so-obvious difficulties in detecting the presence of such negative energies are that our present instrumentation is designed only to measure positive (real) energy in a real-positive space-time frame. We might not even recognize a particle of negative or imaginary energy if we encountered it due to the subjectivity in perspective interpretations discussed earlier.

Returning once again to the depths of interstellar space, it was pointed out that astrophysicists claim to have located quasars separating at velocities greater than that of light. Perhaps this seemingly impossible violation of nature can be explained by the same relative judgments regarding the tachyon?

One theory regarding these separating quasars is that the cataclysmic explosion of a supernova causes their violent dispersal. These violent forces are assumed to have profound effects on space-time by dramatic changes in the gravitational constant.

Within stars, there are two pervasive forces at work. First, there is fusion of hydrogen into helium, which is an expansive force. Second, there is gravity, pushing in against the continual fusion reactions. The delicate equilibrium between these two forces is what allows the star to continue its existence. However, in stars of sufficient mass, say five times or greater than that of our sun, interesting things begin to occur as the star ages.

As the star begins to exhaust its finite quantity of hydrogen, the fusion process diminishes and relation to the force of gravity and the equilibrium is thrown out of balance. As this process accelerates, the star's gravity overwhelms the fusion reactions and starts to collapse the star. If the star is not of sufficient mass, it may be reduced to a neutron star, where all the protons and electrons are squeezed out and only neutrons remain. The resulting neutron star is extremely dense, where a cubic inch of it could weigh many million of tons.

If the original star was massive enough, the gravitational collapse will continue and crush the remaining neutron star out-of-existence resulting in a black hole. The localized gravitation has grown to such a magnitude that even the surrounding space is transformed from its normal linear structure to a dramatically curved manifold.

So severe is this localized space curvature or "warping" that a barrier known as an "event horizon" is formed from which nothing entering can escape due to the gravitational forces. Space-time warping around a black hole is so immense that even photons are pulled in and cannot escape, hence the name "black hole."

What is particularly intriguing here is that the gravitational collapse has so radically warped space around the formerly existing neutron star that time itself has now been altered. For example, where the surface of the now, non-existent neutron star once stood there is a region known as the "Swartzchild Radius." If you were to fall past the "event horizon" towards the Swartzchild Radius, the fall would take forever as time in that region has been so dramatically dilated by the warping of space. And you thought that your days are long now!

Within the core of a black hole, singularity is produced, which essentially means that whatever is sucked into it is virtually crushed out of existence into nothingness by the intensified collapsed gravity. However, following the concepts of flat space-time physics, singularity was impossible. Only within the immensely curved space-time world of the black hole is such an occurrence possible (Misner, 1973). Strangely enough, modern astronomy now believes that most galaxies (including our own) have super massive black holes at their cores, acting as gigantic engines, swallowing up vast amounts of interstellar matter and eventually spitting out new paired-particles.

Considering that such awesome power does indeed exist, perhaps the previously discussed exploding and separating quasars are being blown out into warped space-time, therein seeming to achieve velocities greater than that of light as viewed by distant observers such as ourselves.

Effects of superluminal velocities might occur because the normally linear space-time into which the quasar is exploding is no longer as it was, but is now curva-linear. The space has been collapsed, warped, and for all practical matters shrunken by the dramatic changes in gravitation. It could then be that the quasar is being driven through warped space-time, which gives the appearance of being infinitely fast for there is no longer as much space for the quasar to travel through, therein negating the time required to do so. This is an over simplified view of the gravitational lensing effect spoken of earlier.

However, if you were within the exploding quasar material itself (don't try this one at home), the velocity you would measure as your own would not exceed that of light due to your relative perceptions. For you, as an active participant could not detect the warping of space-time about you or the supposed temporal reversal or nullification induced by such velocities.

It would all appear quite normal from your vantage point. Only if you were observing distant stars through and beyond the area you were in, would you recognize the alteration in space-time around you, as we do from Earth. Here once again we see how critical subjective interpretations become regarding the phenomena of time.

These theoretical arguments provide a splendid example of how time is fundamentally a representation of space. For when space is greatly altered or modified, time correspondingly changes. Moreover, if you collapsed or warped space, you shorten time, stretch or lengthen space and you increase time (Sachs, 1972).

With all this discussion of curved space-time and warping effects, we should consider the relationship of special relativity's principle of time dilation to such matters.

In brief, time dilation says that when anything approaches the speed of light, time for it begins to slow down in geometric proportion to the speed at which it is traveling (Bronowski. 1963). In particle accelerators, such as the one mentioned earlier, elementary particles with a normal life span of only several billionth's of-a-second appear to increase their life duration when approaching velocities close to that of light. In theory, if a particle could be accelerated to the exact speed of light, its life span would be infinite. But of course, such has not yet occurred.

Another means of elaborating on time dilation would be to imagine a round trip to the nearest star 4.3 light-years away in which you are instantaneously accelerated to near light speed. A round trip voyage of this nature would take about nine years Earth time.

However, for you aboard the ship traveling at a fraction beneath light speed, time would progress at a much slower rate. When finally returning to Earth some nine years later, you might be only several days or weeks older, while everyone on Earth had aged a full nine years.

In fact, if observers on Earth were attempting to telemetrically monitor your physiological parameters while traveling at near-light velocities to that star, they would encounter difficulty trying even to determine if you were alive.

176

Aliens Above, Ghosts Below by Barry E. Taff

The problem lies in that fact that our earthly instruments are all calibrated to standard Earth time that flows forward at an established rate. For this reason, to observers back on Earth, your heart rate would be exceedingly slow or possibly even non-existent due to the slowing down of your time in relation to theirs.

One might say that your entire interstellar journey takes place between the beats of your heart or the ticks of your watch according to Earth time. But to you aboard the ship, time would appear to pass quite normally, at last sensorally, because all factors are held constant relative to your new world on the vessel.

Unless engineering technology on Earth could adequately compensate for such radical time differentials, communications with a craft at even near-light velocities would certainly be a impossibility. Maintaining telemetric data links with crafts' at superluminal speeds, by the same token, would be beyond even our imagination.

In one sense, the phenomenon of time dilation would turn you into a modern H.G. Wells with his Time Machine novel. But naturally, time travel as experienced with dilation would be limited to a one-way ticket or direction. Or would it?

Is it possible by utilizing superluminal velocities, to complete the entire nine-year Earth-time round trip to the star and then return to Earth seemingly only seconds after you initially departed on your trek? What about returning before you left? In other words, you would have traveled both forwards and backwards in time by moving many times faster than light. Excluding the obvious paradox created by such a feat, there is no other reason why this time traveling experience cannot be accomplished (Bronowski, 1963).

Another enigma of interstellar space that may be directly related to temporal phenomena is the wormhole. This spatio-temporal anomaly is allegedly created by a super-massive black hole (sans the crushing singularity) and is similar only in that an intense warping of space-time occurs.

Theoretically, for no wormholes have as yet been discovered, such a phenomenon would connect two widely separated points in space through a warp induced Einstein-Rosen Bridge effect, points many light years or even parsecs [3.26 light years] apart (Misner, 1973).

In principle, a warp generated bridge connecting two distant coordinates in space would negate the time required to travel from one point to the other, which in space can be immense, even at light speed.

Conceivably, wormhole space-time warping, functioning without the devastating center of singularity, could be a form of instantaneous transference, similar to the phenomenon of teleportation or apports. It is just possible that such holes, bridges and warps in space-time might eventually serve as passages or tunnels for distant interstellar voyages.

Is it possible for us to utilize such unique astrophysical events in our exploration of interstellar space? The question is whether we will eventually be capable of artificially generating such enormously powerful gravitational forces, to harness and control such effects so as to produce highly localized space-time warps. The creation of warps and bridges in space-time would enable us to achieve interstellar and possibly even intergalactic journeys requiring little if no time whatsoever. That is, if we humans could survive the inconceivable forces within such gravitational vortexes, even without singularity.

Until this point we have discussed space-time as being essentially three-dimensional nature. But perhaps space-time only appears as such to us due our limited physical sensory system. Space-time might actually be a multi-dimensional continuum, being viewed as linear or curved only by those whom perceptions are geared and oriented for functioning in the real, physical world.

In Chapter 12 and again in Chapter 14 we learned of a comprehensive paranormal theory incorporating holographic properties related to human brain function as well as four-dimensional space-time.

These "holonomic" functions strongly suggest that at some level we are operating "as one" with Fourier holographic space-time and the universe around us. In contemplating a holonomic, time-like and space-like communication system that theoretically integrates and explains much of the phenomena within parapsychology, traditional concepts regarding EM energy, signal propagation and information theory may no longer apply.

Is the universe a randomly organized system or is it a finely patterned and highly order sequence of events occurring at different levels of space-time? Does the future already exist, simply awaiting our arrival, or do we have control over our destiny? At this point, the function of pattern, chaos and order become crucial regarding the entire concept of time and what lies ahead in the future. For if the universe is not   random, then it may be patterned, ordered and determined.

The holonomic relationship between person and environment may be the key to unraveling the mysteries of psi phenomena. In principle, our brain or mind might virtually be interfering with space-time, relating to those informational bits or elements within our small sector of space and time that correspond to what is occurring in other areas of the universe.

For if information is equally distributed on a spatio-temporal basis, then all information from past, present and the future exists right here and now around us. The same function would apply for information regarding distant locations within real time, but the greater the distance, the greater the perceived displacement in time observed.

In other words, all our "psychic" sending and receiving is done within the space immediately adjacent to our body, which is probably why no form of known energy has ever been detected between biological systems psychically communicating, for it would only be seen in the form of localized field dynamics at either site. If this theory were even partially valid, it would create an instantaneous communication system between biological organisms and their environment by the avoidance of the space between them.

With this system, remote viewing would entail little more than plugging the appropriate spatio-temporal coordinates into consciousness and then accessing the data related to them.

This mode of communication neatly eliminates the need for any radiation (particle or wave) being propagated, as well as the possibility of physically shielding or screening psi functions, for there is nothing to impede, therein erasing all known barriers of time and space.

Another remote possibility is that our brain and/or mind, functioning holographically, similar to that of the surrounding universe, might link-up with informational bits within holographic hyperspace by the collapse or warping of localized space-time. There may be some bio-energetic mechanism analogous to gravity, a "biological gravity" if you will, that can collapse and warp quantum space in and around living organisms similarly, but not identical, to wormholes. Bio-gravitational space-time warping and the resulting bridge would, in theory, allow our holographic brain to reach out for tremendous distances into space and time.

The lingering question, however, even after theoretically identifying an energetic modality that may underlie much of psi phenomena, is whether or not the future's patterns and events are already in existence, and if so, are they mutable.

When precognition does occur, the information perceived during the experience must originate from some source, and it is probable and reasonable to assume that it is emanating from the future itself. That is, once it is cleaned of any inference or deduction. Either it is flowing backwards via an advanced wave potential as previously discussed, or our holographic brain perceives equally distributed information that directly corresponds to future space. If either of these theories are plausible, if would appear to reinforce and support the concept of determinism and predestination.

Just as past events and information already exist and cannot be altered, perhaps future events similarly exist and are immutable. But located at different levels of spacetime.

Following this line of thinking, it is also reasonable to assume that all events would be determined by the "patterning" described here, everything from the act of reading this book to that of the birth of a new star deep in interstellar space.

The best example of an "all or none" deterministic concept would be to digress to the earlier discussion concerning extraterrestrial observers viewing light coming to them from Earth. These alien stargazers would not just observe the major events or minor events transpiring here, they would observe everything caught in the long-wave infrared through the visible light spectrum all the way into the shortwave ultraviolet.

The same way a TV show, recorded on magnetic tape captures all of the actions recorded by the camera, not just the gross movements or extra-loud words. The question now is whether we are able to somehow reconstruct future light or future interference pattern information existing within present space-time. If accomplished, it would allow us to observe the future in entirety.

Let's say for one moment that we acknowledge and accept the notion of determinism and predestination. The question then haunts us as to what might be patterning or ordering us and how such might be accomplished. Perhaps the ordering structure creates holographic interference patterns of information within our brains that are related to memory, but in this instance they are of the future and are what guide us into it. Such a mental impression could be defined as a pre-memory, or premory, and might possibly explain déjà vu, as some people experience it.

These memories of the future would generally be subliminal in nature like most forms of psi phenomena, except when occasionally surfacing to conscious level where they might be recognized and referred to a precognition, premonitions, insights, intuitions, foresight, a lucky guess or, everyone's favorite, a coincidence, that which skeptics and debunkers rely on so frequently.

There may be a good reason why more of us are not gifted psychics, able to accurately and reliably see what awaits us in the days, months and years ahead. Beyond the negative reinforcement and fear we have all come to experience when sharing such occasional knowledge with others, our society has never been designed to handle this level of awareness.

Sure, we would all love to go win a fortune in Las Vegas by knowing which slot machine was going to pay off in the seven-figure range or win the weekly Lotto jackpot. But I really do not think that this ability exists within humankind for the distinct purpose of gambling, unless of course that was your destiny.

Although, in Executive ESP, paranormal researcher Douglas Dean discovered that many high-ranking CEO's consistently scored well above chance on precognition tests, that is, as long as they were unaware of the nature of the test. Is this an example of one of those instances where gifted individuals were led into their success by their subconscious paranormal perceptions? We'll probably never know.

Precognition seems to serve a deeply rooted emotional need. One that is more tailored to our subconscious needs and a desire, which is why so many spontaneous instances of precognition involve traumatizing events affecting loved ones.

Indeed, surveys and studies have indicated that the majority of precognitions are those involving events such as natural disasters (earthquakes, floods, volcanic eruptions, etc.), wars, maritime disasters, or family and/or friends being harmed. In a way, precognition seems to operate as a distant early warning system such as radar, and occasionally we consciously perceives those impending threats to our welfare both personal and otherwise.

But you see, it really does not make any difference whether we believe in determinism or in that we are masters of our own fate. For whatever we choose to believe, we must sit back and patiently watch the future unfold. In this matter, we certainly do not have any choice at all. Or do we?

If the future already exists in some form and the past continues to exist, would it be possible to physically visit these other times with some sort of time machine? While it certainly appears possible to view the future and past paranormally, such perception is generally distorted to such a degree that it is for all intents and purposes worthless because we have no way of determining a precognition's accuracy until and unless it occurs.

But what about building a machine that travels through time the way we currently travel through space, but far more rapidly and efficiently?

Well, if our notions of achieving superluminal propulsion are more than ballpark assumptions and pipe dreams (See Chapter 9), then constructing a device that propels us through time at an accelerated rate but not altering one's position in space, is indeed feasible.

What may be required to build a time machine is a method for generating a controlled, highly localized, artificially generated gravitational field. Sort of a quantum wormhole or singularity, that is vertically polarized and rotates both clockwise and counterclockwise.

Precisely how you would go about generating such a quantum gravitational warping of space, where you would come upon the energy to do it, and how you would survive the trip within it, again brings us back to the utilization of the ubiquitous zero point field.

Describing how a machine capable of traveling in time might function based on what we know today, requires delving into some of the most esoteric research ever conducted on earth. This extraordinary type of high-energy work, some of which actually began during the closing years of WWII within Nazi Germany, sets the tone for the genesis of a technology that has the power to transform the lives of literally everyone on earth.

In fact, had the second world war dragged on for several more years, it's very likely that Hitler and the Third Reich would have won, and in the process decimating much of the civilized world.

The evidence compiled by author Nick Cook in his fascinating book, The Hunt For Zero Point: The Classified World of Antigravity Technology, strongly suggests that the Nazi SS were conducting research into unique, non-nuclear energy sources that would have made atomic weapons seem as tame as firecrackers by comparison. Thank God Hitler's SS didn't really understand what they were toying with and that the war ended when it did.

The implications for this technology, if developed apart from its weaponization potential, would allow us to transport people or cargo anywhere on earth in under an hour, to remove the need for any type of internal combustion engine (gasoline, propeller, jet or rocket), to remove the necessity for power transmission lines, to eliminate about ninety-eight percent (98%)

of the earth's pollution and sources of global warming. And, last but not least, bring Star Trek's interstellar propulsion (warp drive) into the very near future. But without a doubt, the most paradigm-shifting change would certainly be time travel.

A time machine might very likely incorporate rapidly, counter-rotating (in excess of 70,000 rpm) matter and antimatter mercury plasmas (volume superconductors?). These mercury plasmas need to be pressurized to around a quarter-million atmospheres (that's 3,675,000 pounds per-square-inch, for those who are counting), which are magnetically suspended, confined and driven by superconducting solenoids within a convoluted, toroidal reactor configuration that is vertically polarized.

There might also be the need for several additional insulated, rotating, high-temperature superconductor rings within the plasma streams themselves to insure the safety of any occupants within such temporal transport vehicles.

Such a high-energy device would, would by its very nature and design, generate a powerful torsion field capable of "frame dragging" the localized gravitational as well as electromagnetic environment, much the way our sun does within our solar system. In theory, this would allow anything within the torsion field to accelerate through time at a far greater rate than the rest of the world.

Now, assuming you could generate and control a stable, non-singularity warping of space, the right-left symmetry of the counter-rotating plasmas would govern movement into the past or future.

Of course, generating and controlling such vast amounts of plasma would not be cheap or easy, especially given the superconducting torus in which they are contained. However, if magnetic confinement fails, as depicted in way too many Star Trek episodes, and the matter/antimatter plasmas came into contact with each other and totally annihilate, the result would be devastation beyond anything human beings have ever known or imagined. In fact, it would make what happened in Tunguska on June 30, 1908 seem like a crude fireworks display.

The last thing anyone on earth, or the moon for that matter, would remember, would be a very bright flash of light, something along the lines of a supernova, a gamma-ray burster or pulsar, and then nothing. This cataclysmic explosion would be roughly equivalent to our sun expanding into a red giant at end of its life cycle in another five billion years or so. This expansion could extend to the orbit of Mars, leaving nothing more than burned-out cinders behind it, disrupting our entire solar system.

To put this magnitude of destruction into perspective, it is important to grasp the fact that one kilogram (2.2 pounds) of antimatter, has enough potential energy if totally annihilated, to lay waste to the entire North American continent, including blowing the atmosphere over it out into space. For our time machine, we would probably require several hundred to thousand kilograms of antimatter!

This is the degree of power that might be required to crack open the zero point field and put its forces to work such as within warp-driven starships or a time machine. Do you think that anyone, or any government for that matter, presently has the wisdom to control and govern such power? If you do, there's some swampland I'd like to sell you that has billions of barrels of oil trapped beneath it. Are you interested? What, you don't believe me?

Think about what was just described because, believe it or not, we are rapidly approaching the point in our technical evolution where harnessing and employing such energies are imminent. Such technologies, are very likely well beyond the "Star Trekian" stage of their development. We all better pray that there are at least some sane people left within these areas of science behind such technology.

Aliens Above, Ghosts Below by Barry E. Taff

On the bright side of this discussion is the possibility that once you open a wide enough fissure within the zero point field, you may not require this degree of power to keep the juices flowing so-to-speak. Then of course, comes the concern regarding closing a forced rupture in the zero point field, and what might occur if this fissure cannot be sealed.

The news recently reported the public concerns about the new Large Hadron Collider, which became partially operational in late summer of 2008 at CERN, outside Geneva, Switzerland. There are those who really believe that operating at energies in the hundreds of teravolts will create a miniature black hole that could gobble up the city as well as the entire earth. What's the probability of this occurring? Astronomical!

The very fact that I am writing this in the early fall of 2008, clearly indicates that the absurd public concerns over the Hadron Collider which went operational around September 9-10th of this year, were totally unfounded. I guess that all the pundits were, as usual, wrong.

There have been many other, equally erroneous, comments uttered regarding the potentially devastating effects of new technology.

The first one that comes to mind involved the testing of the world's first nuclear weapon at the Trinity Site of Alamagordo, New Mexico in 1945. The head of Naval Munitions, an Admiral at the time, was absolutely confident that a nuclear bomb would be little more than what a 2,000-pound "blockbuster" bomb was at the time. He went on to order the men working on the nuclear device to wrap it within a large iron drum enclosure to demonstrate the utter foolishness of such monumental expectations.

The admiral in question was so absolutely confident of his belief that he told President Truman and the Secretary of War (James V. Forrestol) he would resign his commission if the "damn thing" even worked. Thankfully, the weather at the bomb test site was so hot at the time that the workers decided to ignore the admiral's orders.

Needless to say, the bomb worked and the admiral resigned his commission as promised. Another equally absurd belief on the part of scientists was that the detonation of a hydrogen bomb (fusion, not fission) might actually cause the earth's atmosphere to fuse, causing the entire planet to explode along with the weapon. Yeah, that happened?

Demonstrating how ignorance effects one's judgment is the belief, by some, that nuclear weapons will detonate only at certain specific geographic regions of the earth and that their efficacy is also directly tied to such energetic "vortices".

There is one other incident demonstrating the incredible lack of insight on the part of well-educated or informed individuals.

Almost ten years to the day before NASA astronauts landed at the moon's Tranquility Base with Apollo 11 in July of 1969, the head of Cal-Tech (a physicist in his own right), made the absurd pronouncement that we will never go to the moon because such a feat is literally impossible. I guess he was wrong, wasn't he? What is it about such people at high levels of education and authority making such foolish statements?

Speaking about creating your own personal wormhole, there is interesting work going on at the Nova Shiva laser facility at Lawrence Livermore Laboratories in Berkeley, California. The off-the-record word was that this super powerful, inertial confinement fusion setup appears to have already cracked open the zero point field.

They have seen evidence that vast quantities of non-thermodynamic energies are "leaking through" from vacuum space (the zero point field?) significantly exceeding Nova Shiva's power input (breakeven) but not the result of a controlled fusion reaction. Moreover, they have now, theoretically, surpassed the point of breakeven but not to the level of a sustained, commercially viable fusion reactor. If any currently operating technology on earth has the potential to generate an artificial black hole, this may be it.

However, by altering space, you're altering time and vice-versa, thus necessitating control over both spatial as well as temporal coordinates to avoid the pesky problem of appearing in a space where another already massive object already exists, say a mountain or a large building.

You've heard the one about the irresistible force and the immovable object? Well, trust me on this one. This is one instance where you really wouldn't want to test this concept. But strangely enough, that's really not what is at issue here anyway.

For argument's sake, let's say you have built your time machine and after initially testing it as an unmanned temporal vehicle, you have determined that it's safe for human occupation and travel. Now you intend on taking numerous journeys through time and learn the truth about history and when the next depression (don't tell anyone, but it's probably somewhere between 2010-2012, it's hard to be specific at this point) will occur to cash-out your investments and life savings before the stock markets crash and banks close.

Regarding attempts at personal temporal manipulation, the real no-brainer would be to wait until your local state lottery is up say $300 million and then go forward in time to learn the winning numbers.

You then return to the present before the numbers are picked where you go and buy your ticket with those exact numbers. Instant multi-millionaire. You're finally free of being a wage slave! What a life!

The same methodology could be used with horse racing (remember that episode of the original Twilight Zone with the antique box camera that took pictures of events five minutes into the future?), Las Vegas gaming, etc. Needless to say, no one has, as yet, accomplished such a feat. If they did, this type of wagering wouldn't be known as gambling anymore, would it?

But wait, if you travel into the future to learn the winning lotto numbers, you have already passed the point in time where the winning ticket(s) have been purchased, and yours was not one of them as you had not yet learned the correct numbers for buying your ticket. You cannot then return to the past (the time before the lotto numbers were drawn) and buy your ticket because you never did so to begin with. Confused? Does this make any sense? Time travel is not supposed to make sense, which is probably why no one's going to be doing it, if you'll excuse the pun, for quite some time.

My guess is that attempting to travel into the past would result in a situation where you could observe events but not interact with them. It would be like existing within a giant, dynamic hologram, where nothing relative to you possesses any real or rest mass.

Traveling back beyond the point of your birth might be even more problematic. Remember, long before you were born, your subatomic particles and atoms did not exist in the form they do today. So in essence, the act of traveling back that far in time would disrupt all the world lines (cosmic strings?) of every particle within your body, possibly to the point of annihilating you. Talk about having a really bad hair day!

And then, of course, one must consider that before the time machine itself existed with all of its "ultra" diodes, capacitors, transistors, and operational amplifiers, such a device was not in "physical reality" either. I suspect, that if one tried to enter physical space with a physical time machine before its components or occupants existed, the result might be, shall we say, catastrophic in nature.

Perhaps there are different types of space based on the temporal environment you currently exist in. More simply, there might be something akin to "temporal space," a sort of vantage point from where you could look but not touch. This opposed to "physical space," which is where we normally reside. Thus, you might be able to observe historic events in a way far exceeding that of watching a motion picture, but you could not in any way intervene in the affairs of time past because the energy and matter that makes your body yours were never there to begin with.

It's like the old story of going back in time and murdering your grandparents, which means that neither of your parents, nor you, would have ever been born. But didn't you just go back in time to destroy your grandparents? You had to be alive to do that, right? So, there is a major contradiction or paradox here to say the least.

Okay. So we cannot go to say hello to our great-great-great grandfather, nor could we go back to 1937 and attempt to kill Adolf Hitler before the start of World War II as depicted in a 1963 hour-length Twilight Zone episode "No Time Like the Past", starring Dana Andrews.

But what about traveling into the near future to find out which stocks will soar, come back and buy those dollar stocks and eventually make Bill Gates look like a pauper? Well, what sounds good on paper and looks great on the silver screen, does not quite play out in the real world, whether three or four dimensional.

Imagine you are sitting in your time machine right now. You set the controls for a date ten years into the future. You "launch" your vehicle, so-to-speak, and within less than thirty seconds, you "land" in the year 2019.

You leave the machine and discover that not much has changed, except that there are a lot more people and cars. What little gasoline there is teeters around twenty dollars a gallon, and very few people in the United States speak English. I'll bet you can guess what language they do speak?

You eventually find some old friends who are shocked to discover that you are still alive, for they believed you literally disappeared off the face of the Earth a decade ago.

Equally strange, is the fact that you do not look your age, and your clothes look like they came out of a really cheap thrift shop and they're not UV resistant.

After a brief visit with your "old" friends, you check out the stock market and learn what has happened during your ten-year absence. You take voluminous notes and are prepared to return your point of origin and be "king of the world."

You once again enter the time machine that you have carefully hidden, and reset the controls to return to one minute after you originally left. You again "take off" and wait for "touchdown" back in 2009. Hmm, that's strange. Nothing happens. Your chronometer shows that you are back in the present, but you cannot return to normal "physical space."

The problem here is that basically you did not exist for ten years, at least not in normal space. The Earth and everyone on it moved through ten years of time without you. You cannot then go back and be where you were not.

That would be equivalent to taking an airliner to New York while at the same time driving your car all the way across the country. You cannot do both, can you? And of course, if the future and past exist only at an informational level relative to us, then physical time travel would truly be impossible.

Aliens Above, Ghosts Below by Barry E. Taff

Don't even waste your time thinking about parallel universes, dimensions or other such rubbish. The TV series Sliders was clever and well written, but it's pure science fiction. The above scenario is one that, based on theory, would likely play out if and when we ever develop time travel.

This is not to say that we cannot travel to the 24th century and witness the starship Enterprise explore the galaxy or the year 802,701 A.D. and visit Weena and the Morlocks. There is absolutely nothing prohibiting us from doing that, except perhaps the lack of currently available technology.

However, returning to the temporal coordinates you originally left might only be achieved, if while visiting the past or the future, you never attempted to enter (or is it re-enter) physical space while there.

How depressing, all this knowledge and technology and you still have nowhere to go. It's sort of like having hundreds of cable TV channels and there's still nothing to watch. Wait a minute; don't we already have this situation? Man, this is depressing isn't it?

So, contrary to what we have read about in books since 1895 and seen in the movies most of our lives, time travel may be a one-way ticket. It might be a great way to avoid paying your taxes or escape being pummeled by an asteroid impact, but I for one would not want to leave the certainty of here and now unless I knew for a fact that my destination was at least as hospitable as where and when I left.

I guess we will all just have to lay back and let the future unfold as it was intended to. Can you imagine the chaotic mess if we humans started arbitrarily roaming around through time, altering what was and preventing what will be? Although I don't think such a finely ordered universe would allow such to occur.

We systematically destroy and cannot control the limited domain we currently call home. How do you think we would behave in this expanded realm?

Perhaps if we had successfully achieved time travel in the recent past we would not even exist today for having destroying ourselves long ago? Maybe the reason we cannot travel in time, or interstellar space, for that matter, is that, at present, we are not supposed to?

A whole lot of questions, and very few, if any, answers. I guess that only time will tell. Remember, once we can move through time as easily as we currently move through space, we literally have "all the time in the world" to ponder its significance, don't we?

REFERENCES

Alfven, H., Antimatter and Cosmology, Scientific American, April, 1976

Bronowski, J., The Clock Paradox, Scientific American, February, 1963

Burbridge, G., and Hoyle, F.,Antimatter. Scientific American, April, 1958

Collier, R.J., Burkhardt, C.B. and Lin, L.H., Optical Holography, New York, Academic Press, 1971

Cook, N., The Hunt For Zero Point: Inside The Classified World Of Antigravity Technology, Broadway Books, N.Y., 2002

Gamow, G., The Principle of Uncertainty, Scientific American, January 1958

Kozyrev, N., Possibility of Experimental Study of the Properties of Time, JPRS 45238, NTIS, Springfield, VA; U.S. Department of Commerce, 1968

Misner, C.W., Thorne, K.S., and Wheeler, J.A., Gravitation, San Francisco, W.H. Freeman, 1973

Sachs, R.G., Time Reversal, Science, 1972, Vol. 176, pp. 587-596

Taylor, J.G., The Shadow of the Mind, New Scientist and Science Journal, September, 30, 1971, pp. 735-737

Taylor. J.G., Faster Than Light, Journal of Paraphysics, 1969, Vol. 3, pp. 136-145

Terletskii, Y.P., Paradoxes in the Theory of Relativity, New York, Plenum Press, 1968

Terletskii, Y.P., The Arrow of Time, Journal of Paraphysics, 1973, Vol. 7, pp. 72-75

Tiller, W.A., Consciousness, Radiation and the Developing Sensory System, Stanford University, Department of Materials Science, 1972

Chapter 14:
A MEMORY OF THINGS TO COME

Even if time travel were restricted to simply watching past events as they occurred, without the ability to interact with them, wouldn't it be an incredible experience to see what transpired before you existed or after you die? Perhaps, even to prevent your own death, if it was premature.

Imagine the excitement and awe of "virtually" living through events of the distant past such as the great flood, the building of the pyramids, the birth of Jesus Christ, the burning of Rome, the landing of Ezekiel's flaming chariot, and what about a more recent occurrence like the Roswell Crash and what really occurred in Dealy Plaza on November 22, 1963?

What untold secrets and hidden knowledge might be revealed from having an undistorted glimpse of such tragedies as JFK's, RFK's, or Martin Luther King, Jr.'s assassinations? Even though such disasters most likely could not have been prevented due to the temporal constraints described in Chapter 13, wouldn't it be intriguing to try? To discover precisely how temporal continuity would prevent you from interfering with what "was". With such gross limitations imposed on retrograde time travel, we would at least be free of any potential injury at the hands of past events. Or would we?

And what of the future? Of what practical use would an instrument be that could display precise images of events, similar to a television, which have yet to occur? We know through logic, reason and rational thought that one cannot alter past events, as we have already discussed.

But this raises the question of whether future events are equally closed to human intervention (or any extraneous intervention, for that matter). Could one affect the outcome of scenes depicted in such a time viewing machine? Can man control his destiny? Can he change the shape of things to come?

It is highly unlikely that our contemporary or near-future technology will develop sufficiently to allow mechanized time-displaced viewing, let alone physical time travel in the immediate future. The very concept of transcending time seems to locked firmly within the realms of science fiction for the simple reason that it apparently contradicts established physical laws, theories and principles that have remained fairly consistent throughout the course of man's existence on this planet.

Of fundamental significance at present is the principle of causality. A relatively simple principle, which states that the cause of any event must inevitably precede its effect. Things that have already transpired must always remain behind us in the past, closed to effect, while future events remain basically unpredictable via technological means.

In other words, time appears to demonstrate no physical deviation or variance to human perception. Time's arrow moves but in one direction for us, forward.

Modern technology has become so preoccupied with electronically duplicating human physical functions, especially cerebral ones, it has all but ignored the one possible mechanism that might free us from our third-dimensional prison and allow some degree of freedom of movement within the fourth dimension.

Nature has, as usual, already beaten technology to the punch in that it has equipped us with a built-in time-displaced viewing and traveling device----one considered by science to be the most sophisticated and highly organized three pounds of matter in the known universe.

A group of over 10 billion differentiated cells that remain, for the most part, deeply entrenched in mystery, and still largely unexplored. Therein lays, perhaps, the greatest enigma in nature, the mind, possessing all the faculties by which time can be transcended.

Interestingly, the human brain, or more precisely, the mind, appears to be capable of predicting what a machine cannot. For instance, if we examine the reasons why machines cannot precisely predict future events, one fact discovered is that the nature of our physical universe seems random, and it is this randomness that underlies our current belief in free will as opposed to predestination.

The greatest major stumbling block regarding a machine's ability to predict specific details of the future is the Heisenberg Uncertainty Principle. This principle quite simply states that at our present stage of technology, we are incapable of foretelling and analyzing the exact position and momentum of certain elementary particles (Brownian movement) in relationship to one another.

Such information appears to be mutually interdependent, making it virtually impossible to ascertain through present scientific means. The activity of such elementary particles is thought to be absolutely random. However, experiments with this most random process in nature, the quantum process, indicates that it is definitely predictable. Not by a machine mind you, but by the human mind.

Certain gifted individuals have been able to accurately predict the random atomic decay of radioactive Strontium 90 enclosed in special devices (Schmidt, 1969). According to current physical theories in particle physics, however, the process of foretelling the quantum breakdown of a radioactive isotope is insoluble.

Radioactivity can be measured and predicted instrumentally only on a macroscopic scale; we can determine how many atoms in a given sample will decay in a given time. But we cannot say which atom will next decay, nor when a given atom will decay, as it could happen now or perhaps not for a million years.

Assuming that brain's capacity to predict this quantum breakdown process is not a misinterpreted function or product of psychokinesis, there may be something inherently unique within the human psyche that at the present time cannot be clinical reproduced.

If all aspects of the physical world we live in are indeed governed by the quantum process, which is psychically predictable, would it not then be safe to assume that any event in nature is predictable by the same mechanism?

The paranormal ability to perceive events displaced in time has two fundamental names or categories, depending upon where in time the data supposedly originates. If the event has already occurred in the past and is extrasensorily perceived, it is then referred to as retrocognition. Conversely, if the event has not yet taken place and is foretold accurately, free of logical inference and deduction, it is termed precognition.

Information about the past that is available to a person at any given time does not mainly consist of their sense data. Indeed, we usually do not think of sense data as giving information about the past because of the finite time required for any known type of signal to propagate across space and affect our senses.

Instead, our information about the past comes either from inferences we draw from observations we make or through the poorly understood process known as memory, through which we can bring into present awareness observations that we, or others, have made previously and which have somehow been stored in our brains.

A plausible analogy regarding information about the past and future would suggest that if information about the future is available to us at all, the main source of it could well be observations that we will make in the future and which are then stored in our brains. It might be expected that whatever the mechanism of precognition, it could work more easily on the future state of the percipient's own brain than on the world outside.

In other words, precognition could basically be a "remembering" of things future, an analogy to memory rather than a perception of future events. Moreover, an analogy to sense perception of the very recent past. We might refer to this information process as precall, the inverse of recall, and technically define such a function as a pre-memory or premory.

Of particular interest here is the occurrence of refabrication in memory. The best example of this is when one is asked to remember an event from the relatively distant past that was of little or no significance to us. A person may experience difficulty in accurately recalling the details, so the brain automatically fills in what he or she expects to have occurred, such as the room furnishings, clothes of those present and conversations that took place.

Almost invariably, this refabricated memory is incorrect and the individual asking for the remembrance is somewhat shocked as to how poor and inaccurate the other person's memory is. This type of information processing is extremely common and is not to be thought of as abnormal or pathological.

This is the way our brain happens to work. Like has been said of nature, our brain abhors a vacuum. It is just that a majority of the population is not in possession of a photographic memory. Only the most relevant and emotionally significant or recent information appears to remain directly available to conscious memory.

Precisely the same type of information distortion occurs within paranormal perception. In terms of signals that are presumably propagating from some source in space-time, this distortion is referred to as "noise," as opposed to the signal. Much, if not all, paranormal information is loaded with this noise, which is commonly known as "primary process" material.

It is assumed that when sensory input reaches the brain, an oscillatory variation of some internal patterns in the brain occurs, which is related to input. This oscillatory pattern persists for some period of time in at least part of the brain. When a person remembers the stimulus, the stored oscillatory pattern is reconstructed and influences another part of the brain, bringing memory into consciousness, or at least something accessible to consciousness.

This is, of course, a very sketchy description of one model for short-term memory. There are indications that long-term memory involves distinctly different mechanisms.

Suppose that the oscillatory pattern set up by an external stimulus has a retarded wave potential associated with it, which propagates forward in time and in addition possesses an advanced wave potential, propagating backwards in time. More simply, signals are sent out in both directions of time from an event, into both the past and future (Tiller, 1972, Feinberg, 1974, Dean, 1974).

Since the retarded part of the oscillation allows memory of the past to occur and is known to persist for at least some time without great attenuation, it is possible that the advanced oscillation would be able to propagate for a corresponding time into the past before the stimulus occurs.

So at least over this period of time by a process similar to memory of the past, it may be possible for the advanced patterns to be brought into conscious focus, so that one would "remember" the future stimulus connected with the advanced pattern.

If the retarded oscillatory pattern is correlated with short-term memory, and if the latter has a relatively short term of operation, then we could expect that the advanced pattern would also have a similarly short range into the past. This would imply that precognition is effective only for events in the not very distant future, perhaps on the scale of several hours to weeks.

Within this time period, precognition would be expected to show a "decay" curve similar to that shown by ordinary memory.

Thus, precognition becomes easier as the percipient becomes closer to forthcoming events. Signals would then attenuate across time as conventional signals attenuate across space. The further away from the signal source or event in time one happens to be, the lower the probability if perceiving it.

If this model of precognition is correct, there should be little or no spatial dependence of the primary event or signal source and the ability to precognize it. This is because precognition would operate on the future state of the percipient's own brain rather than directly on the distant event.

For example, if there were a supernova explosion in a distant galaxy, whose light will reach Earth twenty years from now, precognition would be able to give a warning of the explosion before the lights reaches Earth about as well as it could disclose an event that occurs in the percipient's immediate vicinity. Distance between percipient and event, therefore is irrelevant.

In accordance with current knowledge in behavioral science, we would expect the same kinds of external and internal stimuli that are known to affect ordinary memory, such as drugs, fatigue, age, training and altered states of consciousness, to have similar effects on precognition. This particular aspect offers an intriguing possibility that will be explored later.

One major inconsistency in this model is that it should not be possible for a person to precognize an event that will occur after his or her death, since no sensory input about that incident could ever reach the brain.

This conclusion is independent of the length of time that the advanced oscillatory pattern can propagate into the past. It is consistent with some beliefs and one old legend to the effect that prophets cannot foretell their own deaths, but it is inconsistent with other legends.

Contradicting this imposed limitation are such prophecies as those of the 16th- century French physician Nostradamus, who accurately foretold events that occurred hundreds of years after his death. Of even greater interest here is the manner by which Nostradamus purportedly observed the future. In his work Centuries, he describes a crude sort of time viewing machine consisting of fire, water, air and a glass tripod.

It was this seemingly dubious instrument that supposedly provided Nostradamus with his detailed future imagery. Unfortunately, heavy religious persecution forced Nostradamus to phrase his predictions in allegories, riddles and rhymes. Or perhaps he too experienced primary process distortion within his precognitive visions and cloaked such "noise" in a convenient form?

Of equal merit at contradicting short-term precognition is the outstanding incident surrounding Morgan Robertson, author of Futility and The Sinking of the Titan. In 1898, Robertson within these books, almost perfectly describes the ill-fated maiden voyage of the Titanic in 1912.

In his recurring dream that lead to the books, Robertson's primary process distortion dropped the "ic" off Titanic and called his gigantic ocean liner Titan. His discussion of the Titan's size and displacement, it striking an iceberg in the north Atlantic during April and the more than 1,500 people who drowned, is certainly beyond anyone's idea of coincidence.

I for one believe that the fourteen years between the publication of the book and Titanic's sinking should certainly not be considered a short-term precognition.

Moreover, according to this physical theory, one can only precall things which one will eventually sense or learn via someone else's report. That is to say, the probability of anyone precognizing a totally removed event that is never directly known about or experienced is theoretically quite small.

However, once again, research has indicated that exactly this kind of experience can occur. Most frequently, it involves an event that has strong, subjective emotional significance and overtones for the percipient, even though he may never learn of it. More simply, this is what researchers refer to as "need relevance." This variable appears to be an important factor mediating paranormal perception.

Before the validity of this "precall" hypothesis can be tested, the logical question to be asked is: "Why are future memories or premories not more frequent? Most individuals do not generally experience difficulty remembering recent past events, so why is the same then not true of precalling future information?

Again drawing from psychology, the answer may deal with our conditioning to a positively time-ordered environment with respect to cause and effect. Responding continually to such a world would very likely cause normal sensory cognition and memory to overshadow, if not completely overwhelm and nullify the differentially weaker precall information, preventing it from being recognized unless it carries an intense, emotionally significant impact for the percipient.

More simply, in a normal waking state of consciousness during which people are continually bombarded by sensory input, premories might take on the flavor of a hunch, gut feeling, premonition or intuition, and automatically be dismissed as an overactive imagination.

That is, unless and until the event does occur as perceived. If one's conditioned beliefs do not incorporate such phenomena as reality, then a "premory" might be looked upon as a lucky guess or even a unique coincidence. It most probably would take some form of altered state of consciousness, inhibiting normal sensory input and shifting the mind away from the outside world to allow relatively unobstructed precall. That is where our demonstration of a real premory begins.

One of the most efficient and successful methods of safely altering a person's consciousness to induce or aid in the generation of mental psi imagery, is Ganzfeld stimulation. Ganzfeld literally means "homogeneous field."

This technique involves placing halved ping-pong balls (or specialized goggles) over a subject's eyes and seating them directly in front of a bright red light (like a photographic safety light) in an otherwise darkened room. Continuous "white noise," a sound like that of softly pounding surf, is played through headphones.

In this condition, the subject has no access to visual or auditory stimulation. The translucent ping-pong hemispheres (or goggles) illuminated by the red light create a totally homogeneous visual field and after several minutes, subjects often report an inability to determine whether their eyes are open or closed. The color being viewed changes and their spacetime orientation is altered (Avant, 1965).

The reasons for using this particular induction technique are quite simple. For example, we know that Psi or ESP often surfaces in consciousness via mental imagery. Ganzfeld stimulation creates or induces similar images.

As was briefly mentioned earlier, Psi rarely occurs in waking consciousness among most individuals because it is submerged in the bombardment of normal sensory stimuli that affect us daily. The Ganzfeld stimulation blocks our normal access to sensory stimulation and the subject is more apt to "tune in" to extrasensory impressions.

On the night of Tuesday, February 3, 1976, at approximately 10:49 P.M. (PST), I was conducting an exploratory telepathy experiment with the aid of Ganzfeld stimulation. The subject, on what was to be a most eventful evening, was a very attractive 27-year old woman, Karen, who by profession was a freelance photographer.

She had previously expressed an interest in working with the Ganzfeld, and the fact that she claimed to have experienced some intense, although spontaneous paranormal phenomena during her youth added to the decision to test her with this technique.

After attaching the ping pong hemispheres over her eyes, turning off the room lights and switching on the red light in front of her, Karen was instructed simply to think out loud; to describe all her impressions and imagery. She was told that her free verbal responses would be recorded on tape so there would be no question about what she had said after the session.

A set of headphones was then positioned over her ears and the white noise generator was turned on and adjusted to gently drown out extraneous sounds in her immediate environment.

Within seconds, Karen began to utter verbalizations of detailed and intense imagery, even before the first telepathic "target" was brought out and concentrated on. The stimulus or target in this case was a drawing from NASA of a futuristic space station. It was hoped that under Ganzfeld stimulation, Karen might describe some of the characteristics associated with the agent's impressions while viewing the drawing.

But Karen's responses turned out to be of much greater significance than dealing with the trivial elements of the target drawing. A verbatim transcript of her verbalized imagery follows:

"I see a woman with dark skin and dark hair. She's not black, but dark skinned...she's somewhere south of Mexico...her hair is pulled back and tied...the land around her is very humid and tropical and there is definitely something wrong here.

Everything is coming apart...shaking violently...the ground is splitting and cracking...I guess it's an earthquake or something...buildings are crumbling and collapsing...falling and crashing to the ground...thousands and thousands of people are falling and being buried beneath these buildings that are breaking up...all these people are being crushed and dying...there are many people lying on stretchers, bleeding horribly...terribly injured. The ground is like jelly or water...not solid...are there are loud, horribly loud sounds...like roaring...like a jet engine next to my ears.

Something about the 4th comes in....it's the 4th of the month...the date is really important...I don't know if its this month or when...but I know that it's the 4th of the month. This scene is making me sick to my stomach with all the wounded and dead bodies...the injured children on stretchers...it's awful.

Aliens Above, Ghosts Below by Barry E. Taff

Another series of numbers keeps flashing in my head...three...three o'clock in the morning....all this seems to be happening at about this time in the morning....it's dark outside....I can't really see very well except for the fires....it's so dark...everything is moving....the ground is swaying back and forth really hard....it's making me feel like car or motion sickness, or even sea sickness....can I stop now?...I really feel nauseous and sick."

It took a while to calm Karen down, after which she agreed to continue the experiment. We proceeded to follow through with the planned targets that were prepared earlier. The exploratory Ganzfeld was partially successful, as Karen perceived some salient characteristics of several targets.

The most significant responses, however, were not those of her telepathic "hits," but what she had said earlier. The experiment was far more successful that either of us had realized. Not at telepathy, as desired, but precognition.

It was not until the next morning, Wednesday the 4th of February at about 8:30 A.M. (PST), that the news came in over the radio that there had been a 7.5 magnitude earthquake in Guatemala early that morning. It became immediately apparent what had happened some nine hours earlier with Karen.

Her first impressions, which we regarded as nothing more than sheer fantasy, fabrication of mind or overworked imagination, turned out to be an accurate description of what was going to occur some five hours later more than 1,500 miles away.

To say that Karen was startled upon hearing the news would be an understatement, for she herself did not know why she had perceived those startling images the night before.

Some hard-nosed skeptics and debunkers, of course, have said, and will say, that Karen's impressions were simply random gibberish amounting to no more than mere coincidence regarding the Guatemala earthquake.

Critics pointed out that there are hundreds of earthquakes each year, especially where tectonic plates meet (such as near Guatemala), and the mere synchronistic relationship between Karen's impressions and the event are therefore negligible and meaningless.

As the debunkers continually refer to probabilities as criteria for determining the validity of paranormal phenomena, it is worth briefly noting the statistics involved here. The question we must first ask is just how many serious quakes are there every year, how many of those occur in the region of Guatemala, and what is the ratio of Karen's prior earthquake predictions compared to her accuracy or "hit" rate?

By definition, a major quake registers magnitude 7 or more on the Richter scale and a great quake registers 8-plus. According to the U.S. Geological Survey (USGS), as of 1977, the long-term average is for approximately 16-18 major and one great quake a year.

The USGS's Branch of Seismicity and Earth Structure (Denver, Colorado) computer program for estimating the probability of earthquake predictions (whether scientific or paranormal in nature) uses all known earthquakes from 1963 to 1974 as a database. Unfortunately, this is really too small a sample to obtain extremely accurate statistical probabilities (especially in view of the large number of major and great quakes between 1975 and 1977), so the results here must be viewed with caution.

The United States Geological Survey (USGS) computer evaluation (as of 1977) of Karen's earthquake forecast or prediction stated that for the geological location south of Mexico City, in the magnitude range of 7 to 8, with a time range of 1 day, there are 0.01 quakes of this size in this area and time span.

193

The quake discussed here has a probability of 0.005 (one-half of one percent) of occurring by chance alone. In other words, this prediction has a probability of 0.995 (99.5%) of not being due to chance.

As to Karen's hit record, one does not exist. She has never previously predicted such an event, and has not since. In other words, she is one-for-one.

When we review and thoroughly analyze the startling parallels between Karen's perception and the actual event, it's evident to the most ardent disbeliever that some type of informational reception in advance of the event did in fact occur.

Karen began her verbalizations by describing a dark skinned woman with dark hair somewhere south of Mexico, the surrounding land being very humid and tropical in nature. The quake occurred in Guatemala, which is south of Mexico and is populated primarily by dark skinned (not black), dark haired people. The climate of this region is classified as extremely humid and tropical.

Numerous film clips and photographs of the actual quake damaged area released by the news media showed many children and adults on stretchers, wounded and bleeding. Hundreds if not thousands of buildings crumbled and collapsed, trapping and burying people within their disintegrating structures. Karen's comments about a loud roaring, like that of a jet engine, correspond to remarks made by many of the survivors, who described the intense rumbling sound of the ground during the quake.

The fourth of the month kept coming up in Karen's utterances, a date that she stressed as very important. Indeed it was, for the fourth of February proved to be the exact date of the quake. Her other reference to three o'clock in the morning was approximately when the quake hit.

After this hit-by-hit comparative analysis between the event and Karen's vision, it appears this amazing "coincidence" as some might call it, incorporates not only precise details and the approximate location but the date and time as well. How much more specific can a description be? Believe it or not, most skeptics would probably argue the point that Karen did not actually say Guatemala!

Considering that we are dealing here with a subtle, diffuse and often distorted form of information processing, the precision and accuracy of Karen's vision are remarkable. So remarkable, in fact, that when the tape recording of her voice was replayed on Wednesday (the fourth) evening, it bore a striking resemblance to news reports transmitted from Guatemala itself.

Although not in chronological order, a fascinating instance of precognition happened to this author in 1975.

While staying over my girlfriend Darlene's (from Chapter 6) apartment in West Los Angeles, I had a very disturbing dream. In my dream I'm piloting a TWA 747. The way I recognized this specific carrier was by the aircraft's color scheme…red and white, and of course the letters TWA helped a lot.

I'm in the cockpit looking out where I was able to observe that we were starting our descent and approach for landing in South Africa. As the cruising altitude of airliners is way too low to observe such graphic continental features, it's intriguing that I somehow knew we were approaching South Africa.

Suddenly, the drone of the four large turbofan engines ceased. The flight controls were dead and all the instruments were dark. The aircraft was losing altitude very rapidly,

194

dropping like a stone.

I went through all the normal procedures to re-fire the engines, but to no avail. Suddenly, the aircraft impacted the ground with tremendous force. The violent explosion blew the aircraft apart. The crash and resulting fire was so fierce that it figuratively and literally blew me out of bed, taking Darlene to the floor with me. I was covered in sweat.

After I told Darlene about the dream, I could immediately see the look on her face; that of worry, concern and puzzlement. When I calmed down, I did a little research and discovered that a 747 had, in fact, never before crashed. Remember, this was 1975 and Boeing 747's were in commercial service for only several years.

The problem from my perspective was that I had no information whatsoever as to when said crash would occur. Would it occur within days, weeks or months, and on what particular day at what time? Therefore, attempting to contact the FAA or TWA about my dream would prove to be futile and foolish, if not insane.

Five days later, the first 747 did, in fact, crash. It was a TWA and it crashed in South Africa. Talk about feeling helpless and overwhelmed by the forces around you. What's the point of knowing such things if one cannot intervene to prevent them?

Can you imagine the response of the FAA or one of major airlines if such a call was placed today in the aftermath of 911? How soon to do think it would be before the FBI would be at my door with guns drawn? I wonder if such a precognitive event as this will ever be put to the test in today's homeland security environment? How would such an event be played out given the current, overly paranoid concerns (and perhaps for good reason) of our government?

Speaking about preventing catastrophic events, another event, but this time a far more personal incident occurred to this author in the early spring of 1971.

I was a senior in college and met a beautiful girl in one of my classes named Sharon, who bared a striking resemblance to the contemporary actress Jane Krakowski. We began dating and everything seemed just fine. In many ways, Sharon was one of the better relationships I've ever had. She was one of the few blonde women I've ever dated. We were compatible in almost every way and shared many interests. But then came the dreams.

In these dreams I had about Sharon, I always found myself in the backseat of a late-model car. Sharon was in the passenger seat and although I did not see myself behind the wheel I assumed that I was the driver even though I was unable to distinguish even the car's dashboard layout.

We turned down the street Sharon lived on in Northridge, and as we approached the culdesac upon which her home rested, a speeding car came out of nowhere and hit us head on. The impact was extremely intense.

All I remembered about the other vehicle was that it was dark in color and medium sized. The car Sharon and I were in suffered extensive damage, leaving Sharon's broken and bloody body lying motionless before me.

The recurring nature of this dream was very disturbing for obvious reasons. After several days of these recurring nightmares, I broached the subject with Sharon and, as expected, she was not pleased. But not for the reasons one might expect.

Unfortunately, Sharon believed that I was fabricating this dream simply as a cheap way of ending our relationship. Sharon felt that as I lived in West Los Angeles and she lived all the way out in the northwestern San Fernando Valley, I simply didn't want to drive all that distance to see her.

In those days, the price of gasoline here in Los Angeles was around twenty-eight cents ($0.28) per gallon for high octane (I know, depressing, isn't it?), so the cost of fuel was not a concern. What was of concern was Sharon's well being as well as my own.

As this matter dragged on, Sharon became so upset that she just walked away from the relationship for what she felt were very obvious reasons. I really couldn't blame her, could I? What would I have done if the situation were reversed? Would I have believed her any more than she believed me? Probably not.

A short time later, Sharon was out on a date with someone else, and the dream I had, did, in fact, occur, with one significant exception; I was not in the car during the accident. Sharon was badly injured and has required continuous medical care throughout her life. Her date on that evening, the driver of the car she was in, unfortunately did not survive the violent collision.

Apparently, my ego and logic put me in the driver's seat during my dream. I foolishly believed that by no longer dating Sharon I would change the course of the future, thereby preventing the accident.

All that really occurred was that I incorrectly interpreted the precognized event. A very hard dose of reality to swallow at such a young age. So much for changing the shape of things to come!

This particular event somewhat reminds me of one of the original Twilight Zone episodes (CBS, 1959-1964) wherein Russell Johnson (the professor from Gillian's Island) travels back in time and attempts to prevent the assassination of President Abraham Lincoln in April of 1865. Johnson's character discovers that his inadequate recall of the assassination's specifics stops him from saving Lincoln's life at Ford's theater.

The conclusion of this particular Twilight Zone episode, that of Rod Serling's closing narration, is that some aspects of time are open to change while others are not. What if, in the end, we discover that future events are no different than those in the past, and that we have no more power to control our destiny than we can alter events of the past? It would be interesting to learn how such foreknowledge would alter the ways in which we currently live our lives? I wonder what we might do different or as to whether we would stubbornly attempt to alter what as to be?

Another, even more extraordinary precognitive incident occurred in 1978 during the course of one of our psi training groups held at UCLA on Wednesday nights. These training groups, which began in 1971, applied positive feedback and reinforcement incorporating a free-verbal response (FVR) as opposed to forced-choice method, as a learning paradigm to enhance paranormal perception.

In those halcyon times, these perceptions were referred to as telepathy, clairvoyance, precognition and retrocognition, as opposed to the all-encompassing "remote viewing" nomenclature of today. A rose by any other name.

As we had been conducting these groups for seven years, even the continued positive results we were achieving were now boring. You know, that been there, done that, sort of feeling. More specifically, the ability of reaching into another's mind or observing things at a distance, we now perceived as somewhat commonplace and ordinary. Hard to believe, I know. However, when there is high degree of success and continuity with such extraordinary research efforts, one tends to become jaded. I guess that this attitude is just part of being human?

In an effort to make things more interesting, we decided to attempt our first precognitive effort with this group.

We turned off the lights in the Neuropsychiatric Institutes's C-floor observation/conference room and went through our normal progressive muscular relaxation procedure. Once we had attained this hypo-metabolic state, we mentally focused on the "target" person of the next week's first session.

In a way, the verbal reinforcements given during this part of this session were similar to what Christopher Reeve as Richard Collier in Somewhere In Time (Universal, 1980) verbalized when attempting to physically transport himself back through time. Except of course, we didn't expect to physically travel in time, and obviously we weren't producing a fantasy film at the time either.

We began describing the "target" person as a tall, beautifully statuesque, blue-eyed blond girl dressed in a tan business suit. We continued our verbalizations into the centrally placed, amplified, microphone within the otherwise sensory-deprived room as we clearly saw the specific number on the chair in which she was sitting (there were twenty-four chairs in this conference room, each of which was numbered).

As the session continued, we "saw" a very large mansion-like home, within which was a large baby-grand piano. Numerous bits of varying types of personal information continued to flow from our mouths for quite some time. And then, silence.

Vocally piercing the darkened conference room, we all abruptly began describing a tall man wearing all black, with a black hat, black mask, a flowing black cape and an imposing sword. I remember thinking, what kind of crap are we uttering? The session ended and we didn't give much thought to what we had just said because it wasn't relevant yet.

It was now one week later and another group was about to begin. However, on this particular evening, no guest member from the prior week was allowed to bring a visitor. Any new participants on this night could only arrive through third parties who had not been in attendance for the last several weeks, i.e., through independent means.

When each new person arrived they were handed a sealed envelope with a number from one through twelve written on a piece of paper within it. Once in the conference room, we rolled the dice and then asked all new visitors to open their sealed envelopes. Whichever person's number fit the dice roll was the randomly chosen target person for the first session.

We had all pretty much forgotten what we had said a week earlier, so when a statuesque blue-eyed, blond girl's number matched the dice roll, we didn't give it second thought.

I asked this stunning 19-yr old woman, named Toni, to replay the audiotape from the week before and if she heard any statements that directly related to her, stop the tape and comment on them. If the statements were incorrect, let the tape run without interruption. Toni didn't immediately understand what I just said, forcing me clarify this protocol again.

Toni listens, as voices clearly describe her appearance and clothing in detail as well as the exact number of the chair she is seated in. Her look is one of astonishment, although the best was yet to come. When she hears the specific description of the mansion in the hills with the baby grand piano, her eyes open even wider, as those data points were also correct. But those could have been coincidence, couldn't they?

However, then came what I believe to be one of the most fascinating pieces of precognized information that has ever been documented? Let's see if you agree.

Aliens Above, Ghosts Below by Barry E. Taff

When we finished our discourse on the black costumed man with the mask and sword, Toni let out a somewhat muffled scream. There was hesitation in her voice and for good reason.

Toni looked at me and said: "How do you know who I am?" My immediate response was to look at her while shrugging my shoulders, "What do you mean, who you are?" Toni tells our group that her full name is "Toni Williams". We all looked at Toni with blank, expressionless faces, as we did not understand what she was referring to. Who was Toni Williams?

Realizing that our group really didn't know who "Toni Williams" was, she connected the dots for us. Apparently, Toni knew all too well exactly who the masked, darkly dressed, swordsman was. In fact, she knew him for her entire life.

The ornately costumed man turned out to be her father, Guy Williams, the actor who played Zorro in the Disney television series from the late fifties and early sixties. You might better remember Guy Williams from another TV series in the mid-sixties, where he played Professor John Robinson in CBS's Lost In Space.

Toni was speechless and just a little frightened. She looked at all of us as though we were beings from another reality. She sheepishly asked when this tape was made and we told her exactly one week earlier. However, Toni did not even know of, or that she was even coming to our group until several hours earlier that very day!

Toni's question was a simple one. How could we have so accurately described her and her surroundings seven days earlier when she wasn't even aware of us, or of our group?

Indeed, how could we have perceived such an event unless the information pertaining to it already existed? What are the odds of us accurately describing such state specific information about an event one hundred and sixty eight hours before it occurred?

What's the probability of our precisely describing the Zorro character as related to his daughter one week prior to her random appearance and selection as a target in our group? A million-to-one? A billion-to-one? A trillion-to-one? Okay, let's just say astronomical and leave it at that! Does this event sound like we were randomly guessing as to the shape of things to come? Believe it or not, there have been those individuals over the decades that actually believed that we somehow deduced or logically inferred the information described herein. What do you think?

Needless to say, Toni never again returned to participate in one of our research groups, as her one experience with us was more than enough. I can certainly understand how unsettling such an unusual experience can be. But then, as I think about it, maybe I can't.

As we were all very impressed with our first foray into the future, we attempted to replicate our results several months later, little knowing what the full emotional effects of such accurately precognized information would have on some of us.

During this second attempt things went very differently though. All any of us could "sense" was fire, and more fire. We didn't know why this was, but it certainly wasn't worth getting all that upset over. Well, at least, not until the next day.

On that following Thursday, while up in the lab on 2-South of the NPI, I heard the arrival of many fire engines. Racing down to the C-Floor, I discovered that our conference room had apparently caught fire due to a shorting socket that sparked the drapes covering the room's west-facing wall. What a coincidence and shock (oops, there's another pun). And no, I did not start the fire myself to produce a self-fulfilling prophecy.

After these two successful treks into the future, several of our regular group members became depressed and starting having anxiety attacks about the possibility that the future is as immutable as the past, and that free will may be little more than an illusion.

My response to these reactions was simple, "Who cares! We're still going to live out our lives making daily judgments and choices without knowing the shape of things to come whether the future is random and open to change or predestined." For some reason, my attitude regarding such matters doesn't seem to be shared by many others. Why is that?

For some reason, I cannot as yet fathom the belief that reality is random and chaotic. To me personally, my experiences and research strongly suggest that reality is finitely ordered and predetermined, and this belief gives me a sense of inner peace.

Maybe I just can't accept the notion that anything as vast and extraordinarily intricate and complex as the universe could be the result of random, chaotic energy. No way! Or perhaps, I've had way too many precognitive experiences growing up, both in and out of the lab environment to believe otherwise?

In this regard, there is another precognitive event from my past at the UCLA lab that I believe is worthy of consideration.

In early 1978 and I had a very vivid dream about the parapsychology lab I worked in at UCLA. In this dream, we're all at the lab, Dr. Moss, Kerry, John and Francis as well as this author.

Suddenly, the head of the NPI, Dr. West, walked in and began talking about his dislike of the work we were doing. In the midst of his ranting, the entire room began to violently shake, as though we were suffering a major earthquake.

As the shaking continued, the room felt as though it was falling and the entire building was collapsing beneath us. We all attempted to grab onto something in response. Then, the shaking and falling sensations abruptly ceased. These motions were now replaced by others, that of moving horizontally.

All of our attention was immediately drawn to the lab's windows facing west. We were indeed moving horizontally. However, there was an odd wooden plank of sorts upon which sat the rotted corpse of a woman. To her right, was the rotted and mangled corpse of a large German Shepard.

Upon seeing these bizarre "corpses", Dr. West let out a loud scream. He told us that the woman sitting upon the plank was his dead sister and that the dog was her old German Shepard that was also dead.

Then the room's motion entirely ceased. I opened the only door the lab had and stepped out into what should have been the hallway. Surprise! No hallway, no building.

The image we were presented with was right out a horror movie. We were now outdoors. Under a brilliant full moon, the ground appeared as moist, dark, freshly turned earth, with a subtle shrouding of fog hanging over it. Immediately before me were crude wooden steps that led down towards the ground.

Once upon the ground, I turned back and was shocked to discover that our lab's room had turned into a early-to-mid 19th century funeral coach with glass walls and candled lights at each corner. Sitting atop the driver's bench was the rotted corpse-like woman with the mangled German Shepard.

I asked our "corpse driver" what all this was. She or it, immediately answered, "I've brought you here to bury you because you're dead." How nice of her to inform me of such.

I immediately awoke covered in sweat with a feeling that my heart was about to explode out of chest. Can you say high anxiety night terror?

Words cannot convey my emotional reaction to this dream. It goes without saying that my first thought was that perhaps there would be a major earthquake and the entire NPI would collapse causing all of our deaths. Not a pleasant thought.

After I had some time to logically and rationally think about the dream, there was a far more likely possibility that what I perceived was a horror-laden, melodramatic metaphor of our lab dying.

Of course, I had no way of knowing which of these interpretations was correct, although the second one seemed more likely. I discussed my dream with Thelma, and she too thought it was little more than my insecurities about the lab's future producing a fearful dream.

While this may have been partially correct, all of us in the lab were well aware of how Dr. West, the NPI's officials and UCLA' administrators in general, felt about our work.

Even in those early years, there was the formal, academic concern over political correctness. Therefore, we all knew that we, and the lab, were living on borrowed time so to speak, as we had access to all the facilities and services of a conventional lab without any funding whatsoever.

I did not totally subscribe to Thelma's belief that my dream was nothing more than my subconscious fears regarding the lab's inevitable demise, as it was common knowledge to all concerned that the lab's days were numbered. The possibility of our lab's imminent death was no more on my mind at that moment in time that at any other.

After the passage of several days and then weeks, I pretty much forgot about this bizarre dream, and perhaps for good reason. Several weeks' later Dr. West made an unexpected visit to the lab. I'll bet you can guess what happened next?

Dr. West proceeded to tell us that our lab would be shut down and its space given to others who had funding available that would pay for the requisite facilities and services we were getting free of charge. Well, I guess nothing lasts forever, does it?

As Dr. West was leaving the lab I asked him if I could speak with him for a moment and he agreed. I do not know what gave me the courage to ask Dr. West if he has a sister, but I did. His reply was very enlightening.

Apparently, he did have a sister. Naturally, given the content of my dream, I had to ask, "What do you mean, did? He said that she died some time ago. My immediate follow up to his reply was, "May I inquire as to what caused her death?" "She suffered a protracted death from cancer which wasted most of her body", the doctor said. My immediate reply to Dr. West was to give my condolences. He thanked me, but then asked why I asked about his sister and I told him that someone had mentioned it to me some time ago and I was curious.

As I might never again have an opportunity to speak with Dr. West in such a casual manner, I quickly asked him one last question. "Did your sister have a dog?" West looked at me very strangely, cocking his head to one side, probably trying to figure out why I was asking such obscure questions of him.

He thought for a moment, finally answering. "Why yes, she used to have a dog." I immediately followed up with, "What breed of dog?", "A German Shepard, he responded. "What happened to that dog?" I asked. Again, Dr. West looked at me as though I was a police detective conducting an intense interrogation of a suspect.

However, the good doctor answered my final question in saying that his sister's German Shepard was killed in a violent auto accident many years before she herself passed.

I thanked Dr. West for his time and he walked away, never suspecting the real reason I asked such bizarre questions of a literal stranger. Had I told him of my dream, he very likely would have thought that I belonged in the NPI as an inpatient, as he was extremely skeptical about such matters.

Having learned what I just did, it was obvious that my dream had a very common form of distortion called "primary process". In laymen's terms, this is a method by which our subconscious mind colors or modifies information going to our conscious mind that might otherwise be too painful or difficult to deal with. Primary process distortion could be looked at as the noise as related to the signal.

Obviously, the thought of our lab closing was one that was far too painful for my conscious mind to deal with, so my unconscious cleverly cloaked it with the melodrama of a low-budget, Roger Corman, horror movie. This is certainly preferable to dying during an earthquake while in the lab, isn't it?

This type of distortion is extremely common when dealing with paranormal perception. In fact, it's very rare when such does not occur.

Speaking of the old UCLA lab, there was one really strange incident that occurred to me during my time working at this facility. This event is not of the mental type, such as precognition, it is purely physical as in psychokinetic, as in apport.

An apport, which was discussed in earlier chapters of the first section, is when objects disappear and/or reappear from within closed physical environments via an unknown mechanism.

I believe it was late one evening in 1975, I do not recall the exact month or day, but it must have been a weekday, because it involved my being at the lab earlier in that particular day.

It was very late one evening when I realized that I left my pen in the lab. Now before you think I've totally lost my mind, please understand that this was a very special personalized gold pen, with my initials (B.E.T., long before the Black Entertainment Television) and birth date engraved in it. An ex-girlfriend gave me this pen as a gift several years earlier.

I called John, who also worked in the lab, at home and he remembered seeing it by the phone just before he left. Immediately, I was concerned that one of the janitors might pick it up and that would be the last time I ever saw it. We were frequently reminded to never leave anything of personal value in the lab unless it was locked in the isolation booth.

Of course, I could always go back to the campus in the dead of night and go through security in order to get my pen. However, I was too tired to do that at such a late hour.

I decided to just go to sleep and hope for the best. Given my concern over this pen I found it very hard to sleep even though I was exhausted. I was mentally beating myself up over such a foolish act of leaving this special pen behind in the lab.

Take a guess as to what happened next? Just as I was about to fall off into slumber I distinctly felt something hit the bed next to me. It was my pen. Not any pen, mind you, but that one-of-a-kind, personally engraved, gold, Parker T-ball jotter.

Aliens Above, Ghosts Below by Barry E. Taff

Now there are endless numbers of personalized pens on the earth, but how many were of that specific model with my specific initials and birth date engraved on it?

So, we call this an apport, do we? Well, it would be nice if there were a way to replicate this incredible event, which of course, there is not. And let's not even touch upon how such an event might possibly transpire within the physical world in which we currently reside.

Well, at least I got my pen back and that was what the whole thing was about to begin with, was it not? So in the end, the apport served my needs quite well. Although, I have other, far more serious needs at the moment, and nothing is apporting its way into my life. Damn. Why doesn't this physical paranormal stuff ever work when you really need it to?

And wouldn't you know it, several years later while out a case, I lost this pen again, never to recover it. What does that mean? God only knows. Although I really wonder if the Parker pen company would find this story of interest?

There is another incident that while not as state specific in terms of its informational content about the future nevertheless demonstrates a high degree of strangeness associated with it. Perhaps this one could fall under the heading of synchronicity...a seeming acausal linkage between two events in time.

Ever since I was a child and saw a particular character actor on television, Edward Andrews to be specific, I had a very strong impression that I knew him. His appearance, his voice, everything about him was familiar to the point that it started bothering me. I told many of my friends and family members about this and they basically ignored me.

Jump ahead to the middle 1980's and I was called out to a house in Pacific Palisades here in southern California to investigate a potential haunting. The woman calling me was Mrs. Edward Andrews. Yes, Edward Andrews' wife.

I arrived and met both Mr. and Mrs. Edward Andrews. Immediately, Edward looks at me and said, "Do we know each other? You look really familiar?" What was I supposed to say? But wait, there's more.

At some point, their daughter walked in and they introduced her to me. I do not remember her name, but I do vividly recall her nickname, "Taff". Taffy, where did that come from?

When I asked the Andrews' how their daughter came by the nickname of Taffy, they simply shrugged their shoulders. They didn't know. I guess they didn't note any synchronistic link between my last name and their daughter's nickname. But then again, I never told them about my precognitive knowledge regarding Edward either, did I?

What does this mean? I haven't the foggiest notion, although it does bring to mind yet another instance where a personal precognitive event had no direct relevance other than feeding a long-term obsession I have regarding a very specific look in women.

During the early spring of 1998 I had a very specific dream. In the dream, I am going to a local bookstore here in L.A. called the Bodhi Tree, which I've bought many books from over the decades. As the dream continued, I met a strikingly beautiful woman who was my exact physical stereotype in every way. Upon awakening the next morning, my path that day was all too clear.

I had not paid a visit to the Bodhi Tree in quite some time, so maybe this was the impetus to go. As the parking in this bookstore's neighborhood is literally impossible, I ended up parking about five blocks away.

On my way to the Bodhi Tree, I passed another shop called the Crystalarium, located in the southwest corner mini-mall at Melrose and La Cienega Blvd., which sells large geodes and crystals for those folks with lots of disposable income. As this was a relatively new shop I decided to go in see what was so special about this place.

After examining the store's contents, one of the shop's employees came out to see if I had any disposable income, which of course, I did not. When a female voice asked if she could help me, I looked up and was immediately frozen in my tracks.

There before me was the girl I saw in my dream the night before. We started talking and one thing lead to another. Eventually, she asked my name and I asked for her's. She got very excited after learning my name, which kind a freaked me out a bit.

Apparently, I had spoken with her and one of her friends years earlier when they worked together at another job and she had been trying to contact me ever since. However, she and her friend had a falling out and this girl, Laura, didn't have any contact information on me.

As the store was empty except for Laura and I, we talked at great length. I discovered that she suffers from acute agoraphobia (fear of being in public or open spaces), and that with the exception of her working, she never goes out to dinner, movies, plays, museums, beaches, vacations, whatever. She just sits at home reading books and watching movies and videos. Sounds like a real fun date, and a cheap one at that. Yeah, for a corpse.

But given her strikingly beautiful appearance, I suspect that her agoraphobia came from chronically being hit upon by every man that ever gazed upon her. As a man, I cannot even begin to imagine what the emotional toll might be if this had been occurring for many years.

Now just imagine the emotional fallout if said woman was negatively reinforced by her parents and jealous classmates during her formative years, resulting in her having very low self-esteem? We know all too well how often that occurs in our society regarding beautiful women, don't we?

However, as I am not a shut in, and do not suffer from any phobias, except that of being attracted to emotionally disturbed woman, I felt that Laura was nothing more than a accident waiting to happen.

Adding more fool to the fire, Laura and I talked several more times and I discovered that she was currently living with a boyfriend. However, she appeared to be ready, willing and able to jump ship, if said ship was very capable of supporting and caring for her needs, as few as they may be.

Well, at least in this respect, Laura was exceptionally normal, and fortunately for me, my ship was still in dry dock (or in my case, space dock) under construction, waiting to sale as in Star Trek: The Motion Picture (Paramount, 1979).

Finally, Laura suggested that we meet for a drink after work. Wait a minute, isn't there a contradiction here from what Laura had just previously said? Didn't she just say that she can't go anywhere other than work?

As tempting as this offer was, I didn't feel like getting involved in someone's failing relationship, especially as the girl was "dead from the neck up" as far as I was concerned.

There is a reason to my madness of reporting this semi-final (thank God, I know) incident. It is that our subliminal paranormal perceptions may be directing our actions and behavior in some manner, especially if we pay any degree of attention to such perceptions. It may be that our subconscious wants and needs are being met by this ability. In simpler terms, it is that we are unconsciously being drawn towards or pushed away from those elements that are most relevant to our needs and desires.

In the incidents cited above, this theory was clearly demonstrated. The reason I dreamt about Laura is that she is physically what I find to be very attractive and therefore my mind reached out in my dream in order to bring me to that image, even though it would never be fulfilled. Remember, in my dream all that transpired was that I met her, and that's exactly what occurred, and nothing more.

Another personal account of this need-relevant precognition mechanism occurred to this author in the middle 1970's.

I kept having dreams about meeting a young Joan Collins, about my age. In the dreams, she kept calling the name Barry, but she wasn't referring to me. I told my friends, my colleagues and pretty much anyone who would listen about this recurring dream. They got pretty sick of it and I didn't blame them.

First, let me say at the outset, that Joan Collins was my exact physical stereotype, although a little too old for me now (preferably as she appeared in Harlan Ellison's "City On The Edge of Forever" episode of the original Star Trek series or as she looked in the feature film Land of The Pharaohs.

Over the course of several decades, I have had numerous girlfriends who bared a striking physical resemblance to Joan (nine in total), many of whom you've already met in earlier chapters. I guess you'd call this an obsession of sorts, wouldn't you? Well, at least if I have to have an obsession, it might as well be a beautiful one. Beauty yes, but at what cost?

Not long thereafter, we were called out on a haunting case in Encino within the San Fernando Valley. We arrived and rang the doorbell. The woman who opened the door was a dead ringer for Joan Collins, with the exception that her age was the same as mine.

You'll never guess what the first name of this woman's husband was? You guessed it, Barry. Need I say more? What an incredible coincidence. Well, the case (with the younger "Joan clone") was not one of note due to the low frequency and magnitude of activity. However, this woman, whose name is of no consequence, wanted to have an extramarital affair with me. Now that was a surprise. As I refuse to do to another what I wouldn't want done to me, I refused her offer.

My friends and associates stopped questioning my dreams after this one. But that too, was short lived. I guess this does become boring and hard to swallow for those who have not lived with it as long and intensely as this author has?

There is yet another, extraordinary synchronistic link between Joan Collins and this author's life. In the late spring of 1976, an article appeared on the front page of Los Angeles Times' View Section ("Ghost Watch in Hollywood", June 2, 1976, pp. 1, 7 & 14) discussing a haunting case we were investigating in the Hollywood Hills. A photograph of this author was part of that article.

As was usual for mainstream journalism at that time, the article was somewhat cynical and tongue-in-cheek, but did acknowledge the scope and magnitude of the paranormal activity going on at the Hollymont Drive location (see Chapter 1).

Now comes the real high strangeness as related to this author. If you turn the first page of that Los Angeles Times' article over, you find a photo of Joan Collins right on the back of my photograph.

Interesting, as Joan Collins is the one and only image deeply burned into my subconscious at a very young age regarding feminine beauty. But what in the hell does this mean? Perhaps it is nothing more than my seeking order within the otherwise randomly, chaotic world in which we live.

The real question is; from where does this singular obsession originate? The answer to this question lies within the wallpaper and ring tone of my cell phone, and might be discussed in a future book (that assumes that this one ever gets published and sells).

This specific, complicated aspect of my life is far stranger than anything you've read in this book thus far. Therefore, this necessitates my evaluating the merits and wisdom of discussing it within another publication.

Several years later in 1978, I again began having the same dreams about meeting a young Joan Collins. The only real difference in this case is that this "Joan-clone" was brought to me.

One Wednesday night at one of our psi-training groups, a girl by the name of Margo showed up with her friend Susan who had previously attended. As in the earlier instance, Margo was a virtual physical duplicate of Joan with the exception of her age, which was slightly younger than myself. Her beauty was truly breathtaking. She almost didn't look real. More manufactured, than alive.

Needless to say, we began dating and had a very brief relationship. While there was intense physical attraction between us, Margo unfortunately came from an extremely dysfunctional family, in which her father abused her physically and emotionally at every turn. In fact, Margo's first marriage ended in dismal failure because she married a man just like dear, old dad. What a surprise?

So, as I was not her father, nor a man who would abuse anyone, let alone a woman for any reason, the relationship went nowhere fast. She ended our attempt at a relationship because I was not behaving correctly, that is, abusively.

Years passed, and in October of 1990 while taking a shower one morning, Joan or should I say Margo, entered my mind for no apparent reason. Oh please, not again?

The next day, Margo calls. She had heard my colleague, Barry Conrad, on a local radio talk show during which he gave out his phone number. Margo called Conrad telling him that she was an-ex girlfriend of mine and he gave her my new phone number. So far, so good. But wait, there's more.

We got together for dinner and one thing led to another and wouldn't you know it, we once again ended up in a very short relationship. Margo had grown even more physically beautiful in the ensuing twelve years than she was originally.

Unfortunately, her emotional side or maturity had in many ways regressed. She was even more terrified at the prospect of a relationship with a "normal", non-abusive, man. Well, it was fun while it lasted. Maybe the next Joan-clone will work, although given my backfround with such young duplicates of Joan, I wouldn't bet on it.

In the late summer of 2002, the dreams of meeting a young Joan began anew. In many respects they were identical to the others, but with far less intensity.

Aliens Above, Ghosts Below by Barry E. Taff

I met the next Joan-clone at a Halloween party that same year. Karen was engaged to an acquaintance of mine who was a producer. While talking with Karen at the party, I found myself riveted to her beauty of which she was not aware, so I thought.

I commented on how absolutely beautiful she was. Her response to me was one of disbelief, astonishment and indifference. It was very apparent to me that Karen was extremely insecure and suffered from very low self-esteem. This same old thing is getting real boring, isn't it? What is it with this look?

And of course, Karen was interested in me because of the research I've been doing for the last four decades. This in and of itself should have warned me that the path ahead was a dark and potentially dangerous one. But, as I'm an adventurer of sorts, I had to learn more about this obsessive attraction to a singular female image.

I did not see Karen again until the fall of 2007 when she had been married for several years. She was now even more stunning than she was when we first met. I went over to her to shake her hand as I had only seen her on one prior occasion.

She responded to my outstretched hand by giving me a rather intense hug along with a kiss on the lips. To say that I was shocked would indeed be an understatement. Just what I needed from a woman married to what was now a slightly more than a friend.

Making matters even more troubling was the fact that her husband, who had recently hired me to work on a show, was at the other end of the buffet table watching all of this. He was not at all pleased with his wife's way-too-personal greeting to someone she had met only on one prior occasion and that she knew was very attracted to her.

As several of my friends made their way into the dinning room they observed Karen and I talking for quite some time. All of these friends, not knowing who Karen was, believed that she was my date who I brought to the party. Later, they told me that it looked like she was "hanging" on me. Yeah, right.

Making this situation even more emotionally awkward was what I learned sometime later; that Karen's marriage was not going very well as her husband possessed a violent temper and didn't even know the word "compromise".

Perhaps Karen greeted me in such a fashion in order to demonstrate this fact to her husband who was conveniently standing at the other end of the buffet table? Great! Do I really need this in my life? I don't think so.

Several months later I spoke with the wife of my friend whose house the party was at. She informed me that even if Karen wasn't married, she was way too crazy for me to tolerate for any length of time. Well, at least in that regard, nothing has changed as virtually every girlfriend I've had that's been interested in my work was far from being emotionally stable.

Isn't it interesting how all of these precognitive events involve strong emotionally driven situations? That the one thing that consistently gets through from the subconscious to the conscious mind is information that is very relevant to our deeply rooted, emotional wants, needs and desires.

It's the continuity of these events that fascinates me to no end, as the pattern demonstrated by such occurrences is extremely clear, both within what's been reported throughout the anecdotal accounts of parapsychological research literature for 127 years as well as my own life, as you've just read.

It is no coincidence that the majority of precognized episodes reported over the

206

millennia deal with negative, traumatizing events such as sinking ships, earthquakes, wars, floods, murders, plane crashes and other unexpected tragedies.

It is such things that shock us, that get our attention, that stand out from the mundane trappings of daily life. It is such departures from the depressively boring diurnal rhythm that frequently triggers the fight-or-flight reaction within us. These unanticipated voyages into the darker recesses of reality have the most profound effects on what makes us human and are therefore more readily accessible to our extrasensory abilities. They stand out like large chunks of dandruff on a tapestry of black velour.

It is for these reasons that movies, television and the news media generally focus all their efforts on those stories that so deeply terrify our collective psyche. As commented on in the introduction of this book, the media has known all too well about for many decades about the "If it bleeds it leads" programming concept.

That is why the opening segments of all news broadcasts, whether in print or on TV deal with death and destruction, in whatever form it occurs. I wonder if the news media, or the "merchants of death" as I call them, are aware of the possibility that they're literally biting the hand that feeds them, so-to-speak and that there are dire consequences and repercussions to the media's obsessive fixation on such morbidity. It may come in the form of reverse logic.

A long time ago, a great man said that those who do not remember the past are condemned to repeat it. A profound statement if they're ever was one. However, by the media's endless attention on all things that threaten and eradicate life, we have become desensitized to it and are beginning to look at such horror and suffering as normal.

The eventual fallout from such acclamation is causing us to unconsciously emulate and replicate the death that pervades the world around us. In fact, I personally believe that it has gotten to the point where we may literally crave the torment, pain and death in all of its gut-wrenching forms. And just imagine how such continual media blitzes on death and destruction affects young people who are growing up within this insane environment of death-oriented, sensory bombardment?

Part of the problem is that the current wave of terrorism occurring throughout the world seeks exactly this type of validation for their actions from the world's news media. Unfortunately, we're giving it to them on a silver platter. We are positively reinforcing the behavior of such demented individuals. They are learning that such anti-social acts pay off big-time. They are continuously achieving their fifteen minutes of fame.

We have truly become addicted to human tragedy in all its hideous guises, as is evidenced in the merchants of death within motion pictures, television, video-games and of course books.

It appears that we have finally met our one true, greatest enemy, only to discover that it is our own reflection cast in a cracked, darkened and distorted mirror.

Contemporary mass media has created a culture that perpetuates, and most assuredly glorifies misery, suffering and death. It is not that we do not remember the past it is that we have become enslaved to its overwhelmingly heinous nature.

Decades ago television was based on the least objectionable programming possible. Today, given the mass media of cable television and the Internet, programming is the exact opposite (most objectionable) if, of course, they want high ratings and ad revenues. We as a culture better be careful what we ask for in such matters for we are slowly destroying ourselves from within.

Enough of waxing philosophic, let's get back to what really matters; what research tells us about that such paranormal experiences.

Assuming these almost veridical instances of precognition, such as those stated above, constitutes a premory, it certainly is an uncommon one, due to their incredible detail and precision when compared to the majority of precall accounts. Nevertheless, it superficially appears to conform to the model here when considering the temporal proximity and emotionally shocking nature of the event involved.

There is, perhaps, a solution to the physical theory underling the premory hypothesis that resolves the causal anomaly observed above. The explanation centers around theoretical geophysics and states that prior to a major earthquake, there is a tremendous localized pressure build-up in the Earth's crust, which in some regions is chiefly composed of crystalline structured lattices.

When placed under extreme pressure, these crystal lattices can at times, and if the pressure is great enough, generate a relatively high electrical potential. This potential may sometimes be on the order of several thousand or more volts per centimeter. This reaction is known as a "piezoelectric effect," and is the same property once used to operate radios with crystals many years ago.

The theory goes on to state that these sudden, sharp increases in electrical potential from the Earth's crust can severely disturb the surrounding atmosphere and electromagnetic (EM) field aboveground, sending out high-strength wavefronts or fields of EM energy in advance of the actual earthquake (Beal, 1971; Persinger, 1975).

In fact, prior to the Hawaiian earthquake of April 26, 1972, the precursor EM radiation (sometimes known as Rayleigh Waves) grew so intense as to disable the U.S. Navy's Omega Navigational Station in the Pacific Ocean near the epicenter of the impending quake. The spontaneous and radical drifting of the Omega System prior to the temblor has been blamed on the resulting effect of the Rayleigh Waves on the ionosphere; it inexplicably began to fade and in so doing removed the electrically charged "mirror" overhead that normally bounces radio signals back to Earth.

Such propagated fields of EM energy have been known to produce what is referred to as "earthquake lightning" from cloudless skies due to its ionizing effect on the atmosphere.

Another similar effect is known as "sky glow," where the sky literally glows before a major or great quake. In fact, just preceding a great quake in China in 1976, huge fireballs of EM energy were observed skimming the surface of the ground burning virtually everything in their path near the regions of highest stress.

Such atmospheric precursor phenomena have also been observed and recorded in Japan (a major subduction zone) and Russia, due to the high concentration of crystals in the Earth's crust in those regions (Finkelstein, 1970; Beal, 1973; Persinger, 1975).

These traveling wavefronts of high-intensity, low frequency, EM energy, moreover, is suspected of affecting the nervous systems of both animals and humans; to induce irritability and anxiety, resulting in erratic behavior (Persinger, 1974). Interestingly, the USGS National Center for Earthquake Research in Menlo Park, California, had been closely examining this theory in hopes of uncovering an additional earthquake warning device: that of living sensors.

China, for good reason, has been intensively studying animal behavior responses to earthquake precursors for quite some time and has found them to be fairly reliable when used in conjunction with more conventional measurements such as the radon concentration in well water, tilt and creep meters and magnetometer readings.

Aliens Above, Ghosts Below by Barry E. Taff

Perhaps life forms that are semi-frequently exposed to these biospheric effects can learn to recognize and interpret them accurately, like deciphering a previously unknown language or message.

Animals or human beings might begin to understand what a sudden change in the energy field structure around them indicates...to "tune in" on their own nervous reactions and realize that such subtle changes are indicative of impending sharp Earth movements beneath their feet.

Was this the mode of input for Karen's future memory? Lending partial support to this kind of short-range precognition is the data complied by the former New York Central Premonitions Registry, which appears to suggest a majority of precognized events are usually displaced forward in time not more than 6.67 months on the average and generally concern major events rather than trivial ones (Nelson, 1976).

It is already theorized that both animal and human beings are inherently sensitive to subtle energetic precursors of natural disasters, of whatever kind they may be (Beal, 1973; Persinger, 1974 & 1975).

Does the piezoelectric effect with its precursor wave reinforce future memory, or is it just another of the many variables we must further consider, in order to eventually understand precognition?

It is reasonable to postulate that this type of event may have been responsible for Karen's perception. Perhaps the advanced potential and precursor wavefront of radiation conveyed the information as to where and when the quake would occur. Accepting that this particular event constitutes a valid case of premory, Karen could have precognized any event that she would eventually learn through normal sensory mechanisms, such as news broadcasts on the Guatemala disaster.

Yet, it is highly unlikely that any known wave of radiation or field was the causal agent, for a variety of reasons. Of greater likelihood is the possibility that rather than data on the incident being carried from its source through space-time to the percipient's brain by a traveling wavefront of energy, it was already and simultaneously in existence at both points of space and time. A more precise description of this information system is to define it as possessing holographic or, more precisely, holonomic properties.

The holonomic analogy offers a new insight into space-time functioning at the paranormal level due to the equally distributed nature of information within the system. Simply stated, each part, or any portion of a hologram, no matter how small or the fact that it has been fragmented, can reproduce an image of the original whole.

Thus, holograms can be broken into many small fragments, each of which can be used to construct a complete image of the whole (Collier, 1971).

If current theories in cosmology are correct, the physical universe is not infinite and endless; there are boundaries and limits. However, there may be a point at which the physical universe of space-time falls back upon itself somewhat like a sphere, hemisphere or saddle. Such an occurrence might indicate that information of the past, present and future is simultaneously superimposed on or within space.

The resulting "superimpositioning" would create an immense "now," leaving time as an illusion without any objective basis, but nonetheless perceived by living organisms in a unidirectional, three-dimensional perspective of reality. As our bodies, brains and other things around us experience entropy, atrophy, erosion and decay, we naturally perceive such as the movement of time.

This type of space-time continuum could be defined as "hyperspace," and its complex matrix as "geometrodynamics," which coincidentally bears a strong mathematical resemblance to Fourier holographic information processes (Wheeler, 1973).

Drawing from contemporary technology, we find that some ten trillion bits of information can be usefully stored holographically in a cubic centimeter! It has been estimated that holography could permit the entire Encyclopedia Britannica to be stored on a space the size of a postcard, or the entire Library of Congress in a single small filing cabinet. Holography's ability to store vast amounts of information in a relatively small space may perhaps supply the key to unravel psi's enigmas.

With the hologram, many images can be superimposed on a single piece of film utilizing successive exposures. Each or several images can then be retrieved without being affected by the other images.

This overlaying of images, or multiplexing is done by using a different spatio-temporal frequency carrier for each picture or pattern, just as innumerable radio messages can be transmitted between two sites simultaneously by the use of different carrier frequencies. Moreover, since the film is three-dimensional (to an extent) there is still another degree of freedom in multiplexing, that of angle.

It may be these properties of holography provide us with the first physical model of an information system that does not ostensibly possess physical components or operate in accordance with the known laws of physics.

In theoretical holographic hyperspace, space-time may consist of sequentially encoded information patterns at different spatio-temporal coordinates and vectors serving as frames, gratings or frequencies.

The similarity between a proposed finite, physical universe and holographic processes is that both systems have relatively limited spatial capacity yet can store seemingly infinite volumes of information. The latter factor is especially significant in relation to paranormal perception.

Within hyperspace or hyperspace, time as we consciously perceive it would be measured as the linear distance in terms of light velocity between any two spatial coordinates as observed by those at either site.

Thus, observable real-time (which is not directly perceptible) would be a multi-dimension continuum in which information from what call "eternity" might mutually co-exist within the same space, separated by whatever property or mechanism sequentially orders patterns and events.

Perhaps the equally distributed informational nature of holography is a minuscule representation and replication of how one frame of space-time functions in that any sector of space-time, regardless of its diminutive size, may essentially possess all the bits of information or constituent components of all space-time; i.e., all is one and one is all.

Moreover, if an event is occurring at one particular point in space and time, it fundamentally is informationally or perhaps "virtually" transpiring and existing at all points in space-time at a level not yet recognized by science.

Another way of looking at the above premise is that the past, at an informational level still exists, and future information already exists. In essence experiencing life in our linear-oriented, three-dimensional reality would be equivalent to pouring liquid into a glass.

The glass is already there before you pour the liquid and therefore the liquid must conform to the shape of the glass, which in a way is a form of determinism or predestination. However, within the glass there is random movement of water molecules. Thus, we have the duality of generalized determinism and the localized sense of randomness or free will. The best of both worlds! Or, perhaps, the illusion of both.

As discussed in Chapter 11, contemporary neurophysiologists have proposed brain functioning models based on holographic processes to explain memory, pattern recognition, feature analysis, spatial and possibly even visual and auditory perception (Westlake, 1970; Swigert, 1971; Pribram, 1971; Tien, 1971; Taff, 1973).

If indeed, our brains do function holographically, then perhaps we share a unique relationship and have more in common with the universe around us than we overtly realize. That is, our brains may be small-scale models of space-time, acting in unison with its large counterpart...the universe.

Such holographic coupling properties might explain why attempts to shield psi functions with Faraday Cages, Mu-metal and/or superconducting niobium shields have failed and why no signal propagation has ever been detected between persons extrasensorily communicating. The energy we so well understand may not be traveling the between the two individuals and, hence, there is nothing to shield against except space and time itself, which is obviously impossible.

If such holonomic properties truly underlie paranormal mechanisms it would seemingly provide a common basis for such phenomena as telepathy, clairvoyance, precognition and retrocognition; the inter-phenomenal dissimilarities being resolved as differential aspects of one informational network or system providing input and access.

Experienced phenomena would be categorically classified by where and when in space-time one reconstructs (perceives) information in relation to its supposed point of origin. For example, if information has its source in the past, it's referred to retrocognition. If it originates from ahead of us in the future we call it precognition. In real-time, we would call such exchanges either telepathy or clairvoyance. The prior involving another individual, while the latter, is perception independent of a living transmitter or sender.

If it is eventually demonstrated that this model of the paranormal and space-time is a viable one, science will be faced with overhauling and revising many current theories and beliefs regarding psi phenomena, especially pertaining to the aspect of "will" or "volition," in the act of sending or receiving impressions or signals.

The major revision in our belief system would come in discovering that there is no new signal being generated by the agent or sender. Consistent with this revised theoretical model, sending or transmitting a paranormal signal would entail little more than raising the signal-to-noise ratio of what is already in existence, thereby increasing its recognition probability.

For all we know at this time, the background clutter we currently call "noise," might very well be the signal we are looking for!

Of even greater consequence, though, in particular as regard Karen's case, is that her precognition appears to imply a direct contradiction to one of the basic beliefs our physical existence: free will.

In order for Karen to have precisely and accurately precognized the Guatemalan earthquake, which appears to be strongly suggested, the event must have already existed in the future.

Otherwise, what would the probability be of Karen randomly piecing together the proper bits of information that just happen to correspond to the future event? If this were the case, the odds of anyone temporally compiling the precise data in advance of the event would roughly be about a trillion-to-one.

Put more simply, what is one remembering from the future? Certainly,not probabilities? One does not remember probabilities with regard to past events, so why should the future be any different?

Then of course, there are those who speak of alternative, branching futures in which one's fate is determined by the specific course, branch or path taken by an individual, subjective choice.

Implied in this belief is the notion that all the other branches or paths you did not choose led to different futures that occurred either without you or with you in an alternative or perhaps parallel universe. Yeah, right. If you really believe that, I've got a great bridge to sell you.

Back here on Earth we know of only one future, which is the future we all eventually live to experience. There are, of course, subjective interpretations on the precise details of every event, but by and large, there is a high degree of concordance and convergence, regarding the way events play out.

For example, we may question the factual details concerning JFK's assassination (who, how and why), but I assume we all pretty much agree on the fact that he was murdered on November 22, 1963.

Whatever might be transpiring in an alternate reality or universe based on branching futures we never followed, is irrelevant. We will never experience those alleged alternate universes. Even stranger is the fact that even if we did, we would never know it. We only know the future we collectively and eventually live out.

As to the possibility of altering precognized events prior to their occurrence, there appears to be only two rational solutions. One is that primary process material causes sufficient noise and informational distortion of the precognition to allow a change in the outcome of events due to the fact that the future was not perceived entirely accurate.

The second possibility is that the percipient accurately precognizes the future in detail and in the attempt to affect a change in the outcome virtually alters their pre-memory of it.

If their future memory remained intact and they successfully altered the accurately precognized event, their precall of it should never have occurred to begin with. An obvious paradox.

Assuming that the piezoelectric wavefront theory is not a viable one and the holographic distribution hypothesis is of greater likelihood, what are we then to believe concerning freedom of will and choice?

In order for symmetry to be maintained between past and future, it may require that both time states relative to our "present" are invariable, immutable and already mapped out, so to speak...a space-time manifold where one comes upon and encounters the future to experience it, where all future memories are already contained within our brain and simply require and await the proper set of stimuli to evoke them into consciousness thereby guiding us into our future.

Aliens Above, Ghosts Below by Barry E. Taff

Evidence collected from parapsychological research laboratories around the world overwhelmingly supports the existence of precognition.

In pursuing answers to the paradoxical riddles posed by this phenomenon, we may stumble onto a solution that is not quite what we are ready, willing or able to accept, especially in science.

We may discover that fear is the greatest obstacle hindering our awareness of the shapes of things to come. Shapes that may not yield to human intervention. Shapes that may have dictated our destinies long before man walked the face of the Earth. Shapes that might inevitably tell us of our controlled existence in the universe, an existence where knowledge does not give one power or free will, simply the illusion.

Perhaps the answer to the penultimate question regarding an open or closed future is quite simple. As discussed earlier, how deep is the water (or the illusion) in the glass?

It is intriguing to discover that we know more about the space above our head than the space contained within it. The final frontier of time and space lies within our brain, the last refuge for the most unique force in the universe. A force that may eventually be our ticket to ride in a real time machine!

REFERENCES

Avant, L.L., "Vision in the Ganzfeld," Psychological Bulletin, Vol. 64, 1965

Beal, J.B., "Electrostatic Fields, Electromagnetic Fields and Ions Mind/ Body/Environment Interrelationships," Paper presented at the 6th Annual Meeting of the Neuroelectric Society, Vol. 6, February 18-24, 1973

Collier, R.J., Burkhard, C.B. and Lin, L.H., Optical Holography, Academic Press, N.Y. 1971

Dean, E.D., "Precognition and Retrocognition," in Psychic Exploration, Edgar D. Mitchell (Ed.), G.P. Putnam's Sons, N.Y., 1974

Feinberg, G., "Precognition--A Memory of Things Future," in Proceedings of an International Conference: Quantum Physics and Parapsychology, Geneva, Switzerland, August 26-27, 1974, Parapsychology Foundation, Inc., N.Y., 1974

Misner, C.W., Thorne, K.S. and Wheeler, J.A., Gravitation, W.H. Freeman & Company, San Francisco, 1973

Nelson, R., "From the Central Premonitions Registry," Parapsychology Review, Vol. 7, No. 3, May-June 1976, Parapsychology Foundation, Inc., N.Y.

Persinger, M.A., (Ed.) ELF & VLF Electromagnetic Field Effects, Plenum Press, N.Y., 1974

Persinger, M.A., "Geophysical Models of Parapsychological Experiences," International Journal of Psychoenergetic Systems, Vol. 1, No. 2, 1975

Pribram, K.H., Languages of the Brain: Experimental Paradoxes and Principles in Neuro-Psychology, Prentice-Hall, New Jersey, 1971

Raucher, E.A., "Information Transfer at Velocities Which Exceed the Velocity of Light," Lawrence

Aliens Above, Ghosts Below by Barry E. Taff

Berkeley Radiation Laboratory, UCB, 1975, unpublished proposal

Schmidt, H., "Quantum Process Predicted?" New Scientist, October 16, 1969

Swigert, C.J., "Pattern Identification and Spatial Filtering in a Neuron Network Model," International Journal of Neuroscience, Vol. 2, 1971

Taff, B.E., "It's About Time," International Journal of Psychoenergetic Systems, Vol. 1, No. 2, 1975

Taylor, J.G., "The Shadow of the Mind," New Scientist and Science Journal, September 30, 1971

Tien, H.C., "Psychosynthesis: A TV Cybernetic Hologram Model,"in The Nervous System and Electric Currents, Vol. 2, by N.L. Wulfson, A. Sances, Jr., Plenum Press, N.Y., 1971

Tiller, W.A., "Consciousness, Radiation and the Developing Sensory System," Stanford University, Dept. of Materials Science, 1972

Vaughan, A., Patterns of Prophecy, Hawthorne, N.Y., 1973

Westlake, P.R., "The Possibilities of Neural Holographic Processes Within the Brain," Kybernetik, Vol. 7, 1970, pp. 129-153

END

Chapter 15:
THE PSI/UFO CONNECTION

The "paranormal" as related to psychic research are those faculties and phenomena beyond normality in terms of their cause and effect as currently understood by science. Parapsychology is the branch of science that deals with extrasensory perception (ESP) and psychokinesis (PK), that is, behavioral and personal informational exchanges with the environment that are extrasensorimotor, or not dependent on the senses or muscles. The above definition of parapsychology is a classical one and does not in itself elucidate the numerous subdivisions within each of the two major categories.

Under the heading of psychokinesis, or what is more commonly referred to as "mind-over-matter," falls one of the most enigmatic types of paranormal phenomena----the poltergeist.

As described in Chapters 1, 3, 5 & 6, the term poltergeist translates from German as "noisy, mischievous spirit," and is often linked with haunted houses. Various paranormal manifestations produced during poltergeist outbreaks include unexplained and sometimes violent movement and breakage of objects, interference with and manipulation of electrical devices and appliances, unaccountable sounds and odors, and occasionally apparitions.

As a hardened physical scientist, it is almost inconceivable to consider, let alone accept the possibility of a discarnate (without a body) intelligence influencing and directing the action of energy and/or matter.

Nevertheless, these were the concepts and suspicions of our ancestors in psychical research, for they hypothesized that the causal agent responsible for such phenomena was indeed a prank-playing ghost.

Modern parapsychologists, however, strongly influenced by the success of our physically oriented, technological society, have conveniently provided a new theory for poltergeist activity which suggests that living human agents (technically referred to as "poltergeist agents" or PGA's) are unconsciously and spontaneously emitting some type of energy responsible for the observed phenomena.

The interaction between the poltergeist agent and their environment has been labeled by parapsychologists as, recurrent spontaneous psychokinesis, or more simply, RSPK.

This more conventional hypothesis intimates that this unique energy is generally discharged by pubescent and/or adolescent children experiencing intense emotional conflicts and turmoil in and around themselves. An adjunct to this hypothesis states that the psychodynamic environment, such as the interrelationships between family members, is directly related to the onset, orientation and magnitude of the phenomena. 1, 2, 3

Although some aspects of the poltergeist were covered in Chapters 1, 3, 5, & 6, there is a far deeper and more enigmatic aspect to this mystery than meets the eye. With the current sophistication of electromagnetic remote sensing systems (not remote viewing), one would suspect that the RSPK theory was developed as a result of actual and direct measurement of this energy as it is being emitted from the suspected poltergeist agent during the course of observed phenomena.

Unfortunately, this is not the case. What seems to have occurred is that the RSPK hypothesis was arrived at through a process of backwards reasoning. In other words, it has been established that pubescent or adolescent children were almost always present during outbreaks of poltergeist activity or, more precisely, that the psychokinetic manifestations seemed to occur particularly around these types of individuals. 1, 2, 3. Subsequently, it was reasoned that these children were the causal agents of the psychokinetic displays.

What is important to note here is that the "energy" referred to within RSPK hypothesis as being responsible for the abrupt movement of massive objects (anywhere from twenty to several hundred pounds) does not appear to conform to the properties associated with the four known forces in nature, especially electromagnetic.

One of the basic principles of thermodynamics as related to all forces is that when energy is used to do "work," such as the movement of an object, heat is generated. Specifically, "work" is accomplished when energy produces "force." Force is simply defined as mass times acceleration. Therefore, in order for energy to move an object, it must generate a force exceeding the rest mass and inertia of that object.

Now here is the paradox: the energy, in particular electromagnetic, required to produce a force sufficient to move a massive object should generate such intense heat, say through ionization, that people in the immediate vicinity would be severely burned long before the object began to move.

No such heating or ionization effects have ever been detected or observed. Conversely, if anything, the environment appears to show a temperature drop. It should be made expressly clear here that whatever energy is responsible for these physical phenomena, it has not yet been detected, measured or quantified. 4, 5

There are other forms of energy, such as gravitation, strong and weak nuclear forces and perhaps even electroweak, but their very nature prohibit them from being considered viable candidates for this phenomenon.

The RSPK theory is being used to explain virtually all types of haunting phenomena ranging from poltergeist activity to the appearance of apparitions. However, it is necessary to make the following distinctions.

Generally, haunting phenomena can be divided into two categories: first, events that seem to occur in a haphazardly random fashion; second, events that occur in a controlled manner, seemingly directed by some intelligence. 6

An example of non-directed, random type of activity is when a glass flies off an unoccupied table and strikes the wall, while a television turning on to the same station each night by itself best exemplifies directed type of action. While the RSPK hypothesis may account for the random movement of objects, this cannot explain the controlled manipulation of large amounts of energy or matter.

Psychokinetic experiments within the laboratory seem to reinforce this position because volitional PK produces the movement of small, light objects over extremely short distances, 7, 8, opposed to the spontaneous movement of large, heavy objects over relatively great distances, as documented in numerous poltergeist cases. 9

If we eliminate RSPK as being the operative force underlying seemingly intelligent or directed production of large-scale physical phenomena, what then is left?

One alternative is to consider the same concepts presented by our predecessors in psychical research, namely, discarnate intelligence (disembodied consciousness) such as a ghost or spirit. Another alternative is to consider the possibility of a totally unknown or missing variable that may explain the phenomena.

Over the past one hundred and twenty three years of organized psychical research in the western world, some of the following dissimilarities have been noted between hauntings and poltergeists.

Hauntings are usually visual and auditory. Poltergeists are usually motor displays. Additionally, individuals capable of producing small-scale psychokinesis within laboratory environments demonstrate high levels of fatigue, while large-scale RSPK activity does not appear to physically weaken its supposed perpetrator. Hauntings can persist for years, decades, even centuries, while poltergeists are generally short-lived and burn themselves out rather quickly.

But most important, hauntings are usually linked with a specific house or locale, while poltergeists focus on a specific individual. However, what is not yet known is whether the poltergeist agent is the generator of the phenomena or simply a charged-coupler to an external power source such as surrounding geophysical forces or a discarnate entity.

In other words, the poltergeist agent is unconsciously absorbing energy from a supposedly non-physical source. They are then transforming this energy and re-emitting a force that physically affects the environment.

Although the phenomena associated with both hauntings and poltergeists have been well-established 10, 11, 12 the nature of their true source and mechanics remains a complete mystery.

It's become dismayingly clear upon a comprehensive examination of both the research and anecdotal literature related to apparitions 13, 14 ghosts and hauntings 15, 16 that it is one enigma of nature that does not easily, if at all, lend itself to empirical evaluation due to its randomness, scarcity and general lack of predictability and consistency.

Combining these features with the fact that one cannot bring such research into a controlled laboratory environment, further supports the supposition that the causal element in this situation is an almost total unknown. Because it cannot even vaguely be operationally or functionally defined, therefore, it remains, as it always has been----a phenomenon.

In terms of scientific methodology, the attempt to explain one unknown in terms of another unknown is not only undesirable but is considered invalid. However, one method by which science examines a newly discovered phenomenon is by analogy. This technique involves looking for similarities between the effects of a newly found phenomenon and the effects of a system already well understood. And through the process of studying similarities in the effects between known and unknown systems, we can then learn more about the cause of the latter.

At the same time, it is important to grasp the fact that all true science begins with systematic observation of things we do not understand. This naturally and eventually evolves into the aforementioned analogy method.

Considering the uniqueness of the properties associated with ghosts, hauntings, poltergeists and apparitions, it did not seem likely or probable that an analogous system would be discovered.

However, during the past forty years certain aspects of another system have been found to overlap with the area of the paranormal under discussion here. The system I am referring to here is UFO encounters. Numerous cases from the files of UCLA's former Parapsychology Laboratory, suggests an interrelationship between these two systems of phenomena.

Aliens Above, Ghosts Below by Barry E. Taff

In Chapter 9 (Abduction Central) the cases of Allan of Canoga Park, Judy of Hollywood, Teri from Bel-Air, and Mrs. Valdez from Sunland, clearly demonstrate the high degree of correlation between phenomena manifested in both paranormal and UFO abduction cases.

In the most simplistic of terms, it appears that these individuals who have been abducted, frequently experience some form of paranormal "fallout" (telepathy, precognitive dreams, poltergeist outbreaks and spontaneous healings) following their encounter.

At the other end of the spectrum, it also appears as if those individuals who have intense paranormal experiences, e.g., poltergeists, out-of-body experiences (OBE's), etc., have a greater probability of having an encounter with UFOs. The penultimate question here is; is there really any difference between these two types of phenomena other than their possible source or origin?

Unfortunately, most of these cases that start as paranormal and turn into abductions or start as abductions and evolve into paranormal experiences produce little in the way of hard, physical evidence. What we are invariably left with are anecdotal accounts that occasionally have multiple witnesses and corroborative testimony. However, once in a great while something physical is captured on film or videotape that partially compensates for the lack of anything tangible.

In February 1977 our lab received a call from a Mrs. Olsen of Catalina Island. She and several of her relatives had independently observed flying balls of light, luminous clouds of vapor and several humanoid apparitions.

One particular photograph obtained during the course of this investigation revealed a strange object not seen by anyone present. The photograph was analyzed by computer image enhancement techniques.

The results of the analysis indicated the object captured on film was 1) traveling horizontally, right to left at approximately 986 mph; 2) the refractive index was that of a metallic object; 3) it was going through what is known as trans-axial motion or pitch, yaw and roll while in horizontal flight; and 4) one aerospace engineer's eyeball analysis resulted in the comment that the object resembled a micro-miniature spaceship with a nodular engine cluster at the rear, a tubular fuselage in the middle and a spherical structure at the front.

What was an apparitional image of this type doing in a supposedly haunted environment?

The aforementioned cases, while interesting in themselves, do not adequately represent the striking number of correlations and parallels existing between the effects of certain paranormal phenomena and UFO encounters.

One of the first researchers to advance the notion of UFO-paranormal interrelationships was Dr. Jacques Vallee, an astrophysicist and computer scientist from Stanford University. In his books Passport to Magonia and Invisible College, Vallee painstakingly reviews, examines and delineates the commonalities of these two fields of research.

Perhaps the most dramatic similarity between UFO encounters and hauntings is their general appearance. On a visual level, one of the most common experiences reported by the tenants of haunted houses is the appearance of flying balls of light.

This description is also one of the most frequent observations made by UFO witnesses 17 . The flight dynamics of UFOs appear to mimic the movement of objects and balls of light within haunted environments, both display erratic patterns of flight such as sudden starting and stopping, high-speed, right angle turns, abrupt reversals in direction and spontaneous appearances and disappearances.

Intriguing, is the correlation between the visual observation of humanoid apparitions in both hauntings and CE-III and CE-IV UFO encounters. 17, 18.

The aftereffects of UFO encounters quite often involve other areas of the paranormal besides hauntings and poltergeists. All too often, close encounters of third and fourth kind result in rapid healings, subjective telepathic experiences of communication with the occupants of the vehicle and generalized precognitive experiences. 17, 18

Another aspect of this interrelatedness involves the electromagnetic (EM) effects of both UFOs and poltergeist activity on electro-mechanical devices.

Indeed, the most widely known and best documented proximity effect of UFOs is their consistent interference with electrically operating apparatus such as automobile ignition systems, lights, radios, overhead power lines and jamming TV, radio and radar transmissions. 17, 18. In a similar fashion, disruptions of mechanical as well as electronic equipment, is almost standard operating procedure for poltergeist phenomena.

One of the suspected candidates for such UFO EM effects is microwave radiation. Air Force tracked UFOs have been monitored radiating or emitting a frequency of approximately 3,000 megahertz with a pulse width of two microseconds, a pulse repetition frequency of 600 hertz, and a sweep rate of four rpm with vertical polarity at a one megawatt power level. 17

What is particularly fascinating about the discovery of UFOs emitting high- powered microwave field is that such radiant energy is known to have extremely potent psycho-biological effects on both animals and humans. 17, 19.

Such effects include the generation of first and second degree skin burns similar to sun burns, an effect often reported during a close encounter with UFOs. Such microwave radiation exposure can directly affect the central nervous system (non-thermally) to induce irritability and anxiety to the point of directly interfering with the T-wave of the heart, causing an increased pulse rate, spontaneous hormonal secretions and even cardiac arrest.

The biological effects of microwave radiation have also been known cause the formation of cataracts within the eyes; breakdown blood cells and sharply raise the white count; cause permanent, irreversible chromosomal and DNA damage, and cause cellular tissues and membranes to literally explode 19.

One case in the late 1970's reported in the now defunct APRO (Aerial Phenomena Research Organization) Bulletin described an instance in Kansas where a UFO was about to land and was approached by a local farm dog. The next day, the dog was found dead beneath the area where the UFO had hovered.

The necropsy revealed that the dog had literally been cooked from the inside out, All the fatty tissue had liquefied and dissolved through the pores, only to re-solidify on the outside of the dog's skin killing it.

The most accurate definition of the method of death was given as high-power microwave irradiation (like that from a microwave oven). Though such radiation effects are hazardous, it is unlikely the UFO intentionally destroyed the dog.

It is more probable to assume that animal simply wandered too close to the vehicle and was caught in its power field the same way an individual would be scorched from accidentally standing too close to the exhaust of an operating jet engine.

Because some UFO CE-III & IV's have resulted in witnesses reporting they've heard some voices in their head telling them what to do or not to be afraid, it is more than coincidental that a technique for inducing auditory hallucinations or impressions directly into the brain, bypassing the ear, has been developed using microwaves. Known as the Frey Effect, 19.

This technique can cause an individual to hear humming, pops, whistles, and even voices if the proper pulse envelope of microwave radiation is aimed at their heads. The ears hear absolutely nothing, but inside the head it is as though an inner voice is speaking. This is technically known as auditory nerve induction.

Because animals are known to exhibit far greater sensitivity to such energetic effects, even at low-power levels, it is understandable that they usually react long before humans to the presence of a UFO. Curiously, animals are also acutely sensitive to the presence of hauntings and poltergeist phenomena. Might this not also indicate an approaching wavefront of some type of low-level energy?

Although the pattern emerging here is far from being understood, it should be emphasized at this point that not all UFO cases evolve into episodes of paranormal experiences and vice versa.

The examination of the interrelationships between UFOs and paranormal phenomena is designed as an attempt to gain further insight into the source and nature of the phenomena as a whole, rather than trying to explain one with another.

One of the most demonstrable EM effects UFOs have on the environment is the generation of a powerful magnetic field. 17.

Interestingly, and pointing directly toward another associative aspect, the effects of both natural and artificial magnetic fields on human biology and behavior have been widely studied, although they are nowhere near to being understood. 20, 23.

There are strong indicators that the magnetic fields generated by UFOs affect individuals in such a way as to trigger various phenomena.

Geomagnetic perturbations such as disturbances in the earth's magnetic field caused by cosmic ray bombardment, high-energy solar protons, solar flares (sunspots), solar maximas and internal terrestrial effects, appear to be temporally and spatially correlated to the stimulation and irritation of the central nervous system.

During such geomagnetic perturbations there have been significantly higher admissions to psychiatric hospitals and more erratic ward behavior within such facilities. 24-26. Additionally, there appears to be a cursory relationship between geomagnetic polarity reversals and the sudden extinction of life forms. 27, 28

In addition to affecting the emotional behavior of individuals, geomagnetic perturbations have demonstrated a high degree of correlation with RSPK or poltergeist activity. 2.9 The dependent variables here appear to be geographic location, altitude and population density.

Is it mere coincidence that geomagnetic perturbations have been linked to erratic behavior, that they have been correlated with RSPK, and that erratic behavior is the most readily identifiable characteristic of the poltergeist agent's emotional make-up? And I guess it's just probability that the personality of a PGA is typified by extreme swings in mood, high levels of generalized anxiety and irritability, repressed hostilities and difficulty in working out stressful, internalized conflicts. 2

Even more intriguing is the fact that over the last decade, haunted and poltergeist plagued locations have demonstrated a highly unstable and anomalous magnetic environment as measured by highly sensitive, magnetometers.

Equally suspicious is the fact that PGA's appear to be hypersensitive to environmental 60-cycle magnetic fields such as those produced by household appliances like hair dryers, digital clock radios, computers, etc. Are these rare individuals possibly functioning as inductive magnetic capacitors that when discharging, disrupt even local gravitational fields?

Perhaps haunting/RSPK activity derives its power from tapping into the earth's geomagnetic field that is somehow coupled or mediated by living human agents, discarnate intelligences or some complex bio-holographic animation mechanism as described in Chapter 1 (A Haunting Thought)?

It is generally assumed that such unstable personality traits as discussed herewith are a precondition to the manifestation of RSPK activity. In other words, it is the troubled and emotionally turbulent consciousness of the agent that triggers the onset of poltergeist outbreaks.

In lieu of the possible effects of known energy on the human organism we are confronted by the haunting thought (if you'll excuse the pun) that we may be looking at this entire process backwards.

Quite simply, rather than the personality of the agent producing the energy responsible for RSPK, it may be that some as yet undefined energy that cannot be metabolized or synthesized is creating the erratic personality through a ratchet effect. In more simple terms, some people are so acutely sensitive to environmental energies that it drives them "crazy" in a literal sense.

Four alternatives are suggested here: a) either the poltergeist agent is hypersensitive to external forces such as natural or electronically generated microwave/magnetic fields which indirectly cause them to generate the phenomena, or b) they themselves possess an over abundance of this energy which produces the erratic behavior and phenomena, c) there is a totally unknown force at work here that somehow is coupled to the known forces in the physical world, d) extraterrestrial and/or discarnate intelligences roam far and wide, occasionally influencing our reality in a manner we cannot yet understand and e) the parallels and correlations are simply the result of dissimilar causes producing nearly identical effects...yeah, right.

Although, it is not impossible for different causes to produce similar, if not identical effects.

The issue that lays before us now is whether or not these correlational aspects suggest a deeper, more profound meaning to this whole spectrum of phenomena. The question now is whether or not such similar effects arise from similar causes?

Are UFOs machines that electromechanically produce energy analogous to the unknown paranormal energy associated with hauntings and RSPK activity?

Are there forces of nature, technological or otherwise, which we have yet to discover and that can produce the phenomena described herein. On the other hand, is there an intelligence----either extraterrestrial in reference to UFOs or discarnate in relation to hauntings----that is volitionally affecting our behavior and environment?

Are we as human beings in some way being modified or altered through our encounters with UFOs and/or haunting/poltergeist activity?

If so, why? If these two systems are operating through similar sources, does an encounter with one of them make us more susceptible to experiencing the other?

Answers to these numerous questions will be forthcoming only through the continued and dedicated research of investigators in both fields.

END

REFERENCES

1. Roll, W.G. Poltergeist phenomena and interpersonal relations. Journal of the American Society for Psychical Research, Vol. 64, No. 1, January 1970, pp. 66-69

2. Roll, W.G., The Poltergeist, Nelson Doubleday, N.Y., 1972

3. Owen, A.R.G., Can We Explain the Poltergeist? Taplinger Publishing Company, 1964

4. Persinger, M.A., Geophysical models of parapsychological experiences, International Journal of Psychoenergetic Systems, Vol. 1, 1975, pp. 63-74

5. Taylor, J., Superminds, Viking Press, Inc., 1975

6. Myers, F.W.H., Human Personality and Its Survival of Bodily Death, 1903, (1961 Ed. By University Books, Inc.

7. Rhine, L.E., Mind Over Matter: Psychokinesis, Collier Books, N.Y., 1972

8. Schmidt, H., "Psychokinesis." in Psychic Exploration: A Challenge for Science, Mitchell, E.D. and White, J., (eds.), G.P. Putnam's Sons, N.Y., 1974

9. Roll, W.G. & Pratt J.G., The Miami disturbances, Journal of the American Society for Psychical Research, Vol. 65, No. 4, October 1971, pp. 409-454

10. Taff, B.E. & Gaynor, K., "A new poltergeist effect," Theta, Vol. 4, No. 2, 1976,   pp. 1-7

11. Bayless, R., The Enigma of the Poltergeist, Ace Books, N.Y., 1976

12. Hasted, J.B., Bohn, D.J., Bastin E.W., O'Regan, B., and Taylor, J.G., (untitled report) Nature, Vol. 254, 1975, pp. 470-473

13. Defoe, D., The History and Reality of Apparitions, AMS Press, N.Y. 1973

14. Tyrell, G.N.M, Apparitions, MacMillian, N.Y., 1962

15. Barden, D., Ghosts and Hauntings, Fontana Books, Great Britain, 1965

16. Owen, A.R.G., Science and the Spook, Garrett Publications, N.Y., 1970

17. McCampbell, J.M., Ufology, Jaymac Company, CA, 1973

18. Vallee, J., The Invisible College, E.P. Dutton, N.Y., 1975

19. Cleary, S.F. (Ed.) Biological Effects and Health Implications of Microwave Radiation, U.S. Department of Health, Education and Welfare, BRH/DBE 70-2, September, 1969, NTIS Document No. PB 193898

20. Barnothy, M.F., (Ed.) Biological Effects of Magnetic Fields,: Vol. 1, Plenum Press, N.Y., 1964

21. Barnothy, M.F., (Ed.) Biological Effects of Magnetic Fields, Vol. 1, Plenum Press, N.Y. 1969

22. Degan, I.L., Therapeutic Effects of Constant and Low Frequency Alternating Magnetic 'Fields, NTIS, JPRS, 53091, May 11, 1971, USSR

23. Manganelli, L.A., Biomagnetism: An Annotated Bibliography, Biological Science Communication Project, The George Washington University Medical Center, February, 1972

24. Friedman, H., Becker, R.O. & Bachman, C.H., "Geomagnetic Parameters and Psychiatric Hospital Admissions," Nature, Vol. 200, 1964, pp. 626-628

25. Friedman, H., Becker, R.O. & Bachman, C.H., "Psychiatric Ward Behavior and Geophysical Parameters," Nature, Vol. 205, 1965, pp. 1050-1055

26. Becker, R.O., "Relationships of Geomagnetic Environment to Human Biology," N.Y. State Journal of Medicine, Vol. 63, No. 15, 1963, pp. 2215-2219

27. Morrison, C.G.A. & Funnel, B.M., "Relationships of Paleo-Magnetic Reversals and Micropaleoentology in Two Late Caenozic Cores from the Pacific Ocean," Nature, Vol. 204, 1964

28. Watkins, N.D. & Goodel, H.G., "Geomagnetic Polarity Changes and Faunal Extinction in the Southern Ocean," Science, Vol. 156, 1967, pp. 1083-1086

29. Roll, W.G. & Livington, G., "Geomagnetic Perturbations and RSPK." In Research in Parapsychology, Scarecrow Press, Inc., N.J., 1974

Aliens Above, Ghosts Below by Barry E. Taff

Chapter 16:
TRANSPORT SHOCK

At first, this chapter may seem out-of-place or not in directly associated with the rest of the book. However, as you read deeper into it, you'll discover that what seems like science fiction may in fact, be science fact and not necessarily derived from terrestrial sources. However, whatever the potential source of such alleged technology, if real, it offers to forever change the way every single one of us on Earth lives our lives.

In one of many cavernous laboratories, numerous engineers and physicists from different aerospace companies sit and wait for a technology demonstration. Within the vast complex sit two separate booths that look, very much like ultra-modern telephone booths, each incorporating a large arrayed antenna at one end.

A spokesman steps forward and addresses the gathered assembly of scientists that they are being given the first public showing of electroporting.

A lab technician places a bowl of goldfish into one of the booths, securing it. At the touch of a button, the glass within each booth polarizes and darkens. This is to prevent flash blindness of the observers. The engineers and physicists are given special protective goggles to shield their eyes against the intensely bright light generated by the system during operation. The principal engineer engages the system.

Suddenly the booth containing the goldfish bowl is bathed in an incredibly brilliant blue-white light emitted from an overhead projector mechanism contained in the booths. The goldfish bowl is consumed in and by the blinding light as it vanishes from sight.

An instant later, the other booth whose glass has already darkened is filled with the same scintillating light and the same goldfish bowl materializes on the stand within it. The audience is stunned and left virtually speechless. The lab spokesman comes forward stating "Gentleman, this is 'electroporting.' Are there any questions?" All the bulging-eyed witnesses raise their hands in perfect unison.

This event is not a scene out of an early script for the remake of The Fly, nor is it an excerpt from a developing script for a prequel to a Star Trek motion picture or the continuing TV spin-offs.

The aforementioned event transpired exactly as described, not in the dim recesses of 2050 or 2500 A. D., as might be portrayed in the opening of a new science-fiction novel, but in the fall of 1979!

After having met and talked with one of the engineers present at the electroporting demonstration of 1979, and having the good fortune to meet two additional engineers who were directly involved in the development of this incredible technology, I am hard-pressed to believe what was told to me.

However, the information related to me by the engineer at the 1979 China Lake demonstration was totally corroborated by the two other persons--who were an integral part of the research and development program resulting in electro-portation, otherwise known as electroporting or what might more commonly be known as teleportation.

According to my sources, which must remain anonymous for obvious reasons, the effort to develop real-life "transporters" or "matter energy scramblers" like the ones depicted in Star Trek and The Fly began in the mid-1960's, and was a joint effort of the Department of Energy (DOE), The Defense Advanced Research Projects Agency (DARPA), Sandia National Laboratories, several of this country's leading aerospace contractors and the world's largest communications company (which must remain nameless except for this clue--its head research facility is located in New Jersey and until its recent divestiture, allowed us to effectively reach out and touch, e.g., communicate with each other for many years.)

According to the sources very closely tied to this project, it combined the most advanced technology on Earth, and perhaps some not of this Earth, to successfully attain its goals. Remember, according the Philip Corso's The Day After Roswell, Sandia is but one of the suspected locations where recovered technology from the 1947 Roswell crash might have ended up for reverse engineering.

However, given that today in the year 2000 we still supposedly do not possess the computing power necessary to handle the enormous quantity and speed required for real-time processing of all the atoms and molecules in any object, let alone a living organism, it's highly improbable that Earth-based technology was the source behind electroporting.

If such were the case, the Strategic Defense Initiative (SDI) or "Star Wars" (now, National Missile Defense--NMD) battle management would certainly not be a concern, as the many millions of lines of necessary software code would be a relatively commercial off-the-shelf (COTS) item.

If we could currently process the astronomical (excuse the pun) amount of real-time data regarding electroporting of any object, the recurring failures of endoatmospheric or exoatmospheric homing overlays or incepts within the kinetic-kill vehicle anti-missile program would not be a problem.

Much of the technology and difficulty associated with and encountered during electroporting's development phases closely mirrored those displayed in the 1958 The Fly and it's successful 1986 remake starring Jeff Goldblum.

In the fictional treatment, X-ray holography was used in conjunction with lasers and electron beam technology to successfully scan objects in three dimensions and eventually break down the molecular and atomic structure into sub-atomic, elementary components, which were then converted into waveforms and transmitted at near-light speed through the air (as with TV) to be reintegrated again at the reception booth.

In reality, the atoms and molecules (mass) of the object to be transmitted were somehow converted from matter into energy and back again through the manipulation of rapidly pulsating electromagnetic beams/fields, coherent light and a force analogous to gravity.

Apparently, early results with electroporting were not exactly encouraging, as all too frequently objects disintegrated would only partially reintegrate, as a virtual or real image in the reception booth.

Later, only to decay, diffuse and break down never to reintegrate. This vexing problem was overcome, they say, but an even bigger one persisted regarding the transmission and reassimilation of animate matter.

As seen in The Fly, the single greatest hurdle or overcome was keeping animate (living) objects stable or coherent during transmission. Something unique about living organic systems prevented their successful breakdown, transmission and reintegration.

Meanwhile, more anomalies were occurring, such as the appearance of both the originally transmitted and reassembled objects at the same instant in their respective booths, but in the form of three-dimensional ghost images. However, the transmitted object possessing rest mass frequently never reappeared.

It took considerably more power and control of the technology in order to successfully transport animate matter. There were virtually hundreds of varying parameters that must be kept in balance in order to successfully electroport a living object.

According to my sources, animals were commonly used during the development of this technology, as it was deemed for too experimental and hazardous for use with humans (what else is new)?

Additionally, complex substances that combined different elements were tested for their transport viability. It is not known whether humans were ever put through electroporting, although dogs, cats and monkeys were employed on a regular basis, many of which during the early phases of development never reintegrated.

As the program matured, they ostensibly licked the animate problem, however, but were to encounter another stumbling block----that of controlling the energy used. Even the slightest variation or diminution in the utilized power could have disastrous effects on the electroportation process. This included the power source being utilized as well as the electronics utilized in the system itself.

A particularly strange effect that was reported was that at times, it was actually easier to transport an object----organic, animate or otherwise----through a relatively small amount of dense material than through the atmosphere! Also, transmission of objects was essentially the same as line-of-sight radio transmission or Laser Radar (LIDAR). Unlike Star Trek, a receiving booth was always required for reintegration as opposed to focusing the beam at its coherence length to achieve transport.

In the end, after the expenditure of many billions of dollars on this still "black" project, almost anything could be transported. Size, shape or substance posed no problem. However, an environmental impact study did.

The study concluded that if electroporters were deployed as an alternative means of transporting everything from merchandise to people, few if any of the global transportation industries would survive intact.

Moreover, more than half of the civilized world's work force would be jobless, as there would no longer be any real need for trucks, trains, cars, boats or planes, nor for the people who build, service and maintain them.

The only individuals left driving cars, planes and boats would be those of us who simply wanted them for recreational purposes. There's nothing quite like a 800 horsepower racing car that can pull in excess of 1+g on a good road course. Damn the electroporting, give me my all-wheel drive, Brembo brakes and ground effects.

What about all the companies that supply energy in the form of gasoline and oil for all these suddenly outmoded methods of transportation? These industries would also crumble, as there would not longer be any need to burn fossil fuels to power moving vehicles that pollute air with deadly hydrocarbons, ozone, carbon monoxide, carbon dioxide and nitrogen dioxides.

Sure, it would free us from the dependency on oil and OPEC for energy in the form of transportation, but at the same time it would hurl the world into a depression far greater than that of 1929, a course that it seems we may already be on anyway.

This is not like the invention of the typewriter, where most individuals thought it would put many people out of work only to result in the creation of more jobs.

It is unlikely that all the people unemployed and displaced by the commercialization of electroporting would end up building, servicing and maintaining such technology due to its level of complexity and sophistication.

All the beneficial assets gained through the efficiency of electroporting would be offset by the terrible economic collapse that would inevitably follow. Still, wouldn't it be simply marvelous to step into an electroporting booth, say, in Los Angeles, punch in your destination, Hawaii for example, insert your personal atomic code card (which carries your specific nuclear resonance code which is updated as your use it) and engage the system?

You are instantaneously transported to the receiving booth in Hawaii. No more absurd five-hour flights in poorly ventilated cabins with contaminated air and tasteless food.

Now the real question is, exactly what would one feel as their body is broken down into its constituent components of elementary sub-atomic particles, converted to waves, transmitted at relativistic speed and re-assembled at the intended destination?

Well, if this system really tears apart atoms and molecules, you would literally die and be resurrected every time you were transported. And you thought Lazarus had problems? Talk about a really bad hair day!

Not exactly what one envisions as a pleasant experience, is it? The best guesstimate possible based on what limited information is available suggests that electroporting does not actually tear apart the atomic and molecular structure of the object being transported.

More likely, it is some mechanism that directly converts all the mass of the object into massless energy without physically disrupting the orderly cohesive atomic and/or molecular ensemble. Hmm. That's impossible, isn't it?

I know what you're thinking now. This entire process sounds more and more like some science-fiction story of an otherwise overactive imagination. But before we jump to that conclusion, let's remember that much of the activity manifested by paranormal and/or ufological phenomena seemingly contradicts if not violates what we currently know about the laws governing the physical universe we reside in.

Looking at this matter another way, how would we accept and consider the function of television or cellular phones 1,000 years ago. At that time, nothing within the collective knowledge of human consciousness could have come to grips with such technological marvels.

However, let's for the sake of argument, assume that the electroporting technology does not, in fact, kill you every time you use it. What would happen to one's consciousness during the duration of transport, albeit only a few seconds at the most? As the body, in physical terms, really done exist for a short period of time, what feelings and sensations might accompany such transport?

To really play devil's advocate, what would occur if there was a surge of power during your transmission? Would a brown-out or black-out cause you to reintegrate considerably later than when you attempted transmission? Would you be caught in sub-atomic limbo for hours or days and then suddenly appear at your destination thinking only an instant has passed?

Would a surge upwards in power cause you to accelerate beyond light speed and appear at your destination before you made the attempt to transport? The ramifications sort of resemble the Einsteinian "twins paradox" spoken of in hypothetical superluminal space travel.

The most interesting question or perhaps problem posed by electroporting is the concept in itself. Simply put, electroporting is reversing the well-known Einstein formula E=MC2. For in actuality, we have long ago seen this equation work from right to left--that's what gave us nuclear weapons, matter converted to energy. In order to achieve electroporting, the equation must be made to work in reverse, from left to right, where energy is turned into matter.

The implications involved with such an accomplishment go far beyond the "simple" concept of electroporting.

What is at stake here is the potential to create matter of any type of our raw energy. Put in simpler terms, how about a three-dimensional Xerox machine? How about making an infinite number of copies of any item----a diamond ring, furniture, cars, planes, etc., (people?)---by simply reproducing the patterns of energy in the original?

What at first sounds like the replicators in Star Trek: The Next Generation, and the violation of the conservation of energy principle is in reality, anything but.

All matter is essentially composed of the same building blocks, Molecules are really nothing more than a collection of organized groups of atoms that are themselves composed of even more highly ordered clusters of protons, neutrons and electrons. Protons are built out of a combination of even smaller elementary particles known as quarks, while electrons are the conglomerations of fractional charge carriers built up over time.

Therefore, wood, plastic, brick or metal, even living cells, is actually all made of the same basic ingredients...sub-atomic elementary particles known as quarks and fractional charge carriers.

These elementary units are omnipresent and exist in an almost infinite abundance. So why not use our technology gleaned from electroportation to gather, collate, organize and build these assemblages so that the result is atoms and molecules of specific numbers and weights, which in essence is matter? Such a device might come to be known as a "matter replicator," again borrowed from Star Trek: The Next Generation.

We need not strip the Earth of the remainder of its resources in order for society and modern civilization to flourish and prosper., whether it be trees for wood, or mines for iron, bauxite (aluminum), gold, silver, titanium, etc.

As we have already mastered the ability to turn energy into matter and back to energy again, this next step should not pose any insurmountable difficulty, other than freeing the human race from the requirement of labor. Even food, in all its diversity, animal, vegetable, mineral and fruit, could be produced ad infinitum rather than growing it.

Although, as with photocopying almost anything which is degraded from the original, generating endless copies of three-dimensional matter, might result in a significant reduction of cohesiveness of integrity from the original.

For example, when animals have been cloned, such clones do not live very long due to numerous genetic defects thought to be the result of the imperfect cloning process.

A most beneficial side-effect of this technology is that it would free the entire planet from want, whether it be for basic elemental resources needed for building, fuel or food. The human race need not go to war anymore over the inequity in distribution of resources.

But then again, what would a nation----if not a world----conditioned by a work ethic do if the majority, if not all of its populations no longer need work in order to survive?

228

If manual labor----or labor period----as we currently know it completely disappeared, what would most individuals do with their time? Could the human race live in a potential utopia without greedy special-interest groups and large corporations attempting to manipulate and control advanced processes to still make as much as possible off everyone? What type of beings would we become if all our needs, wants and desires were supplied by society.

Whether electroporting is every commercially utilized and exploited depends on many factors, the least of important of which is the more advanced nations' need for such technology to free their dependency on Third World energy and its inevitable economic recession and inflation.

Perhaps before our culture reaches a pinnacle of technological achievement it needs to be humbled by reassessing its morals and values.

Besides exotic transport devices, there are conceivably other "black" projects, funded by different government agencies and contracted through many of the numerous leading aerospace firms, which could totally alter the way in which we live our lives----projects like the generation of artificial micro-miniature black and wormholes that are created through controlled application of microwaves.

Such artificial black and wormholes could theoretically generate infinite amounts of power pumped through their non-singularity centers.

Other, more ominous projects include the development of anti-matter weaponry, such as anti-proton particle beams and anti-matter bombs. Currently, in government labs located in New Mexico and Oxnard, California, research is continuing at a feverish pace on the most potentially lethal SDI (Star Wars) weapons ever conceived.

Forget about brilliant pebbles, kinetic-kill vehicles, neutral particle beams, mid-infrared advanced chemical laser (MIRACL), chemical oxygen-iodine (COIL) or free-electron lasers. These are systems, with the exception of the airborne laser (ABL) and it COIL, that in all likelihood will never see the light of day, even though our government wants everyone to think they will. In essence these directed energy weapon developments may be little more than make-work projects!

With anti-matter, 100% of the matter is converted to energy. That's over 1,800 times more potent than thermonuclear fusion. Consider that one kilogram (2.2 pounds) of antimatter possesses the energetic equivalent of 500 one-megaton bombs.

That's enough power to easily lay waste to the entire surface land area of the North American continent, not to mention simultaneously blowing the atmosphere over such land out into space. Given that kind of energetic release, consider what occur if such a bomb was sunk deep into the interior of a planet...like Earth!

Unlike other directed energy weapons, e.g., lasers and charged or neutral particle beams, anti-proton beams do not have to directly hit their intended target missile. All that's required is for the anti-proton beam, which would be in a geosynchronous orbit, to fire into a specific "window" in space that the enemy missiles would have to fly through in their launch phase.

Pulsing the antimatter beam weapon several thousand times a second would create a powerful field of anti-protons within that desired spatial window and anything flying through that window would be instantly annihilated.

So much for re-targeting the beam weapon after each shot! In many ways, the anti-proton beam is reminiscent of Star Trek's phasers or photon torpedoes in that when anti-matter is annihilated, it converts all the matter into pure energy, i.e., gamma rays and high-energy photons.

An anti-matter bomb, for reasons already discussed, cannot be tested on Earth. At least our government's military allegedly has enough wisdom to avoid such foolish attempts. The alternative is to send an antimatter bomb aboard a satellite into the asteroid belt between Mars and Jupiter, where an attempt will be made to destroy a relatively large asteroid, say several kilometers in diameter, perhaps.

As there is no atmosphere is space to generate a blast effect through compression, the antimatter's annihilation effects will be put to the test. If the bomb successfully destroys the target asteroid, it might be fully developed and eventually deployed. The question is where?

Hmm. Given the above scenario, isn't our not-so-brilliant military overlooking the most obvious collateral damage potential? Seems to me that violently destroying an asteroid in the belt between Mars and Jupiter would be akin to hitting a billiard ball into many other billiard balls.

The result could, and very likely would, send large pieces of asteroid(s) flying in every direction creating a chain reaction that could reach far beyond the asteroid belt itself.

How about showering wildly careening asteroids throughout the solar system? And if I accurately recall our pre-history, wasn't such a meteoric or asteroid impact the alleged cause of dinosaur extinction?

Well, at least we'll have successfully field tested the most powerful explosive device ever created. What a technological milestone!

Pity, that no one on Earth will live to savor this accomplishment. Or, live to regret it, for that matter. Kiss the human race goodbye?

But then again, just maybe we'll use this incredible power to open a doorway into the zero point field any really learn how to travel amongst the stars and well as through time itself. Nah, no such luck. Will the human race survive long enough for it to create in reality what science fiction has done on the screen? What do you think? What are the odds?

END